W9-DGF-978

Compassionate STATISTICS

Compassionate STATISTICS

Applied Quantitative Analysis for Social Services
With exercises and instructions in SPSS

Vincent E. Faherty
University of Southern Maine

PROPERTY OF WLU
SOCIAL WORK LIBRARD
DISCARD

SAGE Publications
Los Angeles • London • New Delhi • Singapore

Copyright © 2008 by Sage Publications, Inc.

All rights reserved. No part of this book may be reproduced or utilized in any form or by any means, electronic or mechanical, including photocopying, recording, or by any information storage and retrieval system, without permission in writing from the publisher.

For information:

Sage Publications, Inc.
2455 Teller Road
Thousand Oaks,
  California 91320
E-mail: order@sagepub.com

Sage Publications India Pvt. Ltd.
B 1/I 1 Mohan Cooperative
  Industrial Area
Mathura Road, New Delhi 110 044
India

Sage Publications Ltd.
1 Oliver's Yard
55 City Road
London EC1Y 1SP
United Kingdom

Sage Publications Asia-Pacific Pte. Ltd.
33 Pekin Street #02-01
Far East Square
Singapore 048763

Printed in the United States of America

Library of Congress Cataloging-in-Publication Data

Faherty, Vincent E. (Vincent Edward), 1939–
Compassionate statistics: Applied quantitative analysis for social services (with exercises and instructions in SPSS)/Vincent E. Faherty.
      p. cm.
Includes bibliographical references and index.
ISBN 978-1-4129-3982-9 (pbk.)
    1. Social service—Statistical methods. 2. Evaluation research (Social action programs)—Statistical methods. 3. SPSS (Computer file) I. Title.

HV29.F34 2008
361.001′5195—dc22   2007005883

This book is printed on acid-free paper.

07   08   09   10   11   10 9 8 7 6 5 4 3 2 1

Acquisitions Editor:	Kassie Graves
Editorial Assistant:	Veronica K. Novak
Production Editor:	Melanie Birdsall
Copy Editor:	Gillian Dickens
Typesetter:	C&M Digitals (P) Ltd.
Proofreader:	Cheryl Rivard
Indexer:	Naomi Linzer
Cover Designer:	Candice Harman
Marketing Manager:	Carmel Withers

Contents

Acknowledgments

First and foremost, I must acknowledge my wife, Angela, and my two sons, Vincent and David, for their patience in the face of my countless distracted moments when we were together and for their unqualified support as I raced toward the completion of this book. I could not have done this without you.

Then, I must salute the warm and persistent encouragement offered by Kassie Graves, acquisitions editor at Sage, along with the competent technical help from Veronica Novak, senior editorial assistant; Melanie Birdsall, production editor; Gillian Dickens, copy editor; and from the rest of the production staff at Sage who crafted this work into its final product.

Thank you, also, to the professional reviewers of the early drafts—Julie M. Clark, Hollins University; Pallab Mozumder, University of Massachusetts, Amherst; Ce Shen, Boston College; and Cindy F. Dutschke, Texas A&M University—whose knowledge and suggestions helped soften the sharp edges that appeared due to my omissions, generalizations, and downright mistakes. I certainly take full responsibility for the final product, but I know it is a creation that is brightly polished by your wisdom.

Finally, I commend all my former social work students whom I had the pleasure to interact with over the years in Utah, Missouri, Iowa, and Maine. Your probing questions and your insistent demand to make things relevant to social work practice have challenged me to write this book.

1

Introduction, Overview, and Nondefinitions

Figures often beguile me, particularly when I have the arranging of them myself; in which case the remark attributed to Disraeli would often apply with justice and force: "There are three kinds of lies: lies, damned lies, and statistics."

—Mark Twain, *Autobiography*, 1904,
cited on www.quotegarden.com/statistics

Welcome to *Compassionate Statistics: Applied Quantitative Analysis for Social Services (With exercises and instructions in SPSS)*, a book obviously about the one subject that is universally dreaded by most social service professionals—statistics. And rightly so. After all, no matter what your official title is—advocate, case manager, caseworker, counselor, gerontologist, probation officer, parole officer, social worker, or something else—you are in this high-pressure, tragically misunderstood, and severely underpaid profession precisely because you *like people* and not because you love to crunch numbers like your annoying relative, the accountant, who always seems to find you at family gatherings, just to harangue you with his latest insights into public welfare fraud and ply you with his ideas on how to fix it. So, you look at yourself, happily, as not just another number cruncher. Your goal is to provide the absolute best, state-of-the-art services to your clients who are struggling with horrific personal, economic, and social difficulties every day of their lives.

Then again, you might be a supervisor or upper-level administrator in one of those social service agencies that employs those social service professionals in the front lines of the vast array of community-based organizations. Your mission is distinct from that of your staff. What keeps you awake at night is how you can make available to those vulnerable clients a staff that is highly trained and sensitively responsive to their particular needs. And, in the midst of all these human resources issues, you need to run an organization that is effective and efficient in its current operations and yet open to change and dynamic development.

Or, perhaps, you are a baccalaureate or beginning graduate student in one of the thousands of academic programs in colleges and universities throughout society. Your need is different, again. In your busy schedule, where you juggle life and education, sometimes precariously, your goal is to finish your professional education so you will be adequately prepared to join your professional colleagues on those front lines of service. Amid all the exciting content you are exposed to during your years of study, it is entirely understandable that you might hesitate, ever so slightly, and wonder to yourself, as you register for those required courses in research methods and statistics, why your professors are making you take courses with such irrelevant nonsense. After all, you are in your program because you want to help people, not just do research and count numbers!

Well, if you picture yourself in any one of those scenarios just described, my message is simple and straightforward. With apologies to the creators of the Budweiser beer commercial—this book's for you!

Compassionate Statistics: Applied Quantitative Analysis for Social Services has been designed to serve you, the professional social services student, practitioner, or administrator, as you pursue diligently your many roles and responsibilities in today's society. This book will get right to the core of the essential issues you will need to deal with as you collect, process, and analyze those relevant sets of quantitative data in your work. This is not a watered-down version of statistics, but it is, admittedly, an attempt to go beyond the theoretical material usually found in classic statistical textbooks and lift you, very quickly, to the pragmatic, day-to-day realm, where you are right now. In many senses, this book is an extension of the often-stated value premise of the need to *start where the client is*. In this situation, then, *Compassionate Statistics: Applied Quantitative Analysis for Social Services* is starting where, hopefully, you are.

One final point: This introductory discussion is not meant to disparage in any way the wide array of excellent textbooks on statistics, especially those designed for the social service community. They are important contributions to the professional literature and should be consulted by you, as needed, whenever this book assumes too much or moves too quickly for you from the abstract to the concrete. You are encouraged to keep those standard texts in your library and use them, as appropriate, in conjunction with this book. It goes without saying, of course, that you should also hold very close to you any textbooks that you have used (or are using presently) that discuss the methods and processes of social science research and evaluation in general. Consider those as essential tools to conduct any empirical research or program evaluation project.

Structure of the Book and of Each Chapter

Beginning in the next chapter, Chapter 2, you can expect to find the following material in sequential order.

• *Statistical Content.* Against a background that includes a minimum of theory but a maximum of social services examples, the major statistical issues/themes will be presented. This is a fairly standard list of issues/themes that will provide you with the knowledge necessary to conduct basic, first-level research and evaluation projects that require some level of quantitative analysis. Chapters will be kept mercifully short and to the point in order to facilitate the process of engaging you in the acquisition of some new (and difficult) content or, perhaps, reinforcing content that you experienced years before. What you will *not find* in the content is any statistical formula, which would allow you to compute a statistical test by hand. This decision to keep *Compassionate Statistics: Applied Quantitative Analysis for Social Services* free of any mathematical equations or formulas may be criticized by some statisticians as being overly simplistic and, perhaps, even misleading. Hopefully, that is not true. This book on applied statistics is intended, as stated above, to be a supplementary text, or perhaps an introductory one, that offers you practical knowledge and functional skills that you can apply immediately in your role as a student or as a working social services professional. Teaching you to access computerized software in order to analyze the data, rather than have you process statistical formulas on calculators, was a decision made carefully and is based on the goal of helping you *use* statistics in your work, rather than only *understand* its potential.

• *Summary Points to Remember.* Each chapter content discussion will end with a brief, targeted summary section designed to help you recall the essential elements of each chapter.

• *Case Illustrations.* Using selected material drawn from the professional literature, four actual examples of the statistical issue or procedure discussed in the chapter will be included so you can envision how that particular statistical material did actually appear in a professional journal or book. Thus, you will encounter real data and see exactly how those data were analyzed and presented in print. Additional explanatory material is added after each case to clarify further the statistical procedure under discussion. The first of the four case illustrations is presented at the very beginning of each chapter (with the exception of Chapters 1 and 8) so as to provide you with a concrete example of what will be discussed in that particular chapter. Three additional case illustrations appear toward the end of each chapter, after the content has been presented.

• *Activities.* To immediately fortify your newly acquired knowledge with practice, you will be challenged to conduct a series of relevant statistical exercises with data provided in one or more of the data sets in the appendix section of the book. For some chapters, you may be asked to enter these raw data into a new Statistical Package for the Social Sciences® (SPSS) file that you will save for future use; in other chapters, you may be directed to the Sage Web site, where you can download the data to your own computer for statistical analysis in SPSS. There also exists the possibility that your instructor may modify these activities, or add new ones, for your unique learning experiences.

• *SPSS Procedures.* To assist you in completing these activities, you will have access to clear, step-by-step SPSS procedures, including appropriate computer screen images, relating to the specific content of each chapter. In case you have never used SPSS or are a bit rusty on its operations, you will find a thorough, general introduction to SPSS in Appendix A: Getting Started With SPSS at the end of this book. Please note, however, that the SPSS procedures in each chapter, as well as in Appendix A, are not intended to replace a formal SPSS manual or to substitute for the extensive Help options provided within the online SPSS software program itself. The chapter-by-chapter SPSS procedures and screen shots will assist you in completing the assigned activities, but you might need additional SPSS material to analyze your individual research and program evaluation projects. While all SPSS computers screen shots for this book were created in SPSS 14.0, they should be useful for future editions of the SPSS software with only slight visual modifications.

• *References.* Finally, at the end of each chapter, you will find a list of citations, in the American Psychological Association (APA) style format, for each professional article used in that chapter. This will help you easily find the full text of those articles if you ever wish to read about the entire research project beyond the small excerpt included in each case illustration.

Some Useful Nondefinitions

The phrase *nondefinitions* may sound strange, and that is intentional. They are designed to introduce you to some highly complex, and at times confusing, quantitative concepts that are fundamental to your understanding of statistics. Nondefinitions help you ease into some pretty deep waters—sort of like when you get your feet wet before diving into that crashing wave at the beach. By the way, at the end of this book, there is Appendix F: Glossary of Terms, which includes all the technical terms used throughout the chapters. The glossary is the closest thing to a list of formal definitions you will come across. If you find yourself wanting more details about some term, you could return to your research methods book or to that dog-eared standard statistics book you might still have lying around someplace, or you could log on to the Internet (try google.com, ask.com, msn.com, or wikipedia.com).

Hopefully, what you will find helpful in addition to the glossary is a less technical, example-riddled, almost *breezy* discussion of these important terms and phrases, similar to having a simple conservation with a friend. That's what a nondefinition is in this book. They are listed here alphabetically, not necessarily in the order of importance. The suggestion is that you read through these nondefinitions once now, as you start this book, and then remember that they are here in Chapter 1, for your review, as you travel through the rest of the chapters. Happy journey!

Degrees of Freedom

This is a classic example of a statistical word or phrase that does not mean what it sounds like it should mean. *Freedom* in this case refers to the number of ways a **variable** is able to differ or fluctuate. When you put the variable *gender* with two possible categories (female, male) in the same data set as the variable *location* also with two categories (urban, rural), you have several possible combinations (female urban, female rural, male urban, male rural). The degrees of freedom (noted as *df*) should always be reported when you note the output of a statistical test. Now, relax. The SPSS in most cases gives you the *df* number in the output, so all you have to do is note it and record it correctly. The only situation in which you have to do your own computation of the *df* is whenever you run a correlation test. Stay relaxed . . . it is easy. The *df* is the number of subjects minus two ($N - 2 = df$). Remember that and you will never make a mistake when you are computing either of the two correlation tests (Pearson's *r* or Spearman's *rho*).

Dependent and Independent Variables

Think of any typical cause/effect situation. For example, if your right elbow radiates a dull ache all day long whenever it is raining, you might logically conclude that the dampness in the air is somehow causing your elbow to experience such a pain. In any study of two variables, the one that is influencing, pushing, or exerting some power over the other variable is called the independent variable. The independent variable is usually noted as X in a figure or diagram. The dependent variable, then, is the variable being pushed or being influenced in some way. The dependent variable is what you measure as a researcher and is usually noted as Y in figures or diagrams. In the hypothesis, "Women in this group of applicants will score an average of 5 points higher on the state driving test than men," the independent variable would be gender, and the dependent variable would be the test score on the state driving test.

Descriptive and Inferential Statistics

The words say exactly what these terms mean. You will cover a large number of statistical procedures (tests) in this book, some very simple and others quite complex. These can all be divided neatly into two categories or groups of procedures. Those procedures that merely summarize, condense, or describe one or two variables at a time are called **descriptive statistics.** You learn, for example, nothing more than how many men and women answered your survey. You might also discover, from what they told you, how many men voted Democratic, Republican, and Independent in the last election, as well as the voting pattern of the women. That is all you know if you compute only descriptive statistical procedures on your data. If you have a random sample drawn from a population, however, and you use **inferential statistics,** you can generalize or assume whatever you learn about your sample back to the population from which you drew the sample. Thus, building on what you know descriptively about your sample, you will also be able to determine if gender was partially influencing whether your respondents voted Democratic, Republican, or Independent. If you learn that gender did, in fact, influence political party affiliation (for example, women in your sample tended to vote Democratic more than Republican or Independent), then you can generalize those findings to all of the people in your population. This is not crystal ball gazing; it is using the theory of probability and the power of inferential statistics.

Effect Size

This is an issue that is currently gaining importance in social services research and program evaluation because a number of professional journals are requiring, or strongly suggesting, that the **effect size** be reported along with other statistical tests. As you will learn in this book, specifically in Chapter 8, "Probability and Statistical Significance," the p score (probability) will indicate whether a relationship appears to exist between two variables you are studying. The effect size, arising from additional statistical tests, indicates the strength or the magnitude of a relationship that does appear to exist. Moving beyond statistics for a moment and considering a personal relationship you might hope you have with another individual, you could ask yourself two questions: Do I really have a personal relationship with that person, or are we just friends? If you can answer yes to the first question, then the follow-up asks, How strong is that relationship? In a statistical relationship between two variables, the effect size is similar to that second question.

Consider the situation where you want to contrast two or more distinct research studies that were conducted on that same general topic but used different measurement techniques and even different statistical tests. You could perform a valuable function (technically called a *meta-analysis*) if you had access to the effect sizes of all the reported statistical tests. From this perspective, then, the effect size provides researchers with sort of a common denominator when viewing the results of several research or program evaluation studies that are similar in design but not exact replicas of each other.

While there are a large number of recognized measures of the effect size that you can use in conjunction with most statistical tests, the SPSS program unfortunately does not report all of them. For example, one of the most common measures of effect size when comparing two sets of mean scores, Cohen's d, is not presented in the latest version of the SPSS program that is used in conjunction with this book. What follows is a list of other measures of effect size, readily available in SPSS, and the situations in which you would use each.

- **Pearson's r** provides the strength of the correlation between two variables that are measured at the scale level (e.g., the correlation between income measured in dollars and amount of formal education measured in years). This is used in situations where you compute correlations for inferential, and not descriptive, purposes. A strong effect size would result from a Pearson's r value falling between .60 and 1.00, a moderate effect size would result from a Pearson's r value falling between .40 and .59, and a small effect size would result from a Pearson's r value falling between .00 and .39. To remember these numbers, think of a one-dollar bill ($1.00) and ask yourself, How many cents out of a dollar do I have? If you have eighty-nine cents ($.89), that would be strong; if you have fifty-three cents ($.53), that would be moderate; and if you have only thirteen cents ($.13), that would be weak.

- **Spearman's** *rho* provides the strength of the correlation between two variables that are measured at the ordinal level (e.g., the correlation between attitude toward sex education in schools, measured on a 5-point scale ranging from *very positive* to *very negative,* and attitude toward freedom of the press, measured on the same 5-point scale). This is used in situations where you compute correlations for inferential, and not descriptive, purposes. A strong effect size would result from a Spearman's *rho* value falling between .60 and 1.00, a moderate effect size would result from a Spearman's *rho* value falling between .40 and .59, and a small effect size would result from a Spearman's *rho* value falling between .00 and .39.

- *Phi* provides the strength of association between two variables measured at the nominal level and arranged in a 2-by-2 table (i.e., two variables each having only two possible categories, e.g., gender [female/male] by place of residence [urban/nonurban]). The *phi* value is used only in conjunction with the chi-square test of independence of the variables.

- Cramer's *V* provides the strength of association between two variables measured at the nominal level and arranged in a larger than 2-by-2 (i.e., two variables, at least one of which has more than two categories, e.g., gender [male/female] by political party affiliation [Democrat/Republican/Independent]). Cramer's *V* value is used only in conjunction with the chi-square (χ^2) test of independence of the variables.

Typically, the effect size is reported at the end of the notation that provides the summary information from the SPSS output on a particular statistical test. For example, the notation $\chi^2 = 3.78$, $df = 4$, $p < .05$, $V = .56$ means (without going into great detail at this point) that there exists a statistically significant relationship between two nominal-level variables, and the strength of that relationship is considered to be moderate.

One-Tailed and Two-Tailed Research Hypotheses

This distinction comes into play when you decide exactly how to state your research hypothesis, and it depends, literally, on how specific you can be based on your literature review. Drawing from what other research has shown, if you can hypothesize that only a general relationship exists between variables, such as, "In this community, religion affects crime rates as measured by official police records of conviction for the past 12 months," you have proposed a *two-tailed hypothesis,* also referred to as a **nondirectional hypothesis.** On the other hand, if you know much more specific information (again, drawn from your literature review) so that you can hypothesize, for example, that "In this community, Christians, compared to Jews, Moslems, and Hindi, commit 75% of all crimes as measured by official police records of conviction for the past 12 months," then you would be offering a *one-tailed hypothesis,* also called a **directional hypothesis.** This distinction is quite important for you to remember because all of the SPSS inferential statistical procedures you will compute in the exercises as well as in your own research projects assume you have a two-tailed hypothesis. Thus, if you compute a statistical test and the SPSS output indicates you have a probability value (p) of .08, remember that that value is for a two-tailed hypothesis. If, in fact, you are proposing a one-tailed hypothesis, then you should divide the stated p value in half, meaning, in this example, that your p value is actually lower, at .04 (i.e., .08/2 = .04). Sometimes, as in this particular example, that would mean the difference between having established a statistically significant relationship (i.e., $p = .04$) between the variables and discovering the existence of no significant relationship (i.e., $p = .08$).

Parameter and Statistic

Think of a large bowl filled to the top with hundreds of small spheres, such as M&M candies that are each red, blue, yellow, green, or purple in color. In a very specific sense, a **parameter** is some characteristic of all the elements (which together are called the population) that you know by direct observation of each element. So, in this example, that would mean that you picked out each sphere, one by one, and noted exactly how many of each color was in the bowl. That exercise would yield for you the **population parameter** of the variable color for this particular bowl of candy. A statistic, in a similar narrow sense of the word, is some characteristic of only a sample (i.e., a small number) of the colored spheres that you drew out of the bowl and then observed their individual colors. The actual number of each color in your sample would then be the sample statistic of the variable color for the particular sample you drew out of the bowl. In a very general sense, the word **statistics** refers to a set of mathematical procedures used by researchers to understand the underlying characteristics of large bodies of data. Statistics are considered highly efficient because in many situations, the researcher can study only the sample of the data and yet make some determination about the entire population of the data.

Parametric and Nonparametric Tests

In the hierarchy of statistical tests, those known as parametric are considered the more rigorous because of three characteristics: (1) The data used are at the scale level (i.e., interval and ratio), (2) the population under study is considered to be normally distributed (i.e., the range of values approximates the image of a bell-shaped curve), and (3) the number of respondents about whom you have data is considered sufficiently large (e.g., a minimum of 30). Common **parametric tests** include the dependent samples t-test, independent samples t-test, analysis of variance (ANOVA), and Pearson's r correlation.

Less rigorous, but still extremely useful, are those tests considered *nonparametric* because they lack one or more of those same three characteristics: (1) They use nominal- or ordinal-level data, (2) the distribution of values is nonnormal, and (3) the number of respondents is small (less than 30). The chi-square test for independence and Spearman's *rho* rank-order correlation are common examples of **nonparametric tests** found in social services practice.

Population and Sample

For a researcher in social services, a **population** is the total number of individuals (e.g., inmates in a correctional facility), objects (e.g., case records), or interactions (e.g., all behaviors of members in a counseling group) that she or he is studying in a particular project. A **sample,** then, is only a portion of that population that the researcher actually collects data from or about by means of surveys, observations, or calculations. This is a very important distinction to understand because sometimes (e.g., if the population is not large), the researcher might be collecting data on all the respondents and not on just a few. In that situation, the researcher would report the results of the study on a population, rather than on a sample. Also critical for the researcher is to be clear about what type of sample she or he has drawn for the study because a random sample allows for generalization of the results back to the population from which it was drawn, while a nonrandom sample does not. This point will be discussed below under Random and Nonrandom Sampling.

Questions or Hypotheses

Generally speaking, most human service researchers start out a research project by posing to themselves some very broad and unspecific *research question,* such as, "Are voluntary, not-for-profit social agencies more effective than public human service agencies?" or "Why do some social agency clients abruptly leave before their treatment plans have been completed?" or, perhaps, "Is this agency really serving all the needs of the local community?" The next step, ideally, calls for the researcher to delve deeply into the professional literature and review what others have discovered about the issue, as well as talking to colleagues about their perspectives on the question. This process should lead to a heightened overall understanding of the issue as well as a narrowing of the specific aspect of the issue that the researcher chooses to pursue. The result of this arduous, but critical, process should be either a more focused research question (e.g., Are master degree–level case managers more effective with long-term nursing home clients than bachelor degree–level case managers?) or a research hypothesis (e.g., Male professional staff in human service agencies in the Northeast have an average of 2 or more years of additional paid professional experience as compared to female professional staff in the same agencies). Generally speaking, a research question is more vague and less measurable in quantitative terms than is its corresponding hypothesis. For very practical reasons, the various statistical procedures you will encounter in this book are most appropriate for testing research hypotheses and only less so for answering research questions.

Random and Nonrandom Sampling

If literally all the respondents in the study population had an equal chance of being chosen by you as you drew your sample, then you would have a random sample. This demands that you have at your disposal an exact number of respondents (not simply an estimate) and, furthermore, that you take yourself totally out of the selection process. The best procedure to use is a table of random numbers, such as the one in Appendix E of this book, as the basis for your selection.

If you have not followed the rigorous and structured procedure to gain a true **random sample,** then you have in your research project a nonrandom sample. A random sample allows you to generalize your results back to the population from which you drew it; a nonrandom sample does not provide you with this option.

Research Hypothesis, Null Hypothesis, and Alternative Hypothesis

For reasons that have eluded and mystified students for generations, a researcher should formulate three hypotheses once the literature review is completed. Your **research hypothesis** is your "best guess" of what your data will show once they are collected and analyzed (e.g., "Couples who receive formal communication training have a happier marriage compared to those couples who do not receive such training"). The null hypothesis is then formulated in such a manner that you will be able to statistically test whether the variable, formal communication training, has any relationship with the second variable, happier marriage. In the null hypothesis format, the assumption is that there exists no relationship between the variables stated either negatively ("Couples who receive formal communication training do not have a happier marriage compared to those couples lacking such training") or as distinct from each other ("Formal communication training for couples is unrelated to happiness in marriage"). The **alternative hypothesis** is a complete and absolute contradiction to the null hypothesis ("Formal communication training for couples is related to happiness in marriage"). For obvious reasons, some researchers use the terms *research hypothesis* and *alternative hypothesis* interchangeably because they believe that a carefully stated research hypothesis can, indeed, be tested statistically.

Why do such an awkward thing like develop a **null hypothesis?** The reason is so that you can either support your hypothesis by statistically rejecting the null hypothesis or not support your hypothesis by statistically failing to reject the null hypothesis. You may want to read that last sentence again—admittedly, it does sound a bit like "doublespeak."

Please note that supporting your hypothesis is not the same as proving it because you still risk the danger of committing what statisticians call a **Type II error.** In plain language, a Type II error occurs when you reject a null hypothesis in a situation where you should have not rejected it. That sounds confusing, especially when you throw in **Type I error,** which is the exact opposite of a Type II error. More about this fascinating subject below, under the subheading Type I and Type II Errors.

On the practical side, to be able to reject a null hypothesis means that you must exercise more precision in your data collection and then use the appropriate statistical procedures to analyze the data. And that is the main point of the distinction between a research and a null hypothesis.

Theory of Probability and the Bell-Shaped Curve

These are two of the most difficult, yet important, items to explain. Remember that they are related; in fact, the **bell-shaped curve** helps to explain the theory of probability.

In the Mathematics section of the Science Museum in Boston, Massachusetts, you can literally visualize the formation of a bell-shaped curve in one of the museum's dynamic exhibits. Placed there is a large display that consists of a number of clear Plexiglas tubes placed side by side, vertically encased in a wide, transparent rectangular structure. At the top of the display, you can watch a machine dropping small rubber balls every 3 seconds into the display. Each ball hits a central point above the tubes, then bounces either left or right, into one of the tubes near the center, midway out, or at the very end. If you stand in front of the exhibit long enough, you will discover that when all the balls have dropped, most will cluster in the tubes closest to the center, and the rest will have bounced into the tubes further out, left and right, in descending frequency. You must look quickly because once the last ball has landed in a tube, the tube bottoms open up, the balls drop, and the process begins again. Every time, without fail, all the balls together form the shape of a perfectly symmetrical bell without a handle—the bell-shaped curve. In the science museum display, the top of the bell represents the most-filled tubes, nearest the center (the mean or average), as well as the least-filled tubes on each side (the outliers).

This bell image appears every time, without any human or mechanical manipulation, precisely because it is a naturally occurring phenomenon and, as such, can be used as a basis for future predictions.

The theory of **probability,** operating within various statistical formulas, makes predictions about the likelihood that numerical values observed in random samples will be repeated in populations from which the samples were drawn. This ability to predict the odds that something will take place is drawn from the same predictability inherent in any human visualization of the bell-shaped curve. Try all this out for yourself. If you go online to www.stat .sc.edu/rsrch/gasp and scroll down to the section called Educational Applications, you will be able to engage in some interactive exercises that demonstrate all this material. The third applet (exercise) on the list, *The Let's Make a Deal* applet, demonstrates how cunning and counterintuitive the theory of probability is. You will undoubtedly be fooled by this experience. The fifth exercise on the list, *The Central Limit Theorem* applet, allows you to observe the gradual formation of a bell-shaped curve by virtually rolling dice a large number of times and counting how often certain numbers appear. Who ever said that statistics is not fun (sometimes)?

One additional point about the bell-shaped curve: It represents an "ideal" distribution of values (numbers). In other words, it symbolizes a distribution of numbers that is almost perfectly symmetrical so that the mean (average) value is exactly in the middle, closely encircled by the median and mode, while the rest of the values trail off in perfect coordination to the right and to the left. Such a neat distribution of numbers rarely, if ever, occurs as such in real life. This idealized bell-shaped curve image, however, is useful as an illustration against which you can compare actual distributions of numbers collected in research projects that inevitably appear unbalanced and lopsided against their own mean values.

Type I and Type II Errors

Any discussion of either Type I or Type II errors always relates to the broader topic of rejecting, or not rejecting, the null hypothesis of your research endeavor. This is tricky territory for many beginning researchers because of the use of negatives and double negatives in the same context. The basic difference is this: You commit a Type I error if you reject your null hypothesis when you should have accepted it as true, and you commit a Type II error when you accept your null hypothesis as true when, in fact, you should have rejected it as stated. For example, based on the literature and, perhaps, your own observations, you hypothesize that the population of human service administrators in your state will score an average of 75 points or higher on the 100-item XYZ Cultural Sensitivity Test that is recognized nationally as a valid measurement tool. Thus, you believe that the agency administrators in you state are, generally speaking, sensitive to cultural differences in society. To test this belief (hypothesis), you draw a random sample of administrators, survey them by mail, analyze the results from the sample, and then generalize those sample results to the entire population of all the administrators from which you drew your original sample. So far, so good . . . but because of some factors possibly present, you may be committing either a Type I or Type II error. These factors include the following: Your sample was not really representative of the population, your sample size was too small, your response rate was very low, you used an incorrect statistical test, or you used the correct test but you did not have the appropriate level of data for that test.

Continuing the example, assume that your null hypothesis states that "Human service administrators will achieve a score of less than 75 points on the XYZ Cultural Sensitivity Test." You would commit a Type I error if you rejected that statement when it was really true and subsequently declared in your conclusion that, based on your sample results, all administrators in your state would score above 75 points on the test. This conclusion would be overly optimistic due to a Type I error. Similarly, you would commit a Type II error if you accepted the null hypothesis when, in reality, it was false and then went on to declare that all administrators in your state would score below 75 points on that test. This conclusion, then, would be overly pessimistic due to a Type II error. Perhaps the following may help you remember this confusing combination:

1. *Type I error:* Reject null when null is true, thus overly optimistic

2. *No error:* Reject null when null is false

3. *Type II error:* Accept null when null is false, thus overly pessimistic

4. *No error:* Accept null when null is true

Do not lose any sleep over this precarious situation. In fact, you can easily minimize the danger of committing either a Type I or Type II error by following some simple advice: Use a carefully drawn random sample whenever possible, take out as large a random sample as your resources (i.e., time, money, and energy) allow, use follow-up procedures to obtain as high a percent return rate as possible, and understand the requirements as well as the limitations of every statistical test you use in your final analysis of the data collected.

Univariate and Bivariate Analysis

This is a refreshingly simple distinction. If you are conducting a **univariate analysis,** that means you are studying only one variable at a time. Thus, you might first report your findings on the gender of your survey respondents, then on their age at last birthday, then on their income level, and so on. When you perform a **bivariate analysis,** however, you proceed to analyze two variables at one time in order to learn more about their interrelationship. In this case, you want to view the relationship between gender and income status at the same time so that you can discover how many males, as compared to females, are low income, middle income, and so forth. You can compute a bivariate analysis for either descriptive or inferential purposes, but you would logically execute a univariate analysis only for descriptive purposes.

Values and Value Categories

This is an issue of terminology in statistical language. In your research or program evaluation projects, when you study the variable *gender,* that requires that you measure whether your respondents are female or male. If you want to know your respondents' impression of something, you might ask them how much they agree with a statement you provide to them and then ask them to circle one of three choices: agree, undecided, or disagree. Or, you might want to know the exact age of your respondents at their last birthday. In that situation, you would collect from them precise numbers, such as 24, 38, 55, and so on. Those pieces of data that you collect from your respondents are considered measurements in statistics. When those measurements are expressed as words (male/female, agree/undecided/disagree), they are referred to as *value categories.* When the measurements are numbers, they are called *values.* As you will learn next, in Chapter 2, this distinction can also be understood within the context of the various levels of data measurement. In a nutshell, value categories are used with nominal- and ordinal-level data, and values are used with scale-level data.

Words With Special Meanings in Statistics

Be very careful whenever you use any of the following words because they all mean something unique in a context of social services research and statistics.

• *Bias.* In a statistical context, **bias** does not mean prejudice or discrimination. A sample of respondents that you report as having a *gender bias* simply means that you, the researcher, studied only one gender (e.g., females). Therefore, the results, if they can be generalized beyond the sample, can never be generalized to males since no male was included in the original sample. Samples could, if you made that choice, be also biased regarding religion, age, race/ethnicity, and so on. A biased sample means only that it was purposely limited in some manner.

• *Correlation.* Use the word *relationship* unless you have computed one of the correlation tests (Pearson's *r* or Spearman's *rho*) and found a statistically significant correlation.

• *Prove.* Use this word only if you are conducting experimental research and you are able to report that you have statistically rejected the null hypothesis. Even then, you should soften the word by adding some type of qualifier (e.g., "seems to prove . . ." or "appears to prove . . ."). This is not false humility. Instead, it is a realistic admission that social science researchers do not have at their disposal the instruments or the technology to, literally, *prove* an absolute cause/effect relationship between two variables. After all, we work within the arena of human behavior, and that is an environment much too complex and subjective for anyone to try and predict with any hard assurance what the future holds.

• *Significant.* Use only if you can show in an SPSS output that you have true statistical significance at a $p = .05$ or less level. Otherwise, select some other word such as *important, essential,* or *critical.*

• *Valid.* Typically, this word is found in the context of the instrument you used to collect your data. The word implies that your instrument was *accurate* in the sense that it measured what you wanted it to measure.

2

Levels of Data

Nominal, Ordinal, and Scale

Statistics don't lie . . . statisticians do.

—Anonymous

Introductory Case Illustration

In a study designed to examine how much respect African American youth experience from contemporary society, a research team developed a 20-item scale and administered it in a survey to a sample of 200 African American adolescents. The researchers developed their scale at what is called the **ordinal level of measurement.** This particular scale consisted of a number of short statements describing common interpersonal situations, and the adolescents were asked to provide their own reaction to each statement.

The authors note in their discussion of the methodology that "a 4-point rating scale was adopted: 0 = strongly disagree, 1 = disagree, 2 = agree, and 3 = strongly agree" (Leary, Brennan, & Briggs, 2005, p. 465).

Discussion. As a researcher, you will need to distinguish clearly between the various levels of data because they are all measured differently. This is vital since you will be the one who analyzes those data and then eventually explains what they mean to your audience. The above example shows you how a team of researchers explained to their readers that the data they used were measured at the ordinal level, one of four possible levels discussed by statisticians. This chapter will explain fully those four levels.

Y ou really cannot travel very far through the world of statistical analysis without having a solid grasp on what is commonly called *levels of measurement*. In fact, until you are confident about this issue, that world will be quite confusing to you at times. So, this is obviously a good place to start. And it is a good place to come back to later on in this book if you need to refresh your understanding about these terms.

All **data**—that is, all of those "pieces" of information that you collect during your research and program evaluation activities—fit neatly at one of four possible levels of measurement. Picture these levels as stacking up, figuratively speaking, like steps on a ladder, from a low level of precision (Step 1) to a high level of precision (Step 4). Precision in this situation has to do with how exact you are when you measure something. For example, is it specific enough for you to say, "This is a very big round ball," or do you want to be able to say, "This ball is 86 inches in circumference"? The question is, How exact or how precise do you want your description of the ball to be? Clearly, the phrase *very big round ball* is much less precise than the phrase *86 inches in circumference*.

So, the phrase *levels of measurement* is really just another way of saying *levels of precision*. One of your goals as a researcher/program evaluator is to be able to collect your data with as much precision as is practical since the more precise your data, the more understanding you will be able to squeeze out of them during the statistical analysis phase of your project.

Naming the Levels of Measurement

Most textbooks on statistics label these four levels or steps, in ascending order, as *nominal, ordinal, interval,* and *ratio.* Fortunately for you, the Statistical Package for the Social Sciences (SPSS) makes your life a little bit easier by combining the last two levels, *interval* and *ratio,* and creating a new label that is identified as *scale.* It is not such a radical departure from common usage for the SPSS program developers to combine interval and ratio levels into the new scale level since there is very little pragmatic difference between those two levels anyway. Since you will be using SPSS for all of the exercises in this book, you should accept this revised terminology of three levels rather than four and enjoy this small token of statistical simplicity as long as you can.

This whole discussion that follows is intended to help you conceptualize your data at one of the three levels of precision. As you will soon learn, this ability to conceptualize, or *place*, your data at the appropriate level of measurement is a critical part of the process you will engage in whenever you create an SPSS file, enter data into it, and then analyze it for every possible nuance of meaning.

Nominal Level

Nominal, the first level, simply gives a name to your data and, as such, is not very precise. That does not mean that there is some problem with nominal data—it just means that you cannot do very much, statistically speaking, with nominal data other than to count them up and produce a sum or total. So, for example, when you want to study the variable of *gender,* you name the possibilities under that variable as *female* and *male.*

Studying the variable of *religion* could yield the mutually exclusive categories of *agnostic, atheist, Buddhist, Christian, Hindu, Jewish,* and *Moslem.* Other common variables that yield nominal data are race, ethnicity, marital status, geographic location (i.e., urban, suburban, and rural), educational level (i.e., freshman, sophomore), and social agency type (i.e., public, non-profit, and private-for-profit).

On a practical note, if you ever ask research participants to self-report deeply personal issues such as their gender, marital status, or religious preference, it is a good idea to always add at the end of the list one more category, such as *other, please specify.* This *other* category is typically counted and reported as a number and percent along with the main categories. The additional information provided by the *please specify* option is typically reported in a narrative format in the text or in a footnote.

Another way of describing nominal-level data is to say you are simply placing your data into categories or groups whose members all have some logical relationship with each other. So, all men, all women, all Moslems, all freshmen, and so on possess something in common.

When you enter nominal data into SPSS or into any other statistical program, you will assign each category a number as a way to code it so the computer can process the data quickly. Typically, those numbers will be 1, 2, 3, and so forth so that 1 could be the value assigned to *female,* 2 is assigned to *male,* and 3 is assigned to *other, please specify.* At the nominal level, these absolute numbers are meaningless—that is, they have no quantitative value to themselves for they simply represent the names assigned to the data. In other words, 1 is the name given to female, 2 is the name given to male, and so forth. Those numbers could easily be switched so male = 1 and female = 2, with no loss of information. The numbers used to code the data are like those name tags you wear at meetings, the kind that announce, "HELLO my name is. . . ."

An excellent way to determine if some piece of data is at the nominal level is to ask yourself any or all of the following questions: Does the number I assigned to it as a code have any real, quantitative meaning? Is 2 more than 1, or is 1 more important than 2? If I switch the numbers on the categories, would that affect the meaning in any way? If the answer is no, then you are probably dealing with nominal-level data.

Ordinal Level

At the *ordinal* level of data, you achieve a greater degree of precision for now you are able to *rank* or *position* the categories of the variable in some sort of line. With ordinal data, you will be conceptualizing phrases such as "never to always," "lowest to highest," or "absolutely *yes* to absolutely *no*." How many places there are in the line or how many gradations there are in the ranking is a decision that you make as the researcher when you develop your research instrument. Again, it has to do with *precision*. In other words, how much detail do you want? If you want to know simply how much your respondents agree with a statement (e.g., "Social services for children in the United States today are adequate for their needs"), then you might allow one of three possible answers:

1. Agree	2. Not sure	3. Disagree

If, however, you want more distinction, more exactness, in the data, then you might expand your possible answers to five choices, such as the following:

1. Absolutely disagree	2. Disagree	3. I'm not sure	4. Agree	5. Absolutely agree

The rank order that you achieve with ordinal data does not, however, provide you with anything more than a simple *series of points* from one end to another. You will only have an indication that Point 1 comes before Point 2, Point 2 comes before Point 3, and so on, but you will not know anything about the *space* between those points. Think back to your days as an elementary school student when you had to "line up" for some activity and then had to walk one behind each other from your classroom to the library or cafeteria. On a good day (probably when the class clowns were not too active), all your teacher could hope for was that you and your classmates traveled together in some semblance of a straight line to your destination. It would be highly unlikely that your teacher would ever even think of requiring you to walk *exactly 18 inches apart* from each other. Just a simple line of the first to the last student was typically enough to expect. Ordinal-level data work the same way. As a researcher, all you know with ordinal data is that there exists a progression of points (values) from one beginning point to an opposite ending point, but you have not much knowledge about all the spaces between those points. Another way to explain ordinal data is to realize that they provide you more than nominal-level precision of measurement but less than scale-level precision of measurement.

Ordinal-level data are frequently collected in surveys that try to measure attitudes or perspectives on social issues, particularly when a simple yes/no answer might not provide an adequate response. For example, if you wanted to explore the existence of *sexism* within a certain organization, you might start by asking *how serious* your respondents believed it was within the organization (i.e., very serious, serious) or *how often* the respondents observed sexist behavior in the organization (i.e., always, frequently, occasionally). Thus, if you were conducting a *participant observation* project on crowd behavior, you would need to develop a series of ordinal-level rankings of possible crowd behaviors ranging, for example, from *very noisy* to *very silent* and other points in between those two extremes. Similarly, if you plan a *content analysis* project on television violence, you will need to construct an instrument that captures the range of possible instances of physical violence (e.g., from bodily injury to pushing and other points in between). In all of these examples, you would be collecting your research data at an ordinal level.

Scale Level   #3

The final level of data that social science researchers work with is called *scale*. As mentioned previously in this chapter, that particular word, *scale*, is used in the SPSS computer program under the assumption that it can replace the names of two other commonly used terms, *interval* and *ratio*. The developers of the SPSS program decided that for most research situations, there exists little substantive difference between interval- and ratio-level data, so they opted to simplify the matter by declaring that both interval and ratio levels are to be noted as *scale*.

If you are interested in the nuance of difference, here it is. With interval-level data, you know the value of the space (i.e., the interval) between the measurement points, but you also know that there is no absolute zero upon which you can develop any strict mathematical comparisons. The standardized IQ test as a measurement of intellectual ability uses interval-level measurements. With that particular test, you know the numerical value between scores is one point. So, for example, you can say that a person who has an IQ score of 95 has achieved a score that is 5 points higher on the IQ test than someone who scores 90. Often, IQ scores are placed into categories so that you might see a reference to an IQ of 98 as being considered "average intelligence" or an IQ score above 110 as "gifted." While there may be some persons scoring at a "below-average" level, there is no absolute zero on the IQ scale. In other words, no person can be measured with zero intelligence. Following this logic, then, it would be mathematically incorrect to state that the person with the 95 score is 5% more intelligent than the person with a 90 score because the calculation of percentage must originate from some absolute starting point of measurement. Having equal *starting points* is the same as having an *absolute zero*. That is why we have runners and racehorses begin together at the starting line so we can precisely measure who wins the contest.

So, if interval-level data do not have an absolute zero, then you can feel confident to guess that the *ratio* level does. The ratio level provides you with the most precise level of data—so precise, in fact, that you can manipulate ratio data with the most number of mathematical calculations. That may not seem like the most exciting bit of news at this point in the book, but you will, eventually, appreciate this ability to manipulate data as you grow more familiar with the power and the ease of using SPSS to perform those calculations. The most common ratio-level data you will find in social science research include age in years or months, income in dollars, height in inches, weight in pounds and ounces, and time in days, weeks, months, or years. Ratio-level data will appear in social agency files within the context of number of client contacts, length of treatment, number of foster home placements, scores on pre- and posttest measurements of social functioning, and so on.

Summary Points to Remember

- Think of nominal-level data as simply *name tags*. Any nominal variable (e.g., location) is merely categorized into logical units (e.g., suburban, rural, urban). These logical units are called "categories" in SPSS. For **coding** purposes, any number you assign to these units (e.g., suburban = 1, rural = 2, urban = 3) has no quantitative value other than as a simple identifier or labeler or classifier.

- Think of ordinal-level data as simply *points in a line* from a beginning to an end. Any number you assign to each point has some quantitative meaning. You know that 1 comes before 2, 2 comes before 3, and so forth, and the numbers exist in some form of a ranked order from low to high, poor to excellent, never to always, disagree to agree, and so on. Ordinal data typically have an uneven number of choices (i.e., 3, 5, or 7) so that there is a midpoint in the ranking representing concepts such as "not sure" or "undecided."

- Think of scale-level data as possessing *rich quantitative meaning*. Scale data are real numbers in the sense that they mean exactly what they say. For coding purposes, 3 really means 3 and not the third place on a line from 1 to 5, nor does it represent a third category labeled as urban.

- Remember to think of scale-level data whenever you use the SPSS program and you come across what every other statistics book will call *interval* or *ratio* level. And be grateful that your life has been made a bit simpler.

- Try this self-test (no grades assigned and answers are at the end) to determine if you can identify correctly the three levels of measurement. Place N (nominal), O (ordinal), or S (scale) in the space after each statement.

    1. *Actual score* on a 100-item measurement of knowledge of HIV/AIDS (__)

    2. *Agree* or *disagree* on a series of 10 statements regarding racism (__)

    3. *Job title* on a list of 13 possible selections (__)

    4. Answers on an attitudinal survey with five possible choices ranging from *always* to *never* (__)

    5. *Number of home visits* by professional staff recorded in client case records in a nonprofit family services agency (__)

    6. When the choices are *yes, undecided,* or *no,* answers to the following question: Do you agree with the death penalty for anyone convicted of murder? (__)

(*Answers*: 1. Scale; 2. Nominal; 3. Nominal; 4. Ordinal; 5. Scale; 6. Ordinal)

Case Illustration 2.1

In a study of children's emotional and behavioral problems that used the standardized instrument, the Child Behavior Checklist (CBCL), one of the demographic variables reported was *family role* measured at the nominal level. The authors developed the following categories of the variable *family role:* mothers, fathers, foster parents, grandparents, and other. Data were collected by means of a mailed survey that included the CBCL.

The authors reported that "respondents in the two studies were predominantly mothers of the children ($n = 393$, 72.5%). Thirty-five fathers (6.5%) and 106 others (19.6% foster parents, grandparents, or other relatives) were also respondents" (Early, Gregoire, & McDonald, 2001, p. 604).

Discussion. This is a clear example of **nominal-level measurement** of a variable—in this case, the variable *family role*—because the categories within that variable are simple "names," without any inherent mathematical meaning. Thus, when the authors set up the computer program to run the data, they could have assigned the number 1 to mothers, fathers, or any of the other categories within the variable. They could have assigned the number 2 in the same manner. The number 1 has no quantitative power to it in the sense of being the first in importance or the first in line of some order of things.

Case Illustration 2.2

Researchers very commonly collect nominal variables such as race/ethnicity and marital status from their respondents. In a longitudinal follow-up study of female survivors of childhood sexual abuse, using face-to-face personal interviewing, researchers Liang, Williams, and Siegel (2006) reported their findings on these two nominal variables in the following manner: "Of the 136 participants, 83% were African American, 11% were White, less than 3% were Latina, and 2% were Native American. . . . Fifty-five percent had never married, but others were married (18%) or cohabiting (16%), separated or divorced (10%), or widowed (1%)" (p. 47).

Discussion. Some variables, for all practical purposes, will always be nominal because the reality they are measuring is naturally free of any meaningful ranking or quantitative comparisons. Such variables would include (as in this example) marital status but also citizenship, ethnicity, gender, race, religion, location (e.g., rural, suburban, and urban), and organization structure (e.g., for-profit, nonprofit, and public). While it is certainly possible to quantitatively report the number and percent of those who are married, separated, and so forth in a study, the categories themselves (e.g., whether one is married or separated or whether one self-identifies as a Buddhist or a Christian) have no meaningful quantitative structure. One marital status or religious belief is not superior to any other.

Case Illustration 2.3

A recent research project studied 133 grandparents who had primary responsibility for raising their grandchildren. One set of data the authors received was the grandparents' assessment of their grandchildren's health. Data were collected through personal interviews in the respondents' homes. The researchers presented the grandparents with a list of 12 common health problems and then asked them to check as many problems as they perceived their grandchildren had.

Based on these scale-level data, the authors reported that "the average number of health problems was 4.5 (*SD* = 3.09)" (Gerard, Landry-Meyer, & Roe, 2006, p. 366). In this case illustration, the *SD* represents the value of one standard deviation from the average number.

Discussion. In this example, the respondents were asked to indicate the absolute number of listed health problems they experienced in their grandchildren. Therefore, this variable was measured at the scale level because the data produced could be subjected to a high level of quantification and analysis. In addition to the mean and standard deviation scores in the above example, the researchers could produce (in conjunction with other data collected) what was the most frequently appearing health problem, how boys' health compared to girls' health, how the existence of health problems varied across age levels or across ethnic/racial lines, and so on. Scale-level measures allow you to conduct such mathematical comparisons precisely because you have collected data that indicate realities such as the absolute number of occurrences; the actual weight, height, or length; the score on some test or assessment; and so forth.

Activities Involving Nominal-, Ordinal-, and Scale-Level Data

Open a new SPSS file and set up each of the following variables while you are in the *Variable View* window. Assume that you, the researcher, have sent out a mailed survey to a representative sample of community residents.

1. One of the questions on a survey you sent out asked the following: What was your total family income last year as reported to the Internal Revenue Service (IRS)? You received 172 usable responses to your survey. Set up the variable *family income in dollars*. Name that variable *faminc*. Under the column *Measure*, decide whether to keep the default level as *scale* or change it to the correct level (*nominal* or *ordinal*) as appropriate.

2. Another question on your survey asked for marital status. The respondents were asked to check one of the following choices: *married, divorced/ separated, single, widow/widower*, and *choose not to answer*. Now enter in your SPSS file the variable *marital status*. Choose your own name for that variable. Under the column *Measure*, decide whether to keep the default level as *scale* or change it to the correct level (*nominal* or *ordinal*) as appropriate. A third question on your survey asked the respondents their opinion about the availability, in their immediate community, of counseling services for pregnant, unwed adolescents. The choices you provided were as follows: *always available, sometimes available, usually available, rarely available, never available*, and *I have no knowledge about availability*. Choose a name and enter this variable in your file. Under the column *Measure*, decide whether to keep the default level as *scale* or change it to the correct level (*nominal* or *ordinal*) as appropriate.

3. After asking your research participants 15 other questions, your final one is the following: Would you like to receive a summary of the findings of this research project? The choices you provided were *yes* and *no*. Select a name for that variable and enter it. Under the column *Measure*, decide whether to keep the default level as *scale* or change it to the correct level (*nominal* or *ordinal*) as appropriate.

SPSS Procedures

Coding Data as Nominal

OPEN the SPSS program.

CLICK on the *Type in Data* button in the list of choices.

NOTICE that what appears is called a *screen* in SPSS language. You are now visually in the *Data View* screen.

CLICK on the *Variable View* button at the bottom-left corner of the screen.

NOTICE that you are now in the *Variable View* screen.

CLICK on the first empty cell at the top-left corner of the screen directly under the column labeled *Name*.

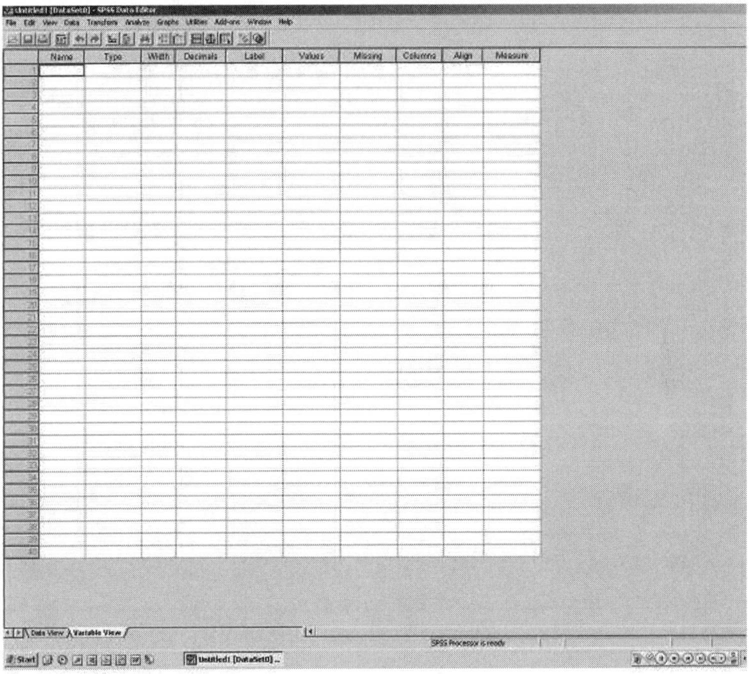

Figure 2.1   Blank SPSS Screen of Variable View

CLICK on the cell under *Name* and TYPE IN the letters *gen*.

REMEMBER that the variable name in this column is merely a short-hand version of the full variable name. Since that shorthand version needs to make sense only to you, choose a simple name that you, and not anyone else, can easily recall, for example, *eth* for the variable *race/ethnicity*. You are required in SPSS to enter in this space a name that begins with a letter, not a number, and contains no space in it. For example, *test1* or *test_1* is acceptable, but *test 1* is not acceptable.

ENGAGE the *Enter* key on your computer's keyboard.

NOTICE that default (i.e., automatic) choices appear spontaneously all across the first row of cells in a horizontal line.

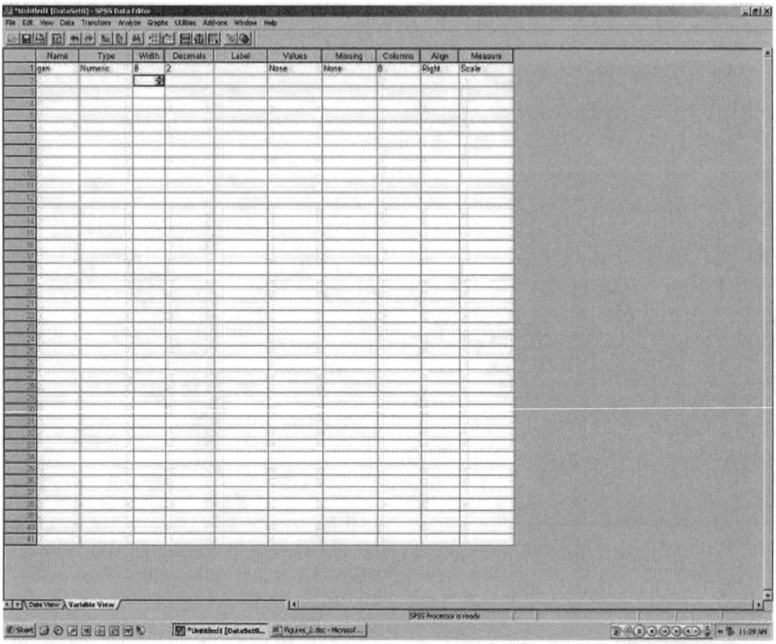

Figure 2.2   Initial SPSS Screen of Variable View of Variable *gen*

DO NOTHING in the cell labeled *Type*. LEAVE the default *numeric* as is.

DO NOTHING in the cell labeled *Width*. LEAVE the default *8* as is.

CLICK in the bottom-right corner of the cell labeled *Decimals*. Then CLICK on the down arrow until the number *0* appears.

REMEMBER that, for visual purposes, you probably do not need any decimal-based numeric values. Social science research typically does not report any numeric value to two decimal places unless you are measuring variables such as grade point average, weight in pounds and ounces, temperature in degrees, height or length in feet and inches, or income in dollars and cents.

ENTER the word *Gender* in the cell under the heading *Label*.

REMEMBER that the *Label* column allows you the opportunity to present the full and complete name of the variable you are entering. Whatever you enter in this cell will be printed as the title of any table or figure that will appear in the *Output* section of all SPSS analyses from this point on. Therefore, choose carefully how you label the variable in this cell for that decision will have long-term implications for the way that your output data look. In the cell with the word *none* already appearing under the heading *Values*, CLICK in the shaded block on the right. The *Value Labels* window will appear. In the space to the right of *Value*, TYPE IN the number *1*. In the space to the right of *Value Label*, TYPE IN the word *female*.

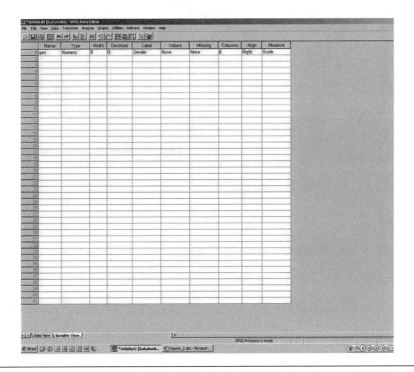

Figure 2.3   SPSS Screen of Label *Gender*

CLICK on the ADD button on the left.

REPEAT the last two steps. In the space to the right of *Value*, TYPE IN the number *2*. In the space to the right of *Value Label*, TYPE IN the word *male*. Do not forget to CLICK on the ADD button on the left.

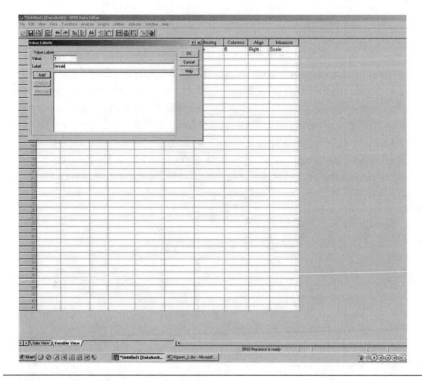

Figure 2.4   SPSS Screen of Value Labels

CLICK the OK button at the top-right corner of the window.

DO NOTHING in the cell labeled *Missing*. LEAVE the default *None* as is.

DO NOTHING in the cell labeled *Columns*. LEAVE the default *8* as is.

CLICK on the cell under the heading *Align*. When the drop-down menu appears, CLICK on *Left, Center,* or *Right* depending on where you want the data to be positioned in each cell when you are in the *Data View* screen.

CLICK on the cell under the heading *Measure*. When the drop-down menu appears, CLICK on the option *Nominal*. You have now completed the coding setup for the variable *gen* measured at the nominal level. If you click on the *Data View* button at the bottom left, you should see a screen that lists the variable *gen* at the top of an empty column.

Coding Data as Ordinal

Once your SPSS file is open, do the following:

CLICK on the *Variable View* button at the bottom-left corner of the screen.

NOTICE that you are now in the *Variable View* screen.

CLICK on the first empty cell at the top-left corner of the screen directly under the box labeled *Name*.

NOTICE that default (i.e., automatic) choices appear spontaneously all across the first row of cells in a horizontal line.

CLICK on the cell under *Name* and TYPE IN the letters *inc*.

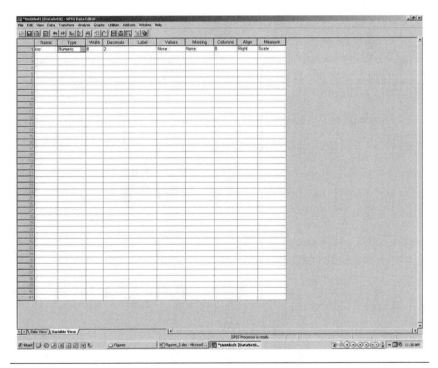

Figure 2.5   Initial SPSS Screen of Variable View of Variable *inc*

REMEMBER that the variable name in this column is merely a shorthand version of the full variable name. Since that shorthand version needs to make sense only to you, choose a simple name that you, and not anyone else, can easily recall, for example, *eth* for the variable *race/ ethnicity*. You are required in SPSS to enter in this space a name that begins with a letter, not a number, and contains no space in it. For example, *test1* or *test_1* is acceptable, but *test 1* is not acceptable.

ENGAGE the *Enter* key on your computer's keyboard.

DO NOTHING in the cell labeled *Type*. LEAVE the default *numeric* as is.

DO NOTHING in the cell labeled *Width*. LEAVE the default *8* as is.

CLICK in the bottom-right corner of the cell labeled *Decimals*. Then CLICK on the down arrow until the number *0* appears.

REMEMBER that, for visual purposes, you probably do not need any decimal-based numeric values. Social science research typically does not report any numeric value to two decimal places unless you are measuring variables such as grade point average, weight in pounds and ounces, temperature in degrees, height or length in feet and inches, or income in dollars and cents.

ENTER the phrase *Income by Ranks* in the cell under the heading *Label*.

REMEMBER that the *Label* column allows you the opportunity to present the full and complete name of the variable you are entering. Whatever you enter in this cell will be printed as the title of any table or figure that will appear in the *Output* section of all SPSS analyses from this point on. Therefore, choose carefully how you label the variable in this cell for that decision will have long-term implications for the way that your output data look.

CLICK on the cell under the heading *Values*. The *Value Labels* window will appear. In the space to the right of *Value*, TYPE IN the number *1*. In the space to the right of *Value Label*, TYPE IN the phrase *Up to 10,000*.

CLICK on the ADD button on the left.

REPEAT this step. In the space to the right of *Value*, TYPE IN the number *2*. In the space to the right of *Label*, TYPE IN the phrase *10,001 to 20,000*.

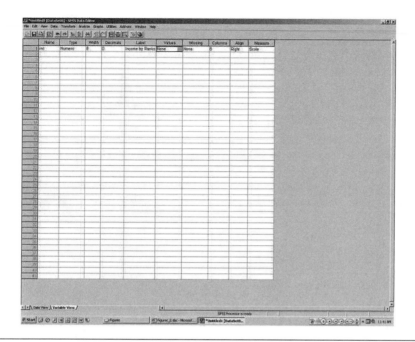

Figure 2.6   SPSS Screen of Variable *Label*

REPEAT this step. In the space to the right of *Value*, TYPE IN the number *3*. In the space to the right of *Label*, TYPE IN the phrase *20,001 to 30,000*.

CLICK on the ADD button on the left.

REPEAT this step. In the space to the right of *Value*, TYPE IN the number *4*. In the space to the right of *Label*, TYPE IN the phrase *30,001 to 40,000*.

CLICK on the ADD button on the left.

REPEAT this step. In the space to the right of *Value*, TYPE IN the number *5*. In the space to the right of *Label*, TYPE IN the phrase *40,001 or more*.

CLICK on the ADD button on the left.

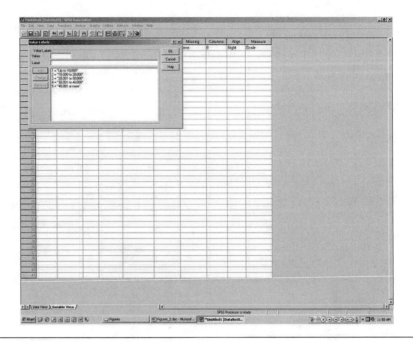

Figure 2.7   SPSS Screen of Value Labels

CLICK the OK button at the top-right corner of the window.

DO NOTHING in the cell labeled *Missing*. LEAVE the default *None* as is.

DO NOTHING in the cell labeled *Columns*. LEAVE the default *8* as is.

CLICK on the cell under the heading *Align*. When the drop-down menu appears, CLICK on *Left, Center,* or *Right* depending on where you want the data to be positioned in each cell when you are in the *Data View* screen.

CLICK on the cell under the heading *Measure*. When the drop-down menu appears, CLICK on the option *Ordinal*. You have now completed the coding setup for the variable *inc* measured at the ordinal level. If you click on the *Data View* button at the bottom left, you should see a screen that lists the variable *inc* at the top of an empty column.

Coding Data as Scale

Once your SPSS file is open, do the following:

CLICK on the *Variable View* button at the bottom-left corner of the screen.

NOTICE that you are now in the *Variable View* screen.

CLICK on the first empty cell at the top-left corner of the screen directly under the box labeled *Name*.

NOTICE that default (i.e., automatic) choices appear spontaneously all across the first row of cells in a horizontal line.

CLICK on the cell under *Name* and TYPE IN the letters *age*.

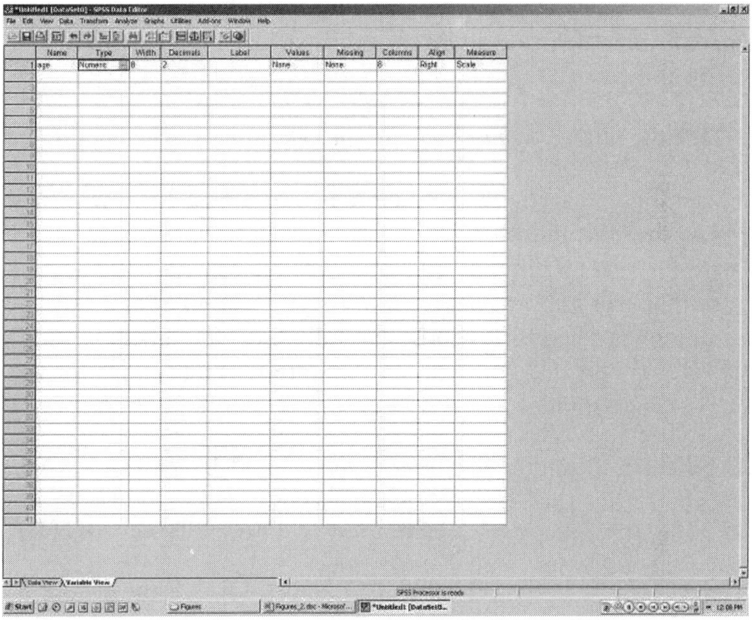

Figure 2.8   Initial SPSS Screen of Variable View of Variable *age*

REMEMBER that the variable name in this column is merely a short-hand version of the full variable name. Since that shorthand version needs to make sense only to you, choose a simple name that you, and not anyone else, can easily recall, for example, *eth* for the variable *race/ ethnicity*. You are required in SPSS to enter in this space a name that begins with a letter, not a number, and contains no space in it. For example, *test1* or *test_1* is acceptable, but *test 1* is not acceptable.

ENGAGE the *Enter* key on your computer's keyboard.

DO NOTHING in the cell labeled *Type*. LEAVE the default *numeric* as is.

DO NOTHING in the cell labeled *Width*. LEAVE the default *8* as is.

CLICK in the bottom-right corner of the cell labeled *Decimals*. Then CLICK on the down arrow until the number *0* appears.

REMEMBER that, for visual purposes, you probably do not need any decimal-based numeric values. Social science research typically does not report any numeric value to two decimal places unless you are measuring variables such as grade point average, weight in pounds and ounces, temperature in degrees, height or length in feet and inches, or income in dollars and cents.

ENTER the phrase *Age in Years* in the cell under the heading *Label*.

REMEMBER that the *Label* column allows you the opportunity to present the full and complete name of the variable you are entering. Whatever you enter in this cell will be printed as the title of any table or figure that will appear in the *Output* section of all SPSS analyses from this point on. Therefore, choose carefully how you label the variable in this cell for that decision will have long-term implications for the way your output data look.

DO NOTHING in the cell labeled *Values*. LEAVE the default *None* as is.

DO NOTHING in the cell labeled *Missing*. LEAVE the default *None* as is.

DO NOTHING in the cell labeled *Columns*. LEAVE the default *8* as is.

CLICK on the cell under the heading *Align*. When the drop-down menu appears, CLICK on *Left, Center,* or *Right* depending on where you want the data to be positioned in each cell when you are in the *Data View* screen.

CLICK on the cell under the heading *Measure*. When the drop-down menu appears, MAKE SURE the option *Scale* is clicked. You have now completed the coding setup for the variable *age* measured at the scale level. If you click on the *Data View* button at the bottom left, you should see a screen that lists the variable *age* at the top of an empty column.

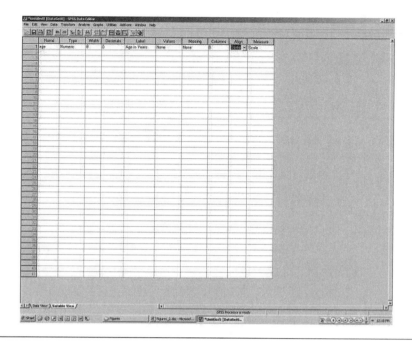

Figure 2.9   Completed SPSS Screen of Variable View at Scale Level

References

Early, T. J., Gregoire, T. K., & McDonald, T. P. (2001). An assessment of the utility of the Child Behavior Checklist/4–18 for social work practice. *Research on Social Work Practice, 11*(5), 597–612.

Gerard, J. M., Landry-Meyer, L., & Roe, J. G. (2006). Grandparents raising grandchildren: The role of social support in coping with caregiving challenges. *International Journal of Aging and Human Development, 62*(4), 359–383.

Leary, J. D., Brennan, E. M., & Briggs, H. E. (2005). The African American Adolescent Respect Scale: A measure of prosocial attitude. *Research on Social Work Practice, 15*(6), 462–469.

Liang, B., Williams, L. M., & Siegel, J. A. (2006). Relational outcomes of childhood sexual trauma in female survivors: A longitudinal study. *Journal of Interpersonal Violence, 21*(1), 42–57.

3

Presenting Data in Tables

I always find that statistics are hard to swallow and impossible to digest. The only one I can ever remember is that if all the people who go to sleep in church were laid end to end, they would be a lot more comfortable.

—Mrs. Robert A. Taft, cited on
www.quotegarden.com/statistics

Introductory Case Illustration

In a Swedish study of individuals who had a history of childhood or adolescent sexual abuse (CASA), the authors produced a table (see Table 3.1) that portrayed the variable of gender broken down by age, ethnicity, education, relation (i.e., nature of the relationship with the offender), and place of residence (Steel & Herlitz, 2005, p. 1144).

Discussion. This is a very common type of table that you should be familiar with as a researcher since you will need to create tables such as this in order to present your data to your audience. This particular example from Steel and Herlitz (2005) is a fairly complex table that contains, quite efficiently, a large amount of information across several variables. Reading across the top, horizontally, you see that the data are first divided into Males and Females columns and then subdivided again, by gender, according to whether the individuals had a history of childhood or adolescent sexual abuse. Scanning down

Table 3.1   Demographic Information for Participants

	Males (N = 1475)		Females (N = 1335)	
	No CASA (N = 1419)	CASA (N = 83)	No CASA (N = 1206)	CASA (N = 185)
Current Age				
Mean	46	43	46	41
Range	23–79	23–77	23–79	23–74
Ethnicity (%)				
Scandinavian	93	94	96	96
European	3	2	3	2
All Other Nationalities	4	4	1	2
Education (%)				
Primary	24	12	21	15
Secondary	54	54	50	57
University	21	32	28	25
Other	1	2	1	3
Relation (%)				
Steady Relation	77	66	78	74
Temporary Relation	9	9	2	10
No Relation	4	15	20	16
Missing	10	10	0	0
Place of Residence (%)				
Large-Sized City	18	27	20	22
Medium-Sized City	29	29	30	29
Small City or Countryside	45	30	42	45
Abroad	8	14	8	4

SOURCE: Steel and Herlitz (2005).

the left side of the table, you learn how all of those reported numbers are further partitioned into variables such as current age, ethnicity, education, and so on. What could be made clearer is the fact that most of the numbers are percentage values, while the mean and range values for the variable, *current age,* are whole-number values.

In this chapter, you will learn how to place your data in tables in a simple and understandable manner.

This chapter and the next, Chapter 4, both cover various ways of presenting what are called **frequency distributions** in statistics. In plain language, frequency distributions are simply compilations of numbers that relate directly to each variable you are studying in your research or program evaluation project. Frequency distributions are quite common in statistical reports since they can be calculated for variables at each of the levels of measurement: nominal, ordinal, or scale. While frequency distributions can be reported very simply and specifically (e.g., exactly how many people surveyed were 21 years old, how many were 22 years old), most frequency distributions in social services research are reported in a *summary* format (e.g., the average age of all respondents, the average ages of males and females). These summary frequency distributions are also called *grouped frequency distributions* in some statistics books.

The reason why you summarize or group your frequency distributions should be fairly obvious by now: You want to do everything you possibly can to assist the consumer in understanding what you are presenting.

Frequency Distributions and Levels of Data

Examples of nominal-level frequency distributions would be the number and percent of females and males who responded to a mailed survey (females, $N = 79$ [52%]; males, $N = 73$ [48%]) or the number and percent of staff by job title in a residential human services agency (administrators, $N = 5$ [7%]; counselors, $N = 33$ [49%]; recreational therapists, $N = 12$ [17%]; teachers, $N = 9$ [13%]; and social workers, $N = 10$ [14%]).

Ordinal-level variables tend to produce frequency distributions relating to rankings that report, for example, the following:

- The personal feelings of respondents about the issue of abortion: always allowed, $N = 33$ (24%); sometimes allowed, $N = 29$ (21%); undecided, $N = 14$ (10%); rarely allowed, $N = 25$ (18%); and never allowed, $N = 39$ (28%)
- The self-reported frequency of alcohol use: several times a day, $N = 123$ (17%); once a day, $N = 144$ (20%); only on weekends, $N = 89$ (12%); once a month, $N = 159$ (22%); and never, $N = 210$ (29%)

Finally, variables measured at the scale level yield frequency distributions that are so precise that they allow the researcher to make meaningful comparisons and inferences across categories. For example, you could report the average age (e.g., 19.3 years), the standard deviation (e.g., 1.67), range of average ages (e.g., 16 to 21), and the average speed (e.g., 69.5 mph) of all citizens stopped by police for speeding violations on a particular day for each town, city, or county in a geographic area. Another example would be to list the average number of days each month of in-patient hospitalization in a large mental health facility, cross-referenced by gender and official psychiatric diagnosis. This latter frequency distribution could provide you with an interesting perspective (a "bird's-eye view") of that mental health facility's hospitalization patterns, particularly how those patterns might be influenced by month of the year, gender, or diagnostic classifications.

Remember that frequency distributions are simply the numbers (numerical values) contained in each variable that you have collected by means of some strategy (e.g., survey, content analysis) during your research activities. Having collected those data, you now want to present those numbers to your readers in some composite and easily understood manner.

Reporting Frequency Distributions

There exist three distinct ways to report summaries of frequency distributions.

First, you can *narrate* the results in a sentence or series of sentences. For example, "Of the 197 people who responded to this survey, 56% ($N = 110$) were female, and 44% ($N = 87$) were male." Narration of frequency distributions is typically recommended whenever you are presenting very simple numbers, without many categories. Narration typically works well for variables with two or three categories, such as gender (female, male), location (urban, suburban, rural), or any variable that is measured by a yes/no response (Have you ever been convicted of a crime?).

Second, you can place the numbers and their corresponding variables in a table, which is the subject of the rest of this chapter.

Finally, you can provide your readers with a figure containing visual graphics representing the numbers and variables. You will learn all about figures in Chapter 4.

Presenting Data in Tables

It is probably safe to say that a number of people, if pressed for honesty, would disclose that they typically give only a quick, cursory glance at any table they come across in professional journals, newspapers, or magazines. Some might even admit to totally skipping over tables as if they were a distraction from the narrative text they are reading. Why do tables get such a bad reputation? The common answers are that tables are boring, useless, or too difficult to understand.

In fact, those charges might be perfectly valid if the reader is presented with a poorly conceptualized and ineptly produced table that comes across as a busy jumble of numbers thrown together awkwardly in columns and rows. But (and this is an essential *but*), if you develop a table with careful forethought and fashion it in a simple, straightforward manner, it can serve as an extremely effective medium for presenting a lot of data in a very efficient, space-saving format. In fact, your audience might even enjoy reading your tables rather than sulk away from them in frustration.

You, as a social service researcher and program evaluator, will come face-to-face with numerical tables in at least two kinds of situations. First, you will be extracting information from tables you find in newspapers, weekly magazines, professional journal articles, government reports, and book chapters. Second, you will eventually have to produce some tables of your own as you complete those final research reports or program evaluation summaries. Throughout the rest of this chapter, you will find enough information to give you the knowledge and skills to be an inquisitive, discerning consumer of other people's tables as well as a careful, meticulous producer of your own frequency distributions in tables.

To get right to the point: Tables should be an effective and efficient way to present a lot of numbers as they relate to one or more variables. Many different kinds of tables are possible, and the full range of formats can be found in most standard textbooks on statistics. For our purposes in this chapter, we will concentrate on two of the most common types of tables that you will come across in the professional social services literature: the *simple grouped data* table and the *complex grouped data* table. You have seen these all your life in newspapers, in magazines, and on television, especially around national election time, when the reporter or commentator wanted to focus your attention on some recent polling data.

Simple Grouped Data Table

A simple grouped data table offers a quantitative view of only one variable at a time. Such a table would provide, for example, an overview of the gender of those who voted in the last national election. The results could be reported in the following manner. "Drawing on the responses from an availability sample of 500 eligible voters in the last national election, Table 3.2 presents the breakdown by gender."

Table 3.2	Number and Percent of Voters in the Last County Election by Gender	
Gender	*Number*	*Percent*
Female	295	59%
Male	205	41%
Total	500	100%

Notice several important points about this table.

First, the one variable (gender) is listed on the left, or vertical **axis,** of the table, while the frequency distributions (in this case, only the number and percent are reported) are presented on the top right, or horizontal axis.

Second, a lead-in sentence precedes the table itself, which provides the reader with some relevant background information, especially where and how the data were collected. In this example, we know that the data came from an "availability sample of 500 eligible voters" who just happened to be at a particular mall on a certain day and also just happened to stop and answer the questions of some researcher. Thus, we know that this was a very localized survey with no random selection of subjects, and therefore it should not be generalized to any other context or any other group. A further discussion of random and nonrandom sampling will take place in Chapters 7 and 8 in this textbook. Indeed, sampling is one of those essential topics that is always included in any standard treatment of social science research, so you might also check the textbook you used in your research methods classes.

Third, the table has a number, "Table 3.2," followed by a title, "Number and Percent of Voters. . . ." The title is simply a very brief phrase that captures the essence of what the table will present. *Not too long and not too short* is a good rule to follow when deciding on a title for your table. Use key words and phrases to transmit what the reader will find in the table. Also, tables should be numbered consecutively within a paper or report of any kind so they can be easily referenced in any discussion that follows. Think of the table's title as a preliminary statement (a sort of "heads-up") to the readers to alert them to what the numbers mean even before they start to look at them.

Fourth, this table has been produced with the Microsoft Word software program commonly found on most computers today, whether those computers are PCs or Macs. The table consists of a series of columns and rows of numbers separated by a few horizontal lines—all possible with any standard word-processing software. You should keep the complete SPSS output for your own use but then create your tables by using any standard word-processing software program. Follow this suggestion and your tables will be picture-perfect.

Complex Grouped Data Table

The second type of table, a complex grouped data table, presents two or more variables, all of which have multiple categories within them. Variables such as *religion* and *job title* or *gender* and *professional degree* are examples of variables that you might want to present in a complex grouped data table.

This type of table, encompassing two or more variables at the same time, is also referred to in statistics books as a **crosstabulation table** or simply a *crosstab* for short. Such a table tells you, for example, that "in the community of Mountain View, a total 10% random sample ($N = 2,057$) of eligible voters in each age category were asked what political party they would vote for if the national election were held today. The results, broken down by age category and political party affiliation, appear in Table 3.3."

Note the following additional points about this table. The word *percent* in the title is enclosed in brackets ( ) as a convenient way to tell the reader that any number in the table that is inside brackets is actually a percentage, based on 100. This is a *code* used by many researchers to avoid using the percent sign (%) everywhere throughout the table. This procedure also simplifies the table so that it does not appear overly elaborate with a lot of repetitive symbols. Become familiar with this procedure—it is very frequently used, and it is something you should consider when creating your own tables. Also, you

Table 3.3 Number and (Percent) of Voters by Age and Political Party Affiliation

Age	Democrat	Republican	Independent	Total
18–29	175 (42)	182 (43)	63 (15)	420 (100)
30–45	185 (46)	170 (43)	45 (11)	400 (100)
46–50	162 (50)	145 (44)	18 (06)	325 (100)
51–65	266 (42)	295 (47)	71 (11)	632 (100)
65+	116 (41)	141 (50)	23 (08)	280 (100)
Total	904 (44)	933 (45)	220 (11)	2,057 (100)

should note that the total numbers and percentages are arranged by rows *horizontally* according to age categories (see the first column on the left), and the final row on the bottom lists the total individual numbers and percent of Democrats, Republicans, and Independents surveyed for this study.

As any textbook in statistics can attest to, there are many variations on the types of tables that are labeled here as *simple* grouped data and *complex* group data tables. No matter what type they are, tables come in a wide variety of shapes and lengths, as the additional case illustrations below will show. When you want to use a table, be creative and make sure that it does what it should do: present numbers and variables in an efficient but easily understandable manner. Try not to get carried away by stuffing *too much* data into any one table, thus filling it with a lot of complicated details. Create several short tables rather than one that is heavily loaded with a lot of variables and numbers. Keep your tables clear and clean, and your readers will compliment you by reading through them rather than skipping over them.

Accuracy in Reporting Frequency Distributions

Frequency distributions carry with them an inherent hazard. If not monitored carefully, they can sometimes present data that are confusing and even misrepresentative. Fortunately, most times these misrepresentations are not deliberate. For example, if you were to report that during the month of February, there was a 300% increase in newly opened protective service cases in one unit of a public child welfare office, most people would interpret that as a very large increase. After all, a 300% increase sounds like a lot. However, a different picture emerges if that high percentage represented the fact that eight new cases were opened in February compared to only two cases that were opened in January (i.e., two cases in February = no increase over January, four cases = 100% increase, six cases = 200%, and eight cases = 300%). So, it is not incorrect, technically speaking, to report a 300% increase in this example, but it is misleading.

A general rule to keep you out of this embarrassing situation is this: *Always report both the number and percent of the total* whenever you provide numbers in a frequency distribution. The same rule applies whether you are presenting your data in narrative format, in tables, or in figures, as you will see in Chapter 4. In a narrative format, you can accomplish this by either starting with the number followed by the percent, as in, "One hundred forty-three females ($N = 45\%$) responded . . ." or starting with the percentage followed by the number as in, "Forty-five percent of the respondents were female ($N = 143$)." In tables, you can simplify your presentation, as well as avoid the issue of misrepresentation, by telling the reader in the title of the table exactly what your list of numbers means. For example, if you state, "Table 4: Percent and (Number) of Professional Staff, by Job Title, Hired During Fiscal Year 2006," then the reader knows that the numbers "15 (12)" in the column opposite the row labeled "Teachers" means that 15% of the staff hired that year were teachers, and that percentage represents 12 newly hired teachers. Of course, you could also choose to represent that row and column as "Teachers 15% $N = 12$" if you were not overly concerned with overloading the reader with a long list of % symbols and N symbols.

A Recommendation About Tables Produced in SPSS

As mentioned above, and as you will soon discover when you generate crosstab tables in SPSS, you will have the ability to easily copy and paste those tables into your final report. Certainly, you will want to copy those tables into a backup computer file or onto a word-processing document for your own use and as a record of your statistical operations. However, consistent with the principle of keeping tables as simple as possible, you are recommended not to copy and paste SPSS tables directly into your final report. The SPSS output tables are full of important information—some of which you need directly, but much of which is background information that the reader has little interest in or a burning need to know. To put it simply: SPSS output tables are much too complex for you to include them as presented in your final report.

You should take out of those SPSS tables all the relevant information you need to create your own table in Word or WordPerfect or in any other word-processing software you use. This is easily accomplished by using common keystrokes to create horizontal lines across the page (there is no need to produce vertical lines) and columns of numbers down the page. Tables produced this way need only one more input from you: a title that provides a number (e.g., Table 3) and a brief statement that denotes what is in the table (e.g., Number and Average Age of Children in Foster care in Agency XXX at Initial Placement and at Case Closure, 2000–2006).

Please note that all the tables produced in this book, either in the chapters or in the case illustrations, are individually created by word-processing software, not copied fully from any SPSS output.

Summary Points to Remember

- Frequency distributions are simply the numbers (numerical values) contained in each variable that you have collected during your research or program evaluation activities.

- A table is one way, but not the only way, to present your data to your audience.

- Tables do require a bit of extra work on the part of the consumer (i.e., the person reading your report), so you, the table creator, should be willing to put in some additional effort too.

- Never simply copy and paste the tables or boxes that appear in any SPSS output window. Instead, create your own tables in Word or any other word-processing program, using the relevant information provided in that SPSS output.

Case Illustration 3.1

In their Table 3: Failure Rates for Clients Receiving SAFE and/or R&R Services, Hendricks, Werner, and Turinetti (2006, p. 712) illustrate clearly the **frequency** and percentage of research respondents who participated in two related treatment programs. In this project, SAFE refers to a 14-day group treatment intervention for spousal abusers, and R&R refers to a second treatment program that used cognitive restructuring techniques. All subjects were measured on their rate of recidivism back into spousal abuse.

Table 3.4	Failure Rates for Clients Receiving SAFE and/or R&R Services					
	SAFE					*Total*
	Completed[a]	*%*	*Incomplete*[a]	*%*	*#*	*%*
Referred to R&R	4 out of 17	23.5	7 out of 17	41.2	11 out of 34	32.4
No R&R Referral	12 out of 134	9.0	12 out of 32	37.5	24 out of 166	14.4
Total	16 out of 151	10.6	19 out of 49	38.8	35 out of 200	17.5

SOURCE: Hendricks, Werner, and Turinetti (2006).

a. Numbers indicate the number of clients recidivating out to the possible number.

Discussion. In this fairly simple and straightforward table, the authors present the numbers and percentage of those who either completed or did not complete each of the two treatment programs. Total numbers and percentage are also provided in the columns on the far right. This is a good example of a basic 2-by-2 crosstabulation table that represents two variables (SAFE and R&R), each possessing only two categories (completed/not completed SAFE and referral to/no referral to R&R).

Case Illustration 3.2

Weiss (2005, p. 382) conducted an international survey of graduating BSW social work students from seven countries on their interest in working with the elderly during their professional career. He offered a comprehensive profile of his 679 respondents across the variables of gender, age, and marital status by their individual countries of residence.

Discussion. This is another clear example of how a large amount of data can be compressed into a small space quite efficiently. In this case illustration, you can quickly view the numbers and percent of 679 students, by country, broken down by gender, age categories, and marital status. Notice also that this table is not the product of any one SPSS output but was produced by a standard word-processing program such as Microsoft Word or WordPerfect.

Table 3.5 Demographic Characteristics of Student Participants, by Country ($N = 679$)

Country	N	Gender				Age				Marital Status			
		Female		Male		20–30		>30		Married		Unmarried	
		n	%	n	%	n	%	n	%	n	%	n	%
Australia	62	49	82	11	18	32	52	29	48	29	49	30	51
Brazil	95	83	94	5	6	63	71	25	28	17	20	70	80
Britain	64	57	90	6	10	41	66	21	34	21	36	38	64
Germany	141	82	66	43	34	102	80	25	20	56	46	65	54
Hungary	101	81	84	16	16	76	80	19	20	36	40	53	60
Israel	138	125	93	10	7	124	92	10	8	47	35	88	65
United States	78	68	88	9	12	72	92	6	8	24	31	54	69

SOURCE: Weiss (2005).

NOTE: Some of the totals among variables may not equal the specified N because of missing data.

Case Illustration 3.3

A simple, straightforward table was included in one study to describe the types of diagnoses for depression that the respondents experienced. In this table (see Table 3.6), the acronym MDE stands for a *major depressive episode*, and respondents may have been placed in the categories of MDE, MDE—partial remission, minor depression, double depression, or no diagnosis (Floyd et al., 2006, p. 287).

Table 3.6 Depression Diagnoses			
	Assessment Time		
Diagnosis	*Pretreatment (n)*	*Posttreatment (n)*	*Two-Year Follow-Up (n)*
MDE	16	2	3
MDE, Partial Remission	2	16	3
Minor Depression	3	0	0
Double Depression	2	0	0
No Diagnosis	0	5	17

SOURCE: Floyd et al. (2006).

NOTE: MDE = major depressive episode; *n* represents number of participants.

Discussion. These authors provide you with an example of a 3-by-5 crosstabulation table that compares two variables (assessment time and diagnosis), one of which has three possible categories and the other has five possible categories. Thus, you can quickly view all 15 possible combinations of the two variables. Notice that the symbol "*(n)*" is a shorthand code to inform the reader that the digits in the columns are absolute numbers rather than percentages.

Activities Involving Data in Tables

1. Using Data Set 1 (Client Demographics and Treatment Results), create individual tables showing the frequencies and percentages of the variables *gen* and *eth*.

2. From the same Data Set 1 (Client Demographics and Treatment Results), produce a table that displays the frequency and percentages of the variable *att2*.

3. Using Data Set 4 (Client Satisfaction Survey), produce a table for the variable *marital*.

4. Create a table indicating the sum for the variables *base1*, *base2*, and *base3* from Data Set 3 (Client Single-Case Evaluation).

SPSS Procedures

Frequencies and Percentages (for Nominal and Ordinal Data)

In either the *Data View* or *Variable View* window, do the following:

CLICK on the *Analyze* menu at the top of the window.

PLACE THE CURSOR over the *Descriptive Statistics* choice.

CLICK on *Frequencies*.

CLICK on the variable(s) you are interested in. Do not mix nominal and ordinal variables together.

CLICK on the right-pointing button in the middle of the window.

NOTE that, for this procedure, you do not have to engage the *Statistics* button at the bottom of the window because the production of *Frequency* and *Percent* are the default outcomes.

CLICK on the *OK* button at the top right of the window.

Applying the SPSS Output

In the output window, do the following:

NOTICE on the left that there is a running list of sections of the output. This is similar to a "Table of Contents" that is automatically produced for all of the output in sequential order. You can return quickly to an earlier procedure or piece of output by simply clicking on any item in the list. This list will be especially useful whenever you run several statistical procedures at one time.

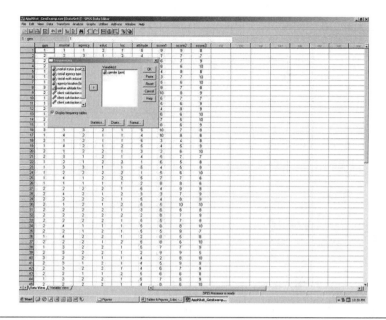

Figure 3.1   SPSS Screen Shot of *Frequencies*

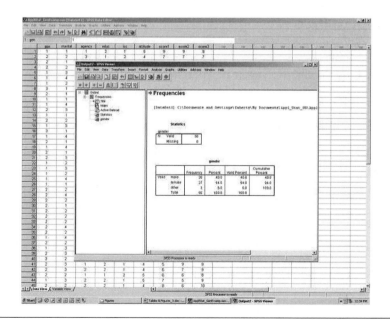

Figure 3.2   SPSS Screen Shot of *Frequencies* Output

On the right of the output window, do the following:

NOTICE that there are the four columns of numbers, labeled *Frequency, Percent, Valid Percent,* and *Cumulative Percent.* For your purposes (i.e., to construct a table in which you present your data), consider only the first column (Frequency) and the third column (Valid Percent). The second column (Percent) is rarely used because it excludes any missing data in its calculations. Likewise, the last column (Cumulative Percent) provides information that is seldom, if ever, considered important to most social service researchers.

INCLUDE only the data found in the Frequency and Valid Percent columns into your table. To return to the *Data View* or *Variable View,* CLICK on the close button [**X**] at the top right of the window.

Sum (for Scale Data)

In either the *Data View* or *Variable View* window, do the following:

CLICK on the *Analyze* menu from the top of the window.

PLACE THE CURSOR over the *Descriptive Statistics* choice.

CLICK on *Frequencies.*

CLICK on the *Reset* button if any variables are appearing in the right box.

CLICK on the variable(s) you are interested in. List only scale-level variables.

CLICK on the right-pointing button in the middle of the window.

CLICK on the *Statistics* button at the bottom of the window.

CLICK on the *Sum, Minimum,* and *Maximum* buttons.

CLICK on the *Continue* button.

CLICK on the *OK* button at the top right of the *Frequencies* window.

Applying the SPSS Output

In the output box labeled *Statistics,* do the following:

NOTICE the number of valid cases (*N*) and the number (if any) of missing cases. Missing cases indicate that one or more of the cells in the *Data View* window is (are) empty.

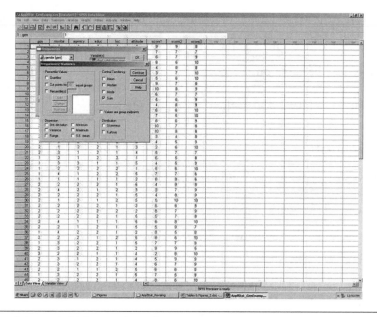

Figure 3.3   SPSS Screen Shot of *Frequencies: Statistics*

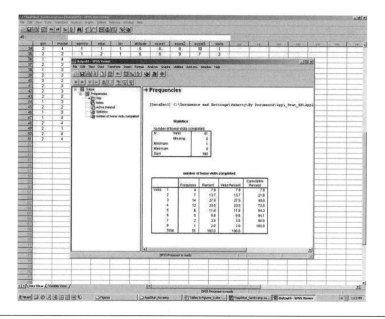

Figure 3.4   SPSS Screen Shot of *Frequencies* Output

NOTICE the values listed for the sum, minimum, and maximum categories.

INCLUDE these values in the table you produce.

IGNORE the table on the bottom that lists the individual frequencies and percentages. To return to the *Data View* or *Variable View,* CLICK on the close button [X] at the top right of the window.

Crosstabulation Table (for Nominal or Ordinal Data)

In either the *Data View* or *Variable View* window, do the following:

CLICK on the *Analyze* menu from the top of the window.

PLACE THE CURSOR over the *Descriptive Statistics* choice.

CLICK on *Crosstabs.*

CLICK on the first of the two variables you are interested in comparing with each other. Include only nominal- or ordinal-level variables.

CLICK on the right-pointing button in the middle of the window to the left of the box labeled *Row(s).*

CLICK on the second of the two variables you are interested in comparing with each other. Include only nominal- or ordinal-level variables.

CLICK on the right-pointing button in the middle of the window to the left of the box labeled *Column(s).*

CLICK on the *Cells* button at the bottom of the *Crosstabs* window. Under *Percentages,* on the left, CLICK in the small box next to the word *Columns.*

CLICK on the *Continue* button. Then CLICK on the *OK* button at the top right of the window.

Applying the SPSS Output

In the output box labeled *Crosstabs,* do the following:

IGNORE the first output labeled *Case Processing Summary.*

NOTICE the number (Count) and the percent (%) values for the variables contained in each cell of the crosstabulation table.

INCLUDE these values in the new table you produce.

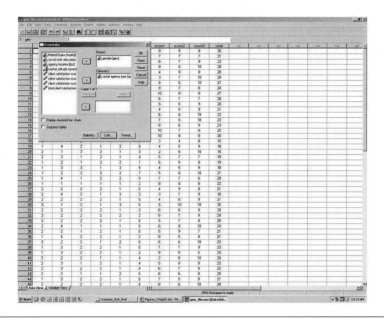

Figure 3.5   SPSS Screen Shot of *Crosstabs*

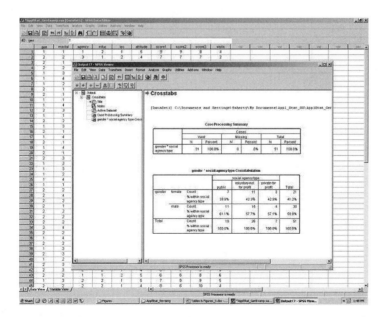

Figure 3.6   SPSS Screen Shot of *Crosstabs* Output

References

Floyd, M., Rohen, N., Shakelford, J. A. M., Hubbard, K. L., Parnell, M. B., Scogin, F., et al. (2006). Two-year follow-up bibliotherapy and individual cognitive therapy for depressed older adults. *Behavior Modification, 30*(3), 281–294.

Hendricks, B., Werner, T., & Turinetti, G. J. (2006). Recidivism among spousal abusers: Predictions and program evaluation. *Journal of Interpersonal Violence, 21*(6), 703–716.

Steel, J. L., & Herlitz, C. A. (2005). The association between childhood and adolescent sexual abuse and proxies for sexual risk behavior: A random sample of the general population of Sweden. *Child Abuse & Neglect, 29*, 1141–1153.

Weiss, I. (2005). Innovations in gerontological social work education in working with the elderly: A cross-national study of graduating social work students. *Journal of Social Work Education, 41*(3), 379–391.

4

Presenting Data in Figures

It is proven that the celebration of birthdays is healthy. Statistics shows that those people who celebrate the most birthdays become the oldest.

—S. den Hartog, cited on
www.elstu.edu/~gcramsey/CorrReg

Introductory Case Illustration

In a comprehensive study of children and adolescents with a dual diagnosis of substance abuse and psychiatric disorders, Bean, White, Neagle, and Lake (2005) tested the effectiveness of an intensive residential psychiatric program as a treatment option. Respondents were studied when they entered the residential program and then, a second time, when they completed the course of treatment and left. As part of the presentation of some of their results, the authors used a *bar chart* to display the amount of reduction in the symptoms of depression and anxiety from the time of admission to point of discharge (p. 57).

Discussion. This is a good example of a simple and clear bar chart that portrays graphically the difference in the number of symptoms before and after the completion of an intensive residential treatment program. Along the horizontal axis, you find the variable *psychiatric symptom* divided into two categories, *depression* and *anxiety.*

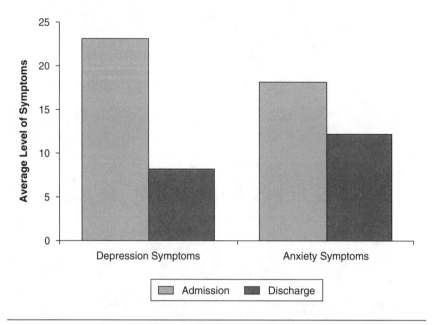

Figure 4.1   Reduction of Depression and Anxiety

SOURCE: Bean, White, Neagle, and Lake (2005).

The vertical axis displays the average number of psychiatric symptoms occurring in the sample of respondents studied in the research project. For comparison purposes, a "key" is exhibited to identify the different bars representing the average number of symptoms at admission and at discharge.

This chapter will demonstrate how to use graphs and other types of figures as alternate ways of exhibiting your data to your audience.

A nother way to present your data (i.e., your frequency distributions), instead of in a table format, is in pictures. We are not talking here about pictures you might take with a digital camera but about *pictorial representations* of data. Granted, these are not usually as detailed or exact as tables, but they do possess two distinct advantages: They cleverly portray large amounts of data, and they grab your attention easier than numbers or words.

Pictorial representations of summarized frequency distributions are called in different contexts *graphs, charts, diagrams,* or *figures.* Practically speaking, these words can be used interchangeably, and we will employ the word *figure* throughout this textbook as a generic label for any type of a nontable display of data.

Since figures present data in a broad, less concrete way than do tables, they provide the reader with a very useful image of patterns or trends in the data. So, what one loses in the close-focused specificity of tables, one gains in the broad-focused generalizations of figures. Therein lies the essential compatibility of both tables and figures in any research report since each produces different outcomes. Whenever you are considering how to present your frequency distributions, ask yourself these questions: Do you want to communicate primarily the explicit details contained in the data? Or do you hope to create some broad, expansive patterns that flow naturally out of your data? Or, perhaps, do you wish to accomplish both effects?

The Structure of Figures

It is important to understand the underlying structure and anatomy of a figure before we begin to describe the different types. All figures are constructed on an intersection of two straight lines known as an *X* axis and a *Y* axis. You have undoubtedly seen many representations of *X* and *Y* axes if you ever took a course in micro- or macroeconomics. The *X* or **horizontal axis** represents all the individual categories of the variable(s) you are studying. If the variable is *location,* the categories could be displayed as *urban, suburban,* and *rural.* The *Y* or **vertical axis** represents the frequency of occurrences of those categories and are stated as either *numerical rankings* (10, 20, 30, etc.) or *percentage rankings* (20%, 40%, 60%, etc.). Figure 4.2 demonstrates the outline of these *X* and *Y* axes.

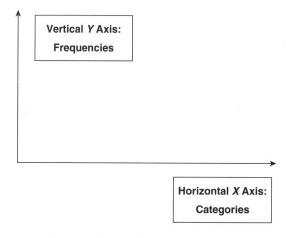

Figure 4.2   *X* and *Y* Axes

)r purposes of simplicity, we will discuss the three types of figures that most commonly appear in social services reports and formal publications: *bar graphs, pie charts,* and *histograms.* There are a number of other types of figures that you can explore further in most formal statistics textbooks, as well as among the optional figures offered to you within SPSS. Some are simply more complex variations on the three basic types presented here, while others (e.g., Pareto charts and stem-and-leaf plots) are used in unique situations.

Bar Graph

A **bar graph** (also called a *bar chart* or a *bar figure*) is usually a vertical series of independent columns that depict the frequencies of nominal-level variables such as gender, race/ethnicity, political affiliation, type of social service agency, and so on. The frequencies reported could be the number of occurrences, the percentage of occurrences, or even both.

The bars, or columns, in a bar chart typically do not touch each other as an indication that they are separate, or discrete, categories of the variable. In practice, however, you will come across some examples of bar graphs whose columns do actually touch one another (as in the introductory case illustration above), so that decision is ultimately yours to make. As an alternative design, the columns of bar graphs could be angled horizontally, which you could do by simply rotating the vertical columns into a horizontal position.

Using the variable *type of social service agency* as an example, it could be displayed graphically as three bars representing the categories of *public, voluntary not-for-profit,* and *private for-profit.* The height of a bar graph, running up the vertical axis, symbolizes the total frequency of occurrence of each category of the variable in your data. Such a bar graph would allow the reader to visualize how many public, voluntary, and private social agencies were included in the sample studied for a research project and to easily compare the differences among the categories by simply looking at the heights of each column.

Pie Chart

A **pie chart** (or *pie graph*) can be used for either nominal- or ordinal-level data, but it is most commonly found representing nominal variables. Visually, a pie chart works best when you are displaying, as its name implies, an array of proportional slices of a perfectly round, 360-degree circle. Pie charts are especially useful when you have a nominal variable with multiple categories that are easily pictured as "slices" but not so many categories that the "slices"

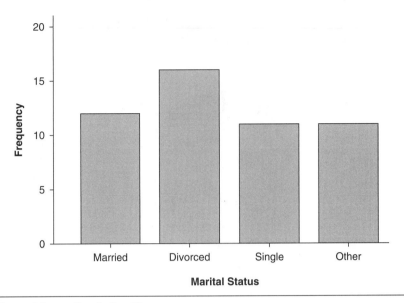

Figure 4.3   Simple Bar Chart

are very small and visually meaningless. For example, you could present clearly the variable *race/ethnicity* in a pie chart with its several possible categories (Asian, African, African American, Hispanic, Native American, White European, and Other). A more confusing picture might emerge if you tried to demonstrate in a pie chart the variable *world hunger* as a percent of the population for each member country of the United Nations. In that situation, your pie chart will have several hundred small and indistinguishable slices, so a table format would probably offer a more realistic option. A general rule is to make sure that the "slices" of the pie are large enough to be distinguishable from the rest of the parts and not so small that their visual presence (and meaning) is lost among the whole composite of parts.

Within social agency contexts, pie charts can serve to highlight many important variables. For example, the slices of the pie would offer a clear proportional representation of the marital status of respondents who answered a mailed survey or the religious identity of all the clients processed through intake in your social service agency last year. You might also exhibit a complex agency budget as a pie chart, thereby indicating the proportional division of resources among staff salaries, rent, utilities, and so forth. Many different subtypes of pie charts are possible, including a dramatic "exploding" pie graph in which one of the slices detaches out from the circle as a means of highlighting one of the categories of the variable being presented.

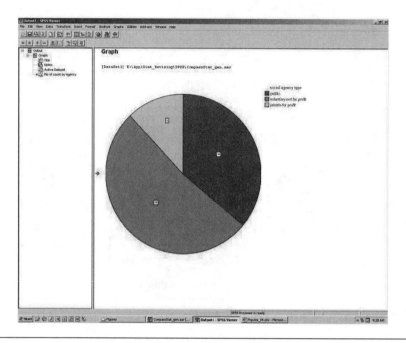

Figure 4.4   Simple Pie Chart

Histogram

The third type of figure discussed here, the **histogram,** looks very much like a bar chart that has been created so that all the vertical bars (or horizontal bars if you chose that direction) touch each other. That is a very important distinction. A histogram, unlike a bar chart, is typically reserved for ordinal- or scale-level data, precisely because the categories of ordinal and scale variables do have some relation or connection to each other. That is to say, the categories are *not discrete* from each other—they have some inherent link to each other based on a ranking of high to low, first to last, and so on (for ordinal) or numerical sequencing of 1, 2, 3, 4, and so forth (for scale). Similar to a bar chart, the height of each bar on a histogram is an indication of the frequency of occurrence of the particular values being represented. For example, if you had access to income data on clients receiving services in an agency, you could clearly represent in a histogram how many of your clients earned between $0 and $10,000, $10,001 and $20,000, $20,001 and 30,000, and so on. Or, suppose you wanted to graphically represent the results of a client satisfaction survey in which you elicited responses to a series of questions with answer choices such as the following:

Agree very much	Agree	Undecided	Disagree	Disagree very much
5	4	3	2	1

Since your data would be at the ordinal level, a histogram would be a logical choice. The fact that the vertical bars touch each other is a recognition that the difference between *agree very much* and *agree* is one of *degree* rather than one of *substance* as you would have in the nominal-level difference between *Asian* and *African*.

When you have scale-level data and not just group rankings, creating a histogram is practical only if you have used a 10-point scale or a 100-point scale measured off in tenths (i.e., 10, 20, 30). The reason for this slight limitation on the application of histograms is clear once you consider that every numerical value (i.e., **score**) will be graphically produced as an individual bar on the histogram. So, if you were trying to present 35 individual scores on a 100-point test, a histogram would portray each score as 76, 81, 82, and so on. Trying to make sense out of an array of more than 10 bars of varying heights can be daunting for most readers, to say the least.

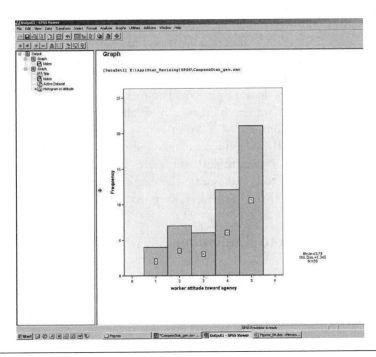

Figure 4.5   Simple Histogram

Creating Figures in SPSS

A few words are in order about technology and, specifically, about the technical ability of SPSS to produce what we are calling graphs, charts, diagrams, or figures. Unlike what was said in Chapter 3 about constructing your own tables in Microsoft Word or WordPerfect, you can (and should) use SPSS to construct any figures you decide to use. In other words, it is highly recommended that you do, literally, "copy and paste" the figures created in SPSS directly into your final report. This will save you an enormous amount of time, allowing you to use the advanced technical capabilities of SPSS to assist you in your figure construction needs. You can find specific procedures for creating figures in SPSS at the end of this chapter.

Narration, Tables, or Graphs

Whether you choose to narrate your quantitative results in a sentence, place them orderly in a table, or graphically represent them in a figure of some kind is ultimately your choice as a researcher. Just keep in mind a few general rules.

First, if you choose to narrate, do it only when you have a small amount of quantitative data, and keep the narration short. No one wants to read long paragraphs with extended sentences full of numbers and percentages and ranges.

Second, if you place your quantitative data in a table, keep it orderly, simple, and uncluttered. Tables that are "too busy" are guaranteed to make the reader's eyes glaze over in less than a few seconds.

Third, if the creative side of your brain wins out and you venture into the world of figure design, do not overdo it. Too many figures, especially if they are radically different from each other, can equally affect the reader's attention span just like a complex table with too many pieces in it.

Fourth, it is perfectly acceptable to "mix and match" and vary your presentation between narration, tables, and figures in your report, within reason. Since the goal is to communicate the quantitative data in a clear and understandable manner to your reader, keep that in mind at all times.

Summary Points to Remember

- Figures are pictorial representations of a set of frequency distributions.
- Figures are typically used only with nominal- or ordinal-level variables.
- Figures are structured along the lines of an X axis (horizontal) and a Y axis (vertical).
- The X axis represents the categories of the variable you are describing.

- The Y axis represents the number or percentage of occurrences of each category of the variable you are describing.

- The bar graph and pie graph are typically used with nominal-level data.

- The histogram is typically used with ordinal-level data.

- You, the researcher, ultimately decide how to present your data: by narration, in a table, or in a figure.

- You should, literally, *copy and paste* into your final report the figures you create by using SPSS.

Case Illustration 4.1

Recently, the U.S. Department of Health and Human Services (USDHHS, 2006) published a comprehensive report on the abuse and neglect of children titled

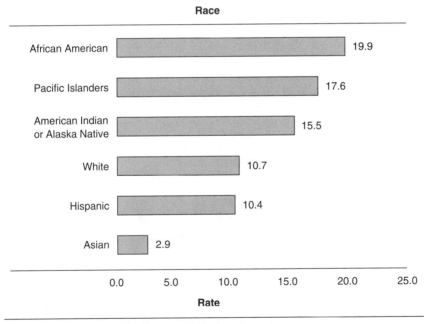

Figure 4.6   Race and Ethnicity of Victims, 2004

SOURCE: USDHHS (2006).

NOTE: African American, Pacific Islander, and American Indian or Alaska Native children had the highest rates of victimization of 19.9, 17.6, and 15.5 per 1,000 children of the same race or ethnicity, respectively. White children and Hispanic children had rates of approximately 10.7 and 10.4 per 1,000 children of the same race or ethnicity, respectively. Asian children had the lowest rate of 2.0 per 1,000 children of the same race or ethnicity.

Child Maltreatment, 2004. Much of the data is presented in graphical format to assist the reader in understanding the mass of information on this serious national problem. Figure 4.6, which follows, is a reproduction of Figure 3.5: Race and Ethnicity of Victims, 2004, by the U.S. Department of Health and Human Services, along with the accompanying explanation of the general meaning of the bar graph (USDHHS, 2006, p. 26).

Discussion. This is a clear example of a bar graph turned horizontally, so that the bars emerge from left to right and the numerical values (in this case, *percentage rates*) also appear on the same perceptual plane. Some researchers believe that this kind of horizontal positioning of the bars assists in understanding since people normally read from left to right. That decision regarding the direction of the bars, however, is entirely in the domain of the researcher/ graph creator.

Case Illustration 4.2

Eastman and Billings (2004) studied the impact of promotional advertising on television during the Olympics, particularly regarding its post-Olympics effect on prime-time television viewing. The authors revealed part of their results, comparing television viewing results after the 1996 Olympics in Atlanta to the 2000 Olympics in Sydney, by means of a simple pie chart (p. 352).

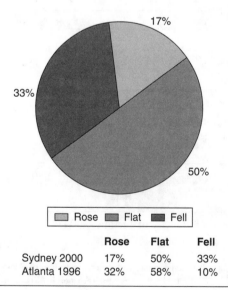

	Rose	Flat	Fell
Sydney 2000	17%	50%	33%
Atlanta 1996	32%	58%	10%

Figure 4.7   Summary Comparison of Proportions of Ratings Changes in Sydney and Atlanta

SOURCE: Eastman and Billings (2004).

Discussion. This is a straightforward, easy-to-understand presentation of comparative data that includes not just the graphical image of the slices of a pie but also their accompanying percentage values. The authors could have chosen to "explode" the 33% slice out of the pie if they had wished to emphasize the dramatic drop in ratings following the 2000 Sydney Olympics.

Case Illustration 4.3

One finding from a study of 258 undergraduate social work students revealed a wide disparity in their attitudes toward research methods courses in their BSW program. After measuring the students' fear of research on a 10-point survey question, the authors chose to display this set of results on a histogram (Secret, Ford, & Rompf, 2003, p. 416).

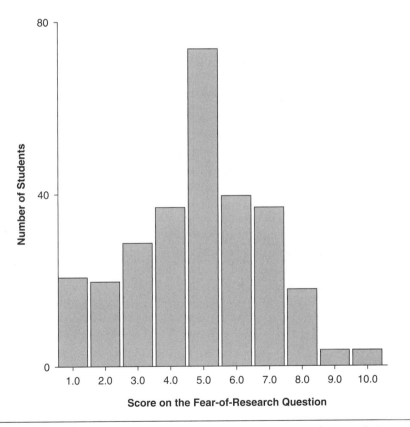

Figure 4.8   Histogram of Research Attitude Measure: Fear of Research Course

SOURCE: Secret, Ford, and Rompf (2003).

NOTE: 0 = *no fear;* 10 = *much fear.* N = 284, M = 4.9, SD = 2.04.

Discussion. While there are other ways the authors could have reported these data (through narration or in a table, for example), a histogram does appear to make an interesting point, almost dramatically. The "urban legend" that all social work students "hate research" is dispelled quickly and firmly by this graphic representation of the findings. As this self-report from one sample of undergraduate social work students suggests, there seems to exist a wide range of attitudes that extend across the span of *no fear* (0) to *much fear* (10), with a pattern that approximates the shape of a normal, bell-shaped curve. Another urban legend bites the dust?

Activities Involving Data in Figures

1. Using Data Set 1 (Client Demographics and Treatment Results), create separate bar charts for the variables *gen* and *eth*. Copy and paste the output into a Microsoft Word document. Remember to add consecutive numbers and individual titles to your figures.

2. Using Data Set 1 (Client Demographics and Treatment Results), create separate pie charts for the variables *rel, mar,* and *clin.* Copy and paste the output into a Microsoft Word document. Remember to add consecutive numbers and individual titles to your figures.

3. Using Data Set 5 (Community Social Needs Survey), create separate histograms for the variables *tax, cut,* and *limit.* Copy and paste the output into a Microsoft Word document. Remember to add consecutive numbers and individual titles to your figures.

4. Using Data Set 4 (Client Satisfaction Survey), create a bar chart for the variable *facil.* Then, create a histogram for the same variable. With the histogram, select the option *With normal curve.* This option is an overlay of a bell-shaped curve, and it provides you with information to help you determine if your distribution is, generally speaking, normal. Discuss with a colleague which figure, the bar chart or the histogram, describes the variable *facil* with the most clarity.

SPSS Procedures

Pie Chart (for Nominal-Level Data)

In either the *Data View* or *Variable View* window, do the following:

CLICK on the *Analyze* menu from the top of the window.

PLACE THE CURSOR over the *Descriptive Statistics* choice.

CLICK on *Frequencies*.

CLICK on the variable(s) you are interested in. Do not mix nominal, ordinal, or scale variables together.

CLICK on the right-pointing button in the middle of the window.

CLICK on the *Charts* button at the bottom center of the window.

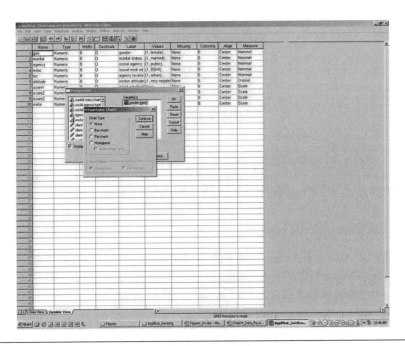

Figure 4.9   SPSS Screen Shot of *Charts* Window

CLICK on the *Pie charts* button.

CLICK on the *Continue* button.

CLICK on the *OK* button at the top right of the window.

Copying and Saving a Pie Chart in Microsoft Word

With the pie chart displayed, do the following:

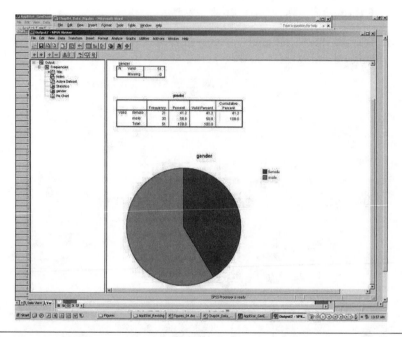

Figure 4.10   SPSS Screen Shot of *Charts* Output for Pie Chart

CLICK on it in the center.

CLICK on the *Edit* menu at the top left of the window and CLICK on *Copy,* PRESS DOWN on *Control + c* on the keyboard, or RIGHT CLICK on the mouse and CLICK on *Copy.*

OPEN a new or an existing Word document.

CLICK on the page where you want to place the graph.

CLICK on the *Edit* menu at the top left of the window and CLICK on *Paste,* PRESS DOWN on *Control + v* on the keyboard, or RIGHT CLICK on the mouse and CLICK on *Paste.*

CLICK on the *File* menu at the top left of the window.

CLICK on *Save* or PRESS DOWN on *Control + s* on the keyboard.

Bar Graph (for Nominal-Level Data)

In either the *Data View* or *Variable View* window, do the following:

CLICK on the *Analyze* menu from the top of the window.

PLACE THE CURSOR over the *Descriptive Statistics* choice.

CLICK on *Frequencies*.

CLICK on the variable(s) you are interested in. Do not mix nominal, ordinal, or scale variables together.

CLICK on the right-pointing button in the middle of the window.

CLICK on the *Charts* button at the bottom center of the window.

CLICK on the *Bar charts* button.

CLICK on the *Continue* button.

CLICK on the *OK* button at the top right of the window.

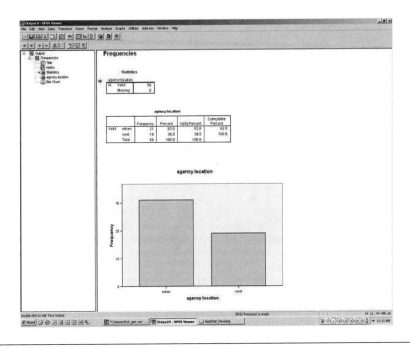

Figure 4.11   SPSS Screen Shot of *Charts* Output for Bar Graph

Histogram (for Ordinal- and Scale-Level Data)

In either the *Data View* or *Variable View* window, do the following:

CLICK on the *Analyze* menu from the top of the window.

PLACE THE CURSOR over the *Descriptive Statistics* choice.

CLICK on *Frequencies*.

CLICK on the variable(s) you are interested in. Do not mix nominal, ordinal, or scale variables together.

CLICK on the right-pointing button in the middle of the window.

CLICK on the *Charts* button at the bottom center of the window.

CLICK on the *Histograms* button.

CLICK on the *With normal curve* button.

CLICK on the *Continue* button.

CLICK on the *OK* button at the top right of the window.

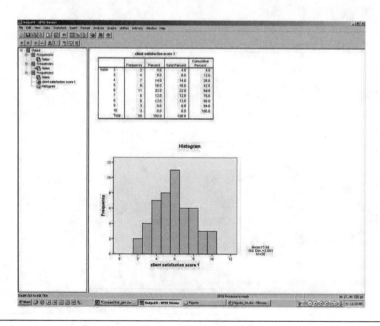

Figure 4.12   SPSS Screen Shot of *Charts* Output for Histogram

(NOTE: There are other options for producing more detailed graphs that can be accessed by pulling down and clicking on the *Chart Builder Wizard* at the top of the window.)

Copying and Saving a Bar Graph in Microsoft Word

With the graph displayed, do the following:

CLICK on the graph in the center.

CLICK on the *Edit* menu at the top left of the window.

CLICK on *Copy* (or PRESS DOWN on *Control* + *c* on the keyboard).

OPEN a new or an existing Word document.

CLICK on the page where you want to place the graph.

CLICK on the *Edit* menu at the top left of the window.

CLICK on *Paste* (or PRESS DOWN on *Control* + *v* on the keyboard).

CLICK on the *File* menu at the top left of the window.

CLICK on *Save* (or PRESS DOWN on *Control* + *s* on the keyboard).

References

Bean, P., White, L., Neagle, L., & Lake, P. (2005). Is residential care an effective approach for treating adolescents with co-occurring substance abuse and mental health diagnoses? *Best Practices in Mental Health, 1*(2), 50–60.

Eastman, S. T., & Billings, A. C. (2004). Promotion's limited impact in the 2000 Sydney Olympics. *Television & New Media, 5*(4), 339–358.

Secret, M., Ford, J., & Rompf, E. L. (2003). Undergraduate research courses: A closer look reveals complex social work student attitudes. *Journal of Social Work Education, 39*(3), 411–422.

U.S. Department of Health & Human Services (USDHHS), Administration on Children, Youth and Families. (2006). *Child maltreatment, 2004*. Washington, DC: Government Printing Office.

5

The 3 Ms

Mean, Median, and Mode

Why are the mean, median, and mode like a valuable piece of real estate? LOCATION! LOCATION! LOCATION!

—Gary C. Ramseyer, cited on
www.ilstu.edu/~gcramsey/CentTend

Introductory Case Illustration

In the current social environment of instability in family life, there exists the increasing phenomenon of grandparents being called upon to serve as the sole caregivers of their grandchildren. A recent study of this trend by Gerard, Landry-Meyer, and Roe (2006) focused on the influence of social support systems in this endeavor, particularly how these community-based resources minimized the negative challenges faced by the grandparents. The researchers collected their data by means of a survey mailed to a purposive sample of 133 grandparents who were recruited from social service agencies. In their published research, the authors reported one of the demographic variables (i.e., *number of grandchildren being raised by the grandparent*) by using the statistical procedure known as the mean. "Fifty-five percent of grandparents reported raising one grandchild, 29% reported two, 7% reported three, and

10% reported raising four or more grandchildren ($M = 1.7$)" (Gerard et al., 2006, p. 366).

Discussion. Reading that the mean, or average, number of grandchildren being raised was 1.7 is pointless in and of itself, since there obviously is no such thing as a ".7 child." That strange number does, however, provide a general statement of the center of the total distribution of numbers of grandchildren being cared for by the 133 grandparents in the study. In the most straightforward manner, a mean value of 1.7 translates as "approximately 2 grandchildren" for each grandparent surveyed. That mean value of 1.7 in this survey could also be used for comparisons to other groups of grandparents in other communities, or over a period of time in the same community, or even as a corresponding measurement considered against state and national averages.

Following up on Chapters 3 and 4, there will be situations where you wish to do something more than simply narrate a description of your data or put those data in some form of table or graph. Statisticians talk about finding the standard, or the typical, or the central measurement in any compilation of data as a way of understanding the whole distribution. Once that mythical *center* is identified, then we can talk about variations on that theme and visualize how the rest of the distribution swirls around the center and also moves away from it.

Just as classical musicians identify the "three Bs" of music as Bach, Beethoven, and Brahms, so, too, can we designate the three pivotal measurements for this center as the "three Ms" of statistics: the *mean,* the *median,* and the *mode.* Within the entire hierarchy of statistical procedures, the mean, median, and mode are undoubtedly some of the easiest measurements to calculate and yet are quite versatile in their ability to simplify our understanding of raw data in a variety of situations.

Statistics textbooks also refer to these three procedures as **measures of central tendency.** This may sound like an awkward phrase, but it makes sense if you picture any set of numbers lined up horizontally from left to right, from the lowest to highest. In that image, the numbers are stretched out in ascending order directly next to each other, so that the number 15 lies to the left of the number 18, which itself lies to the left of the number 23, and so on. Admittedly, this is an odd image since we do not normally think of numbers in that type of alignment; but it helps demonstrate the mean, median, and mode as measures of central tendency.

Illustrations of this image in a social services context could be, for example, the number of presenting problems on a case-by-case basis that were recorded at intake in a family services agency, the ages of children when they are placed by courts in foster care, or the amount of income that clients were earning at intake and then again 6 months after their completion of a job-training program. The point is that any set of numbers that you have access to in any social service agency can be manipulated (remember that *manipulation* is not a dirty word in statistics) by the use of the mean, the median, or the modal procedure. Manipulation, in this context, refers to the process of gaining new information from an existing set of numbers by some sort of new activity, just like you could force more water out of a wet towel the more you squeeze it with your hands in a twisting motion.

We will discuss each of these in the order in which they are most frequently used in social service agency practice.

Mean

The **mean** is the numeric average of all the scores added together as a sum, then divided by the number of cases (i.e., subjects). Mean scores are undoubtedly the most popular statistic that you will find in newspaper reports, on television, on the Internet, and in professional journal articles. The most critical point to remember about any mean score, however, is that it is directly and substantively influenced by the very low and the very high scores on that horizontal distribution of scores we mentioned above. Formally speaking, these high and low scores are referred to as *extreme scores* or **outliers.** So, as long as the scores at the beginning and at the end of the horizontal list of numbers are not so extreme from the rest of the numbers, the mean can be a statistical procedure that produces useful information.

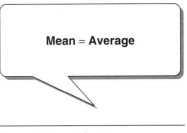

Figure 5.1   The Mean

What does *so extreme* mean in this context? Consider this example. A few years ago, during a class on social research methods, while attempting to demonstrate the differences between mean, median, and mode, a professor asked the students to submit on a piece of paper how much money they had on their person that day in exact dollars and cents. Assume this class consisted of 23 members, evenly divided between traditional and nontraditional students, and took place on an urban, commuter campus. After computing the mean amount, the professor reported a surprisingly high figure, into the range of several hundreds of dollars. As the class discussed this strange phenomenon, one student reported that she worked the night shift at a community group home for adolescents. She further announced that she had come directly from her agency to class and had in her bag her monthly paycheck of several thousand dollars. The rest of the students reported that they had much more modest amounts with them, and no one had more than $50 on their person. That one student with her monthly paycheck, then, explained dramatically why the computed average was so high.

That class discussion serves as an excellent demonstration of how mean scores, especially with a relatively small amount of respondents (or cases), can easily be influenced by even only one extreme case. This influence of outliers on a mean score is technically called, in statistics, the skewness of a distribution of scores. More important, however, remember that a mean score may not provide an accurate picture of your distribution of numbers, if there are one or more extreme scores on either end of the list.

Since the calculation of the mean value involves some very precise numerical values, most statisticians restrict its use to scale-level data only. In practice, however, you will find in the professional literature some examples of mean scores reported for ordinal-level data, especially data collected from 5-point Likert scales (e.g., 5 = *very satisfied*, 4 = *satisfied*, 3 = *not sure*, 2 = *not satisfied*, 1 = *very dissatisfied*).

Median

The **median** score is the exact middle point on that horizontal lineup of numbers that we have been talking about. The median is arrived at by visualizing all the numbers (cases) laid out on a level plane and then by counting in from both ends to the precise midpoint of that distribution. Since some level of ranking or numerical precision is needed, the median value should report only data measured at either the ordinal or scale level.

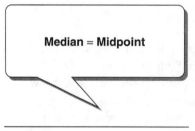

Median = Midpoint

Figure 5.2   The Median

Unlike the mean score discussed above, the median score is *not influenced* by any outliers since each number, no matter what its inherent worth (i.e., 10 or 54 or 117), is counted only as *one position* as you progress in from each end. For example, if you had 27 numbers with increasing values (e.g., 10, 22, 54, 56) stretched out before you on a horizontal plane, the modal number (i.e., midpoint) would be at the 14th spot on that line since you would count in 13 positions from each end. On the other hand, if you had 28 numbers on that line, your midpoint would fall between the 14th and 15th spots on that distribution. Still confused? Take a piece of paper and place 27 numbers (any numbers) on a horizontal line in ascending order. Now find the exact middle (median) so that an equal amount of numbers lies on either side of that midpoint. Now add one more number to either end so you have 28 numbers in a line. Your median score now is an *imaginary point* in the blank space between two numbers. To compute the median point in this situation, simply add those two numbers together and divide by 2—that is your exact middle in that distribution. If the blank space between the two numbers you arrived at was between the numbers 35 and 41, then the median would be 38 $(35 + 41 \div 2 = 38)$.

The median score enables you to report that half the respondents had higher values than the median point and that the other half had lower values than the median point. This may not sound like an earth-shattering event, but it does allow the researcher to analyze the set of numbers under discussion and present some new knowledge about those scores. This new knowledge (new perspective?) has not been influenced in any manner by extremely high or low values at either end of the distribution.

Returning to our example of the professor in the research methods class, the median value of the amount of money the students had in their possession that day would be much lower, probably in the $20 to $30 range. Since the students reported that the most anyone had in their possession that day, other than that one student with her paycheck, was $50, then the midpoint of all the other numbers would undoubtedly fall at some point less than that. The very large value added by that one recently paid student would be counted as only one point in the horizontal list of all the amounts and so would not have any power to influence the median score. The same noninfluential effect of outliers would take place if another student reported that she had no money at all on her person because she walked to campus that day, had only one class, and planned to return home immediately after class for lunch. Thus, her zero amount of money was also counted as only one point in that distribution of values.

Mode

The **mode** is the most frequently appearing score or value as you scan that list of numbers stretched out horizontally from left to right. Unlike the other measures of **central tendency,** you can compute the mode with the nominal, ordinal, or scale level of measurement. For example, you could report the modal computation for the value categories of religion (nominal level), for the value categories of a 5-point Likert scale (ordinal level), or for the values of weight in pounds (scale level).

Unfortunately, the modal score is the most misunderstood of the three measures of association and as such is one of the least used statistical procedures in social science research. The modal score typically produces one of those "so what?" reactions from many readers.

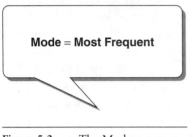

Figure 5.3   The Mode

The lowly modal score, however, can be informative in some contexts. Consider, for example, an urban social service program that targets homeless adolescents by engaging their trust, then coaxing them into a residential shelter, and eventually offering them a comprehensive range of supportive services. By systematically examining the intake data and determining the modal age of the adolescents when they first left home, the administrators would have one critical indicator (but certainly not the only one) of the age group toward which preventive services in the community might strategically be applied. In other words, assume that the modal age for adolescents in a particular community who left home in the past year turned out to be 13 for females and 15 for males. This fact alone would seem to support prevention programs for at-risk adolescents that would be targeted *earlier* for girls than for boys throughout the public and private school systems.

Consider another example. If a particular nursing home discovers that the modal amount of visits by family members for their residents during their first year of placement was 6, then any outreach communications from the nursing home encouraging regular family visits could be initiated not immediately but after, perhaps, the fifth or sixth family visit following the initial placement.

This discussion is not intended to suggest that modal scores (or mean and median scores, for that matter) possess any inherent power to predict the future direction of human behavior. They cannot now and will never be able to accomplish that feat. What is suggested, however, is that the mean, median, and modal procedures can capture the trends of past activity and, armed with that information, can point the way, with only a modest voice, to a possible future. The emphasis here is on the word *possible*.

Think of all the early explorers and adventurers throughout history who ventured forth onto some unknown ocean, over some vast landmass, or up into the limitless abyss of space. Those brave individuals had some information to guide them, gained from past experiences of others. Undoubtedly, they factored this old information into their planning, but they also drew upon new information, plus their own abilities and sensitivities, as they forged forward in their endeavors. Use the information you gain from the computation of mean, median, and modal values in the same manner. The mean, median, and mode all demonstrate a trend—nothing more. But those trends could serve as a useful foundation for your future policy development or program change.

A Demonstration of the Mean, Median, and Mode

Suppose an instructor graded a test for 16 students that was based on 25 points and then recorded the following set of grade scores:

John—18	Brandon—25
Peter—19	Martin—17
Harvey—21	Ayasha—22
Kim—18	June—18
Amanda—16	Harriet—17
Marvin—20	Michael—19
Ivan—24	Jose—22
Ling—23	Marisa—25

You certainly could enter these numbers into a statistical program (such as SPSS) for easy computation, but you could just as efficiently process the data manually or with a simple calculator. Moving beyond the individual names, your first task is to lay out the values (numbers) horizontally, including any repeated values, as appropriate.

16	17	17	18	18	18	19	19	20	21	22	22	23	24	25	25

By adding together all the values (sum = 319) and dividing by the number of cases ($N = 16$), you receive a *mean value* of 19.9 for this distribution of scores.

After dividing the number of cases ($N = 16$) and dividing by 2, you calculate the exact midpoint in this distribution (eight values or spaces in from both sides). That procedure provides you with the exact midpoint in this series of values.

Since that midpoint is the location *between* two values (19 and 20), you conclude that the *median value* for this distribution of scores is 19.5.

Midpoint
16   17   17   18   18   18   19   19   *   20   21   22   22   23   24   25   25

Note that the median is not necessarily one of the values listed. Since there is an even number of cases in this illustration ($N = 16$), the midpoint exists between two values. If you had an odd number of values to consider, then the median would be that particular value found at the exact middle of the distribution. If you ever need an exact median value stated at the level of two decimal places, then this manual approach will not easily suffice. In that specific situation, you are advised to compute the median value using a statistical software program.

Finally, you are able to readily identify the most frequently appearing value in your distribution by simply scanning the horizontal display. In this situation, the *modal* value is 18. In some distributions, you might encounter either a *bimodal* array (i.e., two highest values of equal frequency) or even a *multimodal* array (i.e., more than two highest values of equal frequency).

Summary Points to Remember

- The mean, median, and mode are all measures of the central tendency of a distribution of values (numbers) or value categories (nominal data).
- The mean is the average score, arrived at by dividing the total score by the number of cases.
- The mean is absolutely affected by outliers (extreme scores at either end).
- The mean is most appropriately used with scale data, unless you believe the outliers might distort the data. In that situation, use the median.
- The median is the exact midpoint in any distribution of values.
- The median is not affected by outliers.
- The median is most appropriately used with ordinal data. In practice, however, the mean is sometimes used with ordinal data.
- The mode is the most frequently appearing value or value category in any distribution.

- Some distributions may be bimodal or multimodal.
- The mode is appropriately used with nominal, ordinal, or scale data.

Case Illustration 5.1

In 2006, Buttell and Carney designed a secondary analysis study to evaluate the effectiveness of a 6-month intervention program for men arrested for abusing their spouses. Participants included 850 African American and Caucasian batterers who were mandated by the court to participate. One measure employed was the Spouse-Specific Assertiveness Scale (SSAS) that ranges from 12 (low) to 102 (high) and gauges both assertive behaviors and typical passive-aggressive responses to spousal communication. Thus, lower scores would be considered positive in this context. Participants were measured at two points in time: pretreatment and posttreatment.

The authors noted, "Participant scores were significantly higher on the SSAS passive-aggressive subscale at pretreatment assessment ($M = 34.43$, $SD = 12.41$) compared to the posttreatment assessment sample mean ($M = 31.91$, $SD = 11.32$)" (Buttell & Carney, 2006, p. 126).

Discussion. Since the researchers, in this example, had collected scale-level data, they correctly chose to compute a mean value and standard deviation for the scores. This provided both a central point of comparison (mean) and a measure of variability from that central point (the standard deviation, which will be discussed in Chapter 6). The fact that the authors used the phrase "significantly higher" indicates that they conducted other statistical procedures (not included in this short quotation) that suggest the presence of **statistical significance**. In other words, the finding that there was a drop in scores from pretreatment to posttreatment was probably not due to the phenomenon known as **sampling error** but was due to real change in the respondents.

Case Illustration 5.2

Within the field of medical education, specifically the teaching of human anatomy, dramatic curricular changes have emerged in recent years. Presently, there exist six major didactic approaches that are reportedly used by faculty in medical schools in the United States and Europe. These models of teaching about human anatomy are categorized as follows: direct human dissection of cadavers by students (Dissection); inspection of specimens (Prosection); didactic teaching of content (Didactic); use of static models (Models); use of computer-aided learning, slides, and tapes (CAL); and demonstration of living and radiological anatomy (Living).

Patel and Moxham (2006) report on a study of the attitudes regarding these six various approaches expressed by a nonrandom sample ($N = 112$) of anatomy faculty. They measured their responses on a 5-point ordinal scale that yielded a possible total score of 60 for each curricular category. High scores would suggest a favorable reception of a particular approach to teaching anatomy.

The median ranks (based on 60) for the 6 categories are reported as follows:

Dissection: 47, Prosection: 38, Didactic: 26, Models: 22.5, CAL: 29, and Living Anatomy: 37. (p. 137)

The authors concluded, among other findings, that "the preference for the use of human cadaveric dissection was evident in all groups of anatomists" (Patel & Moxham, 2006, p. 132).

Discussion. In this example, the authors appropriately used the median value because the data they collected were at the ordinal level, which produced a ranking of their attitudes from a high of 5 to a low of 1 on a scale. Since the first category (Dissection) received the highest ordinal ranking (47 out of 60), the authors could present their conclusion as stated. The value of 47 as a median score meant that half the anatomy professors surveyed ranked human dissection higher than 47 on a total possible range from 0 to 60, and half ranked that approach lower than 47 on a total possible range from 0 to 60.

Case Illustration 5.3

As part of a secondary analysis of demographic data exploring whether race and class inequalities exist throughout the criminal justice system in the United States, researchers used the mode as the statistical measurement on one set of data. They discovered, among other things, that young African American males who did not complete high school were at greater risk of spending time in jail than did Hispanic and White youth.

Incredibly, a black male dropout, born 1965–69, had nearly a 60 percent chance of serving time in prison by the end of the 1990s. At the close of the decade, prison time had indeed become *modal* (emphasis added) for young black men who failed to graduate from high school. (Pettit & Western, 2004, p. 161)

Discussion. This is a simple example of how to use a modal value category in a narrative format to illustrate the variable of race. Without providing the readers with any further numerical data, the authors did communicate that their results showed that the most frequently appearing racial category was African American (as compared to Hispanic and White) among those young men who were imprisoned and who did not complete high school. Since the word *modal* is not commonly used, however, this section of data presentation might have been strengthened if the authors had added a brief definition of the term.

Activities Involving the Mean, Median, and Mode

1. Using Data Set 3 (Client Single-Case Evaluation), compute the mean value for the variables *int1, int2,* and *int3.* Narrate the results in a format appropriate for a formal research report.

2. Using Data Set 5 (Community Social Needs Survey), compute the mean and median of the variable *faminc.* Then, looking at the data in the individual cells under this variable in the SPSS *Data View* window, do you think the mean or the median is the better statistic to use so as not to distort the results? Why? Narrate the results in a format appropriate for a formal research report.

3. Using Data Set 4 (Client Satisfaction Survey), compute the mode for the variables *marital, admin,* and *other.* Narrate the results in a format appropriate for a formal research report.

4. Using Data Set 4 (Client Satisfaction Survey), compute the median for the variable *time.* What do the results reveal about this client population? Narrate the results in a format appropriate for a formal research report.

SPSS Procedures

In either the *Data View* or *Variable View* window, do the following:

CLICK on the *Analyze* menu from the top of the window.

PLACE THE CURSOR over the *Descriptive Statistics* choice.

CLICK on *Frequencies.*

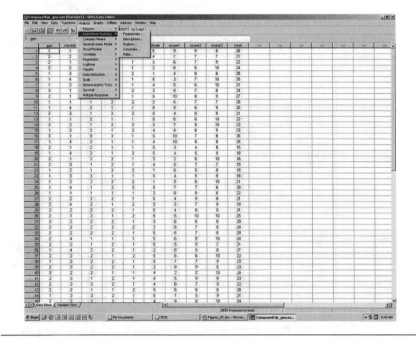

Figure 5.4   SPSS Screen Shot of *Analyze* Window

CLICK on the variable(s) you are interested in. For most precision, use only scale variables. For moderate precision, you may use ordinal variables if they are measured at 5 or more points. For the least precision, you may use ordinal variables measured at only 3 or 4 points. If using nominal data, compute those as a separate action together.

CLICK on the right-pointing button in the middle of the window.

CLICK on the *Statistics* button at the bottom of the window.

CLICK on the *Mean, Median,* and *Mode* buttons. For nominal data, only the *Mode* procedure is appropriate.

CLICK on the *Continue* button.

CLICK on the *OK* button at the top right of the window. To return to the *Data View* or *Variable View,* CLICK on the close button [X] at the top right of the window.

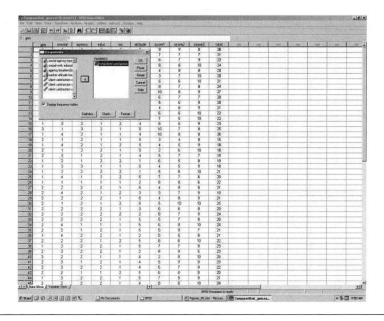

Figure 5.5   SPSS Screen Shot of *Frequencies* Window

Applying the SPSS Output

In the output box labeled *Statistics*, do the following:

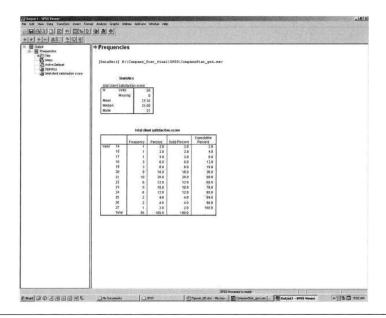

Figure 5.6   SPSS Screen Shot of *Frequencies* Output

NOTICE the number of valid cases (*N*) and the number (if any) of missing cases.

NOTICE the values associated with the *Mean,* the *Median,* and the *Mode.* IGNORE the rest of the output.

INCLUDE the mean, median, and mode values in any figure, table, or narrative summary you produce.

References

Buttell, F. P., & Carney, M. M. (2006). A large sample evaluation of court-mandated batterer intervention program: Investigating differential program effect for African American and Caucasian men. *Research on Social Work Practice, 16*(2), 121–131.

Gerard, J. M., Landry-Meyer, L., & Roe, J. G. (2006). Grandparents raising grandchildren: The role of social support in coping with caregiving challenges. *International Journal of Aging and Human Development, 62*(4), 359–383.

Patel, K. M., & Moxham, B. J. (2006). Attitudes of professional anatomists to curricular change. *Clinical Anatomy, 19,* 132–141.

Pettit, B., & Western, B. (2004). Mass imprisonment and the life course: Race and class inequality in U.S. incarceration. *American Sociological Review, 69,* 151–169.

6

Standard Deviations, Ranges, and Quartiles

Torture numbers, and they'll confess to anything.

—G. Easterbrook, cited on
www.quotegarden.com/statistics

Introductory Case Illustration

Examining the possible relationship between early sexual abuse and later personal behaviors that could be considered sexually risky, researchers selected a random sample of 4,781 Swedish citizens in 1996. From that sample, 2,810 agreed to be interviewed for the study. One variable studied was whether the participant ever experienced child or adolescent abuse (CASA) or not (NO CASA). The ages of the participants, by gender, were reported using both mean and range values.

The researchers described that the mean age of males with NO CASA was 46, covering a range of ages 23 to 79; with CASA, the mean age of males was 43, covering a range of ages 23 to 77. The mean age of females with NO CASA was 46, covering a range of ages 23 to 79; with CASA, the mean age of females was 41, covering a range of ages 23 to 74 (Steel & Herlitz, 2005, extracted from Table 1, p. 1144).

Discussion. The mean value, as you learned in Chapter 5, provides the average value of all the participants in any distribution of numbers. As you can see in this example, the use of an additional measurement, the range, in combination with the mean value, helps to clarify what the whole distribution of numbers looks like. The range is particularly helpful in identifying what are called the *outliers*—those extreme scores found at either end that do influence somewhat the calculation of the mean score. Unfortunately, outliers can sometimes confuse the reader by providing exaggerated information. The range, in other words, can create a sense of balance and order by identifying the extreme outlier data, but that very identification may unwittingly imply to the reader that outliers greatly influence the mean value in either direction. Their influence depends more on the frequency of their appearance in the entire distribution. The point here is that the mean, the range, and all other statistical procedures are not complete in and of themselves—each should be taken in the context of the other measurements reported.

In this chapter, you will discuss several statistical procedures that spread out the distribution of values, away from the mean value. They are all designed to increase your understanding of exactly what is contained within the entire distribution you are studying.

S omewhat less familiar than the three Ms of statistics (i.e., the mean, median, and mode) are three other measurements of the variability within a set of numbers: the *standard deviation,* the *range,* and the *quartiles.* Although they may not be as commonly known (or used) as the mean, median, and mode, they do provide some unique information to any attempt to analyze data quantitatively.

Unlike measures of central tendency discussed in Chapter 5, which capture similarities, **measures of variability** portray how any set of numbers differ from each other. In other words, when you compute the mean, median, or mode of a set of numbers, you sort of *squeeze* them together to produce some recognizable patterns. However, when you conduct one of the measures of variability, you do the opposite: You *stretch* them outwardly, thereby expanding them intentionally to view how different they are from each other. These images of squeezing and stretching do not form a perfect analogy of what really happens, but it is hoped that these representations can serve as a tactic to assist you in understanding and applying the measures of central tendency and measures of variability.

Descriptive Statistics

These measures of variability, along with the **measures of association** (the 3 Ms), are examples of what are called *descriptive statistics*. They portray one variable at a time, highlighting it without exploring any relationship between any other variables. In other words, the statistical procedures presented in this chapter, as well as in Chapter 5, examine each variable individually but from a wide variety of perspectives. Think of what you would probably do if you came upon an intriguing sculpture mounted in the middle of a museum gallery. If you are like most people, you would study intently that work of art by walking around it in a full circle so as to examine it from every angle. Descriptive statistics offer a similar multidimensional perspective to any single variable under study, one at a time.

You can understand the standard deviation, the range, and the quartiles by using the same image of a horizontal list of numbers laid out from left to right, from lowest to highest. This time, however, assume that the numbers on that line represent the ages of nursing home residents at the time of their death for the past year, collected from all nursing home facilities in one geographic area.

Standard Deviation

The **standard deviation** (typically noted simply as *SD*) establishes a common point of reference so that the mean score can be understood more precisely. Every computed mean score of any distribution of numbers you will ever encounter in research has a standard deviation. The standard deviation is simply a number that measures the average distance from the mean value of all the numbers in that distribution. In other words, it points out the typical spread, higher and lower, away from the mean value. So, once you know the mean

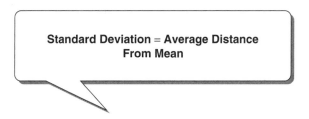

Standard Deviation = Average Distance From Mean

Figure 6.1   Standard Deviation

value, you can speak of "one standard deviation" above and below the mean. And once you know the value of one standard deviation, then you can logically point out the value of two or three standard deviations from the mean by simply multiplying that one standard deviation value by 2 or 3.

The theory behind the standard deviation, which is known as *probability theory,* is drawn from the famous (or infamous) image of the bell-shaped curve that forms whenever you have a normal distribution of values. This complex natural phenomenon is described more fully in Chapter 1 of this book in the section Some Useful Nondefinitions. It might be helpful for you to return and reread the reference (Theory of Probability and the Bell-Shaped Curve) as a refresher before continuing with this chapter.

Welcome back! As the image of the bell-shaped curve visually portrays, in any normal distribution of numbers (i.e., any "idealized" distribution), one standard **deviation from the mean** score marks the two points, one higher and the other lower from the mean, between which 68% of the values (i.e., numbers) will fall. In our example of age at the time of death in a nursing home population, if $M = 76$ and $SD = 2$, you know that for this particular group of nursing home residents under study, the average age at death was 76, and approximately 68% of them died between the ages of 74 and 78 (i.e., $76 + 2$ and $76 - 2$). Continuing this analysis, you could then indicate (again, if the distribution is considered "normal") that 95% of the residents died between the ages of 72 and 80 (i.e., mean plus two standard deviations or $76 + 4$ and $76 - 4$) and, finally, that 99% of the residents died between the ages of 70 and 82 (i.e., mean plus three standard deviations or $76 + 6$ and $76 - 6$).

How could such information be useful to the social service staff (indeed, to all staff) in the nursing home? Granted, this new information is based on only past occurrences of death and is not a predictor for the future. Despite that obvious limitation, however, the social service staff, as well as other professional staff groups, could rationally and programmatically use the information that approximately 68% of residents will probably die between the ages of 74 and 78, 95% between the ages of 72 and 80, and 99% between the ages of 70 and 82. The staff, given that data, might consider focusing additional medical and support services to the residents between the smallest spread of ages (at one standard deviation) as well as to their extended families. Why do this? Because it appears that a great majority of residents (68%), based on past patterns, have died between those ages.

As another example of how a standard deviation score could be useful, consider if a family services agency knew from past client records that approximately 70% of couples experience serious communication problems between the 8th and 11th years of their marriage. That agency could similarly plan to provide community-based educational programming and assertively target those services to couples who have been together for that period of time.

From another perspective, since the standard deviation assesses how dispersed the scores are around and away from the average score, it also provides you with an indication of how *wide* or *tight* that dispersion is from the mean score. Thus, *SD* = 5 would indicate a broader spread from the mean than *SD* = 1. This would not imply any inherent weakness or strength of the distribution of numbers, only that the points between which 68% of the numbers fall are farther away from each other. Generally speaking, the larger the standard deviation, the more spread out is the dispersion of scores from the mean. Stated another way, the smaller the standard deviation, the more do the numerical values approach, or stand close to, the mean score.

One final point: In any formal research report that you create, you are recommended to state the standard deviation directly after you provide the mean score (e.g., *M* = 43.5, *SD* = 2.2). Since these two computations complement each other, both scores jointly can provide a more precise and comprehensive picture.

Range, Minimum, and Maximum

The **range** is the straightforward computation of the distance between the lowest number and the highest number in any data set. From a technical perspective, the range is expressed as a single number, the result of subtracting the smallest value (number) from the highest value (number) in the distribution.

Thus, in a distribution of numbers where 89 is the highest and 43 is the lowest, this is how the range would be computed:

$$Range = 89 - 43$$

$$Range = 46$$

In everyday usage, however, most researchers report the range as two numbers, stated as the lowest to the highest, or vice versa. Thus, in our nursing home example, if the lowest age at which a resident died was 63 and the highest was 99, the range is, technically speaking, 36 (i.e., 99 − 63). Unless you

Range = Highest Minus Lowest

Figure 6.2   Range

are a statistician/purist, most researchers would compute and report the range of ages of residents in that nursing home as "63 to 99" or "99 to 63." This somewhat imprecise representation of the range is actually a reporting of the *minimum* and *maximum* values in a distribution of numbers. As a researcher, it is your choice as to how to report the range value. If you do use the technically correct single number, be prepared to explain what you are stating since it will undoubtedly cause some consternation among your readers or listeners.

One final point to remember: The range is absolutely affected by the outliers since its very computation is drawn from the two outlying numbers on either end. Thus, if the youngest resident to die in the nursing home was 59 and the oldest was 106, those numbers do indicate the range but may not represent equally all the numbers in between. For this reason, if you do report the range, you should also report the mean and the standard deviation values of that variable. Otherwise, you might unintentionally share with your audience some confusing information.

Quartiles

The lonely **quartile** is, without a doubt, the most unreported and least understood value in any distribution of numbers. If you understand that the median score is the exact midpoint in a horizontal array of numbers, then you can easily compute the quartile values on either side of that median value. Thinking in terms of 100, with the median at the 50th point, the *lower quartile* is, then, the number at the 25th point, and the *upper quartile* is the number at the 75th point.

In this context, the word *point* is typically described as a **percentile**. Thus, if you are reporting quartile scores, you are actually noting that 25% of the numbers would fall *below* the lower quartile, while 75% of the numbers would fall *above* the upper quartile. Researchers could also report quartile values as being "at the 25th percentile" (for the lower quartile) or "at the 75th percentile" (for the upper quartile).

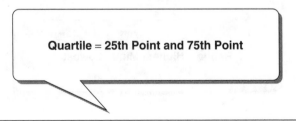

Quartile = 25th Point and 75th Point

Figure 6.3   Quartile

Figure 6.4 represents the points where the median and quartile values would fall in any distribution of numbers, along with the low and high outliers.

The upper and lower quartiles are also referred to as the **interquartile range.** Researchers frequently report the interquartile range along with the median value to demonstrate a relatively stable set of values that are not overly influenced by the extreme scores (outliers) at either end. If you want to convey, for example, the incomes of a group of people, the median and quartile values would provide a more accurate picture than would the mean and standard deviation of the same set of incomes, especially if there were a few very low-wage earners and a few very high-wage earners.

In this example, the median value would represent the exact middle of the distribution of salary numbers, so that half the group earned more and half the group earned less than the median; the lower quartile would represent the wage level of the bottom 25th percentile, and the upper quartile would represent the wage level of the top 25th percentile. This is the reason that the variable of *income* is almost always reported as a median value along with its interquartile range of values.

The statistical computation of the quartile values, as well as the median value, is a complex and tedious task that usually results in a fractional number. For this reason, researchers usually rely on a statistical program, such as SPSS, to perform these calculations, particularly when working with large data sets. For small sets of values (e.g., 10 to 15), you can find the median and quartile values by listing the numbers from lowest to highest and then counting in to the exact midpoint (this procedure was described in greater detail in Chapter 5). That middle point is your median value. Then, find the midpoint for the lower half (lower quartile) and the upper half (upper quartile) by counting in to the exact middle of both that lower 25th percentile of scores and that upper 25th percentile of scores.

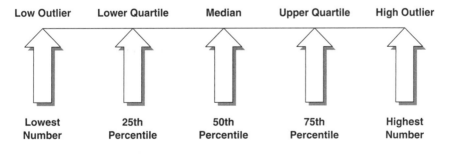

Figure 6.4   Quartile and Median Values in a Distribution

Summary Points to Remember

- Measures of variability indicate how a set of values differs from the mean and median.
- Measures of association and measures of variability are examples of descriptive statistics.
- The "ideal" standard deviation is based on the theory of probability and can be visualized on a bell-shaped curve.
- Since most distributions of values are not absolutely "ideal" or "normal," the image of the bell-shaped curve serves only as a metaphor for comparison purposes.
- Every distribution of values you collect has actual standard deviations that you can compute.
- The standard deviation indicates the average horizontal spread of the values from the mean value.
- Always include the standard deviation value (SD) whenever reporting the mean value (M).
- For a more comprehensive picture, add the range value to the mean and standard deviation.
- When reporting the range, use the more common procedure of providing the highest and lowest numbers. In SPSS language, that translates as the *maximum* and *minimum* values in the distribution.
- The range is affected by the outliers.
- The quartiles differentiate three exact points in any distribution of values: the 25th point (lower quartile), the 50th point (median), and the 75th point (upper quartile).
- The upper and lower quartiles are also called the interquartile range.
- Quartiles are not affected by outliers.
- If you are worried about the influence of extreme outlying values, report the median and interquartile range in addition to the mean and standard deviation.

Case Illustration 6.1

Exploring whether high amounts of financial aid, allocated to developing countries by the World Bank, were exerting negative effects on the goal of reducing poverty, researchers presented one set of summary statistics using quartile measurements.

First, they reported the amount of aid per capita in U.S. dollars for countries grouped into lower-quartile recipients (i.e., bottom 25% of amount received), median-level recipients (i.e., exact 50% of amount received), and upper-quartile recipients (i.e., top 75% of amount received). Second, the researchers reported the amount of aid as a percent of gross domestic product (GDP) using the same quartile categories.

The final report notes that

> there is clearly a group of very high recipients. At the same time the median aid per capita has drifted up over time (from US $11 per person in 1975–79 to US $38 in 1990–95), by the later period the upper quartile had reached $80, so that one quarter of developing countries were in receipt of aid in excess of that amount. While the median aid to GNP [gross national product] ratio has not risen in the same way, the upper quartile has moved up, so that over one quarter of the countries has aid ratios greater than 15 percent in the 1990s. (Lensink & White, 2001, p. 43)

Discussion. To understand quartile deviations, start at the median level and then move up and down from that figure. In this example, the median value indicates the amount of U.S. aid in dollars that exactly half the participating countries receive more than and half the countries receive less than. That point serves as a convenient way to visualize two halves, one greater and the other less than its own value. In reality, no single country may receive that exact dollar amount in aid, but you could picture in your mind the fact that all the amounts of U.S. aid radiate out from that central point. Moving up and down the scale, then, the upper-quartile point is the amount of U.S. aid in dollars distributed to the top 25% of recipients, and the lower-quartile point is the amount allocated to the lowest 25% of recipients. In other words, 75% of participating countries received amounts less than the upper-quartile amount, and 75% of the participating countries received more than the lower-quartile amount. If this is still confusing, refer to Figure 6.1.

Case Illustration 6.2

A recent study examined the relationship between a person's attitude toward a particular music style (in this case, rap and hip-hop music) and his or her social behavior, particularly negative social behavior. A convenience (i.e., nonrandom) sample of 605 young college students completed a standardized instrument that was based on their self-report of their own attitudes and perceptions. One of the demographic variables the researcher collected was their age in years at their last birthday.

The age of the participants was reported as mean, standard deviation, and range values: $M = 20.22$, $SD = 2.80$, and range = 16 to 46 years (Tyson, 2006, Table 1, p. 215).

Discussion. In that very short statement of the mean, standard deviation, and range, you, the reader, know three important aspects of the variable *age* of participants. First, you know that the average participant in this study was slightly older than 20 years of age (i.e., $M = 20.22$). Assuming that this distribution of ages is generally normally distributed (i.e., it is not skewed dramatically high or low), you also know that nearly 68% of the participants had ages between 23 and 17 (i.e., one standard deviation above the mean, or $M + SD = 20.22 + 2.80 = 23.02$, and one standard deviation below the mean, or $M - SD = 20.22 - 2.80 = 17.42$). Finally, you are aware that this distribution of ages is not tightly compacted around the mean age since $SD = 2.80$. In other words, there are "outliers"—those students younger than 17 and older than 23. This might be unexpected for the lower end of the age range but certainly predictable for the upper range since there are apparently a number (at least one) of nontraditional students in the sample (i.e., range = 16 to 46 years of age). If the author had chosen to report the median and modal ages, you would have an even clearer and more comprehensive understanding of this particular distribution of values.

Case Illustration 6.3

The United Nations World Health Organization (WHO) commissioned a series of mental health surveys that were conducted in 14 countries (6 less developed and 8 developed) throughout the Americas, Europe, the Middle East, Africa, and Asia. Data were collected using face-to-face interviews in 60,463 households between 2001 and 2003. The purpose of the initiative was to estimate the prevalence, severity, and treatment of existing, untreated mental health disorders, as defined by the fourth edition of the *Diagnostic and Statistical Manual of Mental Disorders* (*DSM-IV*; American Psychiatric Association, 1994). Some of the results regarding the prevalence of mental health disorders were reported using interquartile ranges. In this situation, you learn the range of values between the 25th point (percentile) and the 75th point (percentile).

The report states that "overall prevalence varies widely, from 4.3% in Shanghai to 26.4% in the United States, with a 9.1 to 16.9 inter-quartile range (IQR, the range after excluding the highest and lowest 4 surveys). Anxiety disorders are the most common disorders in all but 1 country (higher prevalence of mood disorders in Ukraine), with prevalence in the range of

2.4% to 18.2% (IQR, 5.8–8.8)" (The WHO World Mental Health Survey Consortium, 2004, p. 2585).

Discussion. This citation provides another way to use and interpret quartile deviations. Instead of focusing solely on the *points* that exist at the 25th, 50th, and 75th percentiles (as the authors did in Case Illustration 6.1), the WHO report emphasized the range of reported prevalence of mental health disorders between the 25th and 75th percentiles, known as the interquartile range. Thus, you receive in this report a visual image of the middle amount of prevalence of mental health disorders interpreted as a broad swath of numbers that, for effect, minimizes the fact that there also exist countries with prevalence rates much higher and much lower. To highlight that middle range was the decision of the creators of the WHO report and, as such, is neither right nor wrong. It is the type of choice that researchers must make all the time as they render decisions regarding what data to present and how to package those data clearly and creatively.

Activities Involving Measures of Variability

1. Using Data Set 1 (Client Demographics and Treatment Results), compute the mean and standard deviation for the variables *pre, mid,* and *post.* Narrate the results in a format appropriate for a formal research report.

2. Using Data Set 2 (Agency Satellite Offices), compute the range (i.e., minimum and maximum) for the variables *jan, mar, may, jul, sep,* and *nov.* Narrate the results in a format appropriate for a formal research report.

3. Using Data Set 4 (Client Satisfaction Survey), compute the upper quartile, median, and lower quartile for the variables *int, clin,* and *over.* Narrate the results in a format appropriate for a formal research report.

4. Using Data Set 5 (Community Social Needs Survey), compute the mean, standard deviation, range, and interquartile range for the variable *faminc.* Narrate the results in a format appropriate for a formal research report.

SPSS Procedures

Mean and Standard Deviation

In either the *Data View* or *Variable View* window, do the following:

CLICK on the *Analyze* menu from the top of the window.

PLACE THE CURSOR over the *Descriptive Statistics* choice.

CLICK on *Frequencies.*

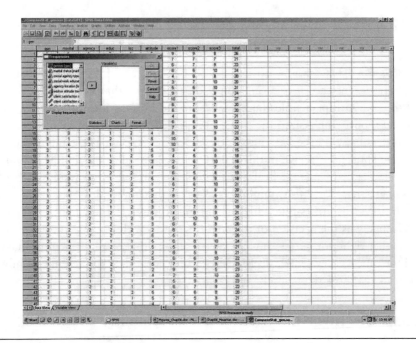

Figure 6.5   *Frequencies* Screen in SPSS

CLICK on the variable(s) you are interested in. For most precision, use only scale variables. For moderate precision, you may use ordinal variables if they are measured at 5 or more points. For the least precision, you may use ordinal variables measured at only 3 or 4 points.

CLICK on the right-pointing button in the middle of the window.

CLICK on the *Statistics* button at the bottom of the window.

CLICK on the *Mean* and *Standard Deviation* buttons.

CLICK on the *Continue* button.

CLICK on the *OK* button at the top right of the window. To return to the *Data View* or *Variable View*, CLICK on the close button [X] at the top right of the window.

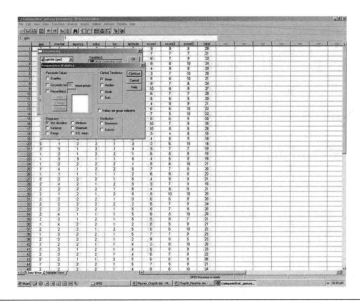

Figure 6.6   *Frequencies: Statistics* Screen for Mean and Standard Deviation in SPSS

Applying the SPSS Output

In the output box labeled *Statistics,* do the following:

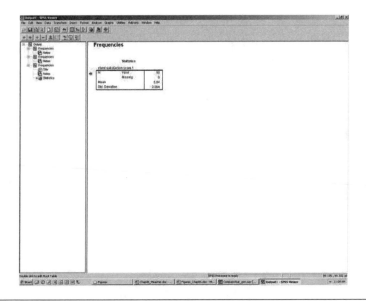

Figure 6.7   *Output* Screen of Mean and Standard Deviation in SPSS

NOTICE the number of valid cases (*N*) and the number (if any) of missing cases.

NOTICE the mean (*M*) value and the standard deviation (*SD*) value.

INCLUDE these values in any figure, table, or narrative you produce.

IGNORE the rest of the output.

Range, Minimum, and Maximum

In either the *Data View* or *Variable View* window, do the following:

CLICK the *Analyze* menu from the top of the window.

PLACE THE CURSOR over the *Descriptive Statistics* choice.

CLICK on *Frequencies.*

CLICK on the variable(s) you are interested in. Use only scale variables.

CLICK on the right-pointing button in the middle of the window.

CLICK on the *Statistics* button at the bottom of the window.

CLICK on the *Range, Minimum,* and *Maximum* buttons in the bottom-left corner of the window.

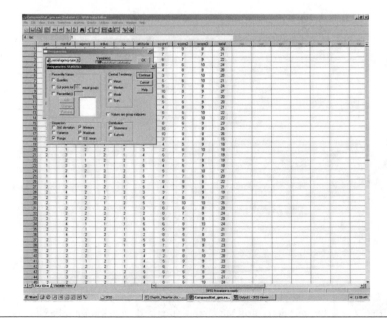

Figure 6.8   *Frequencies: Statistics* Screen for Range, Minimum, and Maximum in SPSS

CLICK on the *Continue* button.

CLICK on the *OK* button at the top right of the window. To return to the *Data View* or *Variable View*, CLICK on the close button [**X**] at the top right of the window.

NOTE that the *Minimum* and *Maximum* values are typically used as the *range* in formal research and program evaluation reports.

Applying the SPSS Output

In the output box labeled *Statistics*, do the following:

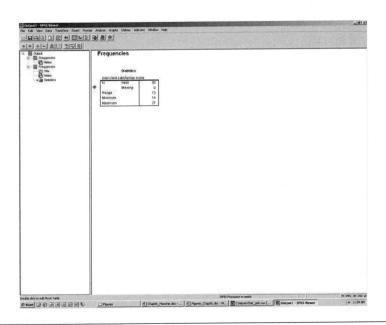

Figure 6.9   *Output* Screen of Range, Minimum, and Maximum in SPSS

NOTICE the number of valid cases (*N*) and the number (if any) of missing cases.

NOTICE the values listed for the range, minimum, and maximum categories.

INCLUDE these values in any figure, table, or narrative you produce.

IGNORE the rest of the output.

Quartiles and Interquartile Range

In either the *Data View* or *Variable View* window, do the following:

CLICK the *Analyze* menu from the top of the window.

PLACE THE CURSOR over the *Descriptive Statistics* choice.

CLICK on *Frequencies*.

CLICK on the variable(s) you are interested in. For most precision, use only scale variables. For moderate precision, you may use ordinal variables if they are measured at 5 or more points. For the least precision, you may use ordinal variables measured at only 3 or 4 points.

CLICK on the right-pointing button in the middle of the window.

CLICK on the *Statistics* button at the bottom of the window.

CLICK on the *Lower Quartile* and *Upper Quartile* buttons in the top-left corner of the window.

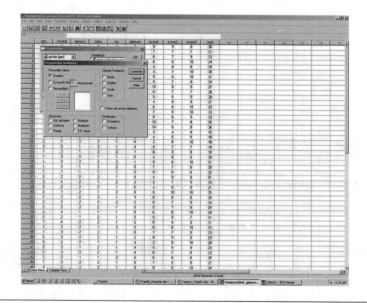

Figure 6.10   *Frequencies: Statistics* Screen for Quartiles in SPSS

CLICK on the *Continue* button.

CLICK on the *OK* button at the top right of the window. To return to the *Data View* or *Variable View*, CLICK on the close button [**X**] at the top right of the window.

Applying the SPSS Output

In the output box labeled *Statistics*, do the following:

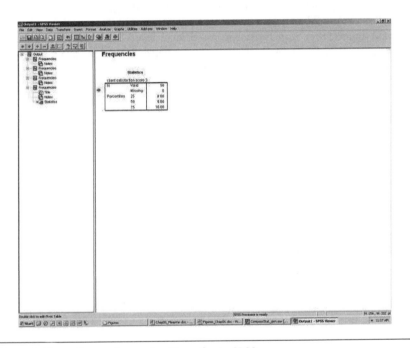

Figure 6.11   *Output* Screen for Quartiles in SPSS

NOTICE the number of valid cases (*N*) and the number (if any) of missing cases.

NOTICE the values listed for Percentiles 25, Percentiles 50, and Percentiles 75.

INCLUDE these values in any figure, table, or narrative you produce.

IGNORE the rest of the output.

References

American Psychiatric Association. (1994). *Diagnostic and statistical manual of mental disorders* (4th ed.). Washington, DC: Author.

Lensink, R., & White, H. (2001). Are there negative returns to aid? *Journal of Development Studies, 37*(6), 42–65.

Steel, J. L., & Herlitz, C. A. (2005). The association between childhood and adolescent sexual abuse and proxies for sexual risk behavior: A random sample of the general population of Sweden. *Child Abuse & Neglect, 29,* 1141–1153.

Tyson, E. H. (2006). Rap-music attitude and perception scale: A validation study. *Research on Social Work Practice, 16*(2), 211–223.

The WHO World Mental Health Survey Consortium. (2004). Prevalence, severity, and unmet need for treatment of mental disorders in the World Health Organization world mental health surveys. *Journal of the Medical Association, 291*(21), 2581–2590.

7

Other Descriptive Statistics

I abhor averages. I like the individual case. A man may have six meals one day and none the next, making an average of three meals per day, but that is not a good way to live.

—Louis D. Brandeis, cited on
www.quotegarden.com/statistics

Introductory Case Illustration

In their study of the prevalence of race and class inequality among prison inmates in the United States, Pettit and Western (2004) cite demographic data originally reported by the U.S. Bureau of Justice Statistics (BJS). Some of these data in this study were reported as simple frequency counts delineated by the variable of race.

The researchers indicated that "the National Longitudinal Survey of Youth (NLSY) figures give the percentage of respondents who have ever been interviewed in a correctional facility by age 35 (whites $N = 2171$, blacks $N = 881$)" (Pettit & Western, 2004, p. 162).

Discussion. Providing to the reader individual sums within categories (in this case, racial categories) is another convenient procedure for clarifying in broad terms the meaning of your data. By presenting whole numbers along with a table of percentages, you get an immediate sense of the size of the participant pool. That information regarding size of the racial categories offers you more detail than what the percentages alone could convey.

This chapter will discuss in greater detail the well-known procedure *sum* plus several additional descriptive measurements that should help you in your responsibility as a researcher to present your findings clearly and comprehensively.

Frequency Count

A *frequency count* is the listing in a column of the number of times (frequency) a value (number) appears in each category of a variable. For scale data (e.g., income in exact dollars), a frequency count provides the number of times the dollar amount of $15,500 appears in the distribution of all incomes recorded in the data set. For ordinal data (e.g., income in rank-order categories) or nominal data (e.g., income using name categories such as "low income," "middle income"), a frequency count presents the number of times a value appears in each ordinal income category (e.g., $10,000–$20,000) or in each nominal income level (e.g., high income). For practical purposes, frequency count is virtually the same as a statement of the *sum* of the values in each category of a variable.

Percent

Typically appearing together with the frequency count and the sum, the **percent** is a statement of the number of occurrences in each category of the variable *based on an absolute value of 100*. The percent symbol (%) or the word *percent* always accompanies the number that indicates the percentage.

Valid Percent

In any table that lists all the frequency counts of the categories of a variable, the *valid percent* indicates the true percentage value, based on 100%, *not including any missing cases* in the distribution. A missing case represents an empty cell in any SPSS data file. This is due either to a data entry error or to the fact that the researcher does not have access to a value for that cell for that particular research participant. If you experience such a situation with missing data, you should use the valid percent number in the SPSS output screen, rather than the value simply stated as *percent*.

Cumulative Percent

As the words imply, a *cumulative percent* is a number, still based on 100%, that indicates the step-by-step summation of the percentage down through a whole list of numbers. The cumulative percent is computed by the addition of each percentage number to the number immediately preceding it on the list. Although this procedure is not commonly reported in social service research projects, it might be useful in situations where the researcher wishes to visualize the progression of increasing percentage points through a distribution of numbers in a sample. Examples might include the birth weight of HIV/AIDS-infected infants or income categories that identify respondents as high income, middle income, or low income.

Sum

In any research context, the *sum* is the aggregate number of all the values in each category of a variable. If the variable is measured at the scale level, the sum reports the absolute total number of values stated in all categories of the variable (e.g., the sum of all the years of professional experience reported by all respondents). In this situation, the sum is equivalent to the *total sum* (see below). However, if the categories of the variable, are measured at the ordinal level (e.g., responses on a 5-point Likert scale) or at the nominal level (e.g., gender categories), then the sum provides only a partial aggregate for each category. The sum should be preceded by the symbol $(N =)$ and followed by the numerical statement of the percentage and the symbol (%).

For example, to report the sum of the variable *gender*, you could state the following: "This sample of respondents included 27 females (47%) and 31 males (53%)." An alternative way to report these data would be, "This sample of respondents was 47% female $(N = 27)$ and 53% male $(N = 31)$." Finally, a third way that you could report the same information to the reader would be, "Forty-seven percent $(N = 27)$ of this sample of respondents were females, and 31 (53%) were males."

Total Sum

The *total sum* is the aggregate number of all the values, not broken down into each category but computed as the aggregate of all the categories taken together. You should use this descriptive statistic only to provide a general overview of the research project (e.g., the total number of respondents to a survey) or to report the total values in all the categories of a variable (e.g., the number and percent of respondents who answered the question about their present marital status as well as the number and percent of those who refused to answer this question). You can employ this total sum statistic in conjunction with the sum statistic discussed above as in the following example: "The gender breakdown of all those who responded to this survey ($N = 58$) indicated that 27 females (47%) and 31 males (53%) participated." In this example, "($N = 58$)" is the total sum, while "27 females (47%) and 31 males (53%)" is the sum.

Skewness

The definition of a **normal distribution** of values (numbers) in a population was discussed in Chapter 1. The visual representation of a normal distribution is the famous bell-shaped curve that appears frequently throughout most standard statistics textbooks. Determining a distribution's *skewness* allows the researcher to judge how close a particular distribution is to what is considered normal from the perspective of *variability along the horizontal axis*. In simpler terms, if you spread out the values of a distribution on a horizontal axis, would the resultant figure stand solid like a near-perfect giant bell, or would the whole shape lean left or right like a wave rushing to crash on a sandy beach somewhere? The amount of skewness of a distribution indicates whether those values are tilting drastically toward the left or toward the right. Any extreme skewness level serves as sort of an early warning indicator that the numerical values you have collected at a scale level may not be normally distributed, and thus a particular statistical test that requires a normal distribution is not appropriate for your analysis. Relax, because the SPSS program offers you a simple way to gauge your distribution's amount of skewness.

Statisticians talk about a nonnormal distribution as "skewed right" or "skewed left" as a tactic to explain this variability from the precise horizontal balance, as seen in a bell-shaped curve. Unfortunately, the meaning of these directional slopes can easily cause confusion. The key to understanding is not the direction of the top of the distribution (i.e., the peak of the wave) but the direction of the tail that you see down near the horizontal plane. Is that tail drifting unusually toward the right? Then that distribution of values is considered "skewed right" or **positively skewed**. If, on the other hand, the tail of the distribution flows oddly off toward the left, that distribution is considered "skewed left" or **negatively skewed**. Most people have to think consciously about this distinction since it is counterintuitive to what your eyes appear to show you.

To provide you with some realistic examples, imagine that you are the administrator of a small residential facility that provides community support services to adults who have recently been discharged from a mental health facility. During the past 5 weeks, you and your staff have been noticing a lot of unusual activity among the residents that seemed to point to symptoms of mental illness. Using the data available in the daily log book in which staff record all atypical behaviors among the residents, you construct a histogram of the number of symptoms per week for the past 5 weeks as a way to understand any pattern that might be present. Figure 7.1 portrays a dramatically decreasing pattern of the total occurrence of symptoms by week, appearing as a nonnormal curve that has a positively **skewed distribution.** An image of a hypothetical normal distribution is overlaid for comparison purposes. Remember that a "normal" distribution of values would start low; increase to a similar mean, median, and mode point; and then drop off to an ending point in a pattern similar to the starting point. This normal distribution, if present, would represent low and high outliers at either end, as well as the average number of weekly occurrences of symptoms during the 5-week period.

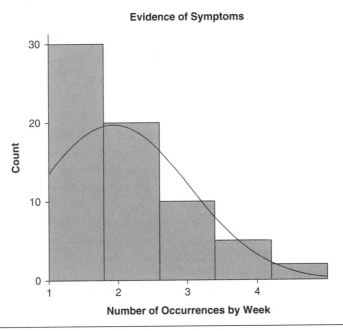

Figure 7.1   A Positively Skewed Distribution With Normal Curve Overlay

If the daily log book revealed instead an increasing pattern of the total occurrence of symptoms over the past 5 weeks, the nonnormal distribution would appear as negatively skewed (see Figure 7.2). An image of a hypothetical normal distribution is again overlaid for comparison purposes.

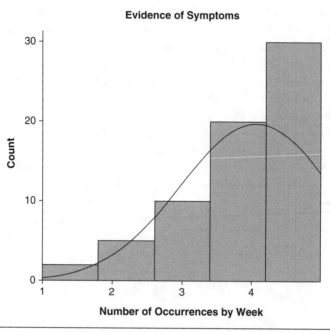

Figure 7.2   A Negatively Skewed Distribution With Normal Curve Overlay

You can consider the amount of skewness to be within the normal range if it computes anywhere in the 0.0 to 1.00 range. Scores between 1.00 and 2.00 should cause you to hesitate and reconsider your options. Specifically, the closer a skewness score approaches 2.00, the more likely you can assume that your distribution is nonnormal.

You may be wondering why it is so important to know whether a distribution is normal; granted, it is not the most earth-shattering piece of news in anyone's life. However, it does have great relevance to your choice about the appropriate statistical test to run on your research data. You will discover more about this in Chapter 15. Here, in Chapter 7, it is enough for you to know what skewness is in practical terms and then be able to compute it with a very simple SPSS procedure. Skewness is rarely, if ever, reported in formal research or program evaluation reports.

Kurtosis

Another possible distortion to a normal distribution, but pointed in the opposite direction to skewness, is **kurtosis.** The good news is that you can analyze any distribution's kurtosis just as easily as you can its skewness. Kurtosis is simply the measurement of a distribution's *peakedness* or *height* in reference to the normal bell-shaped curve. So, in comparison to what you just saw in the discussion of skewness (above), you might say that a distribution's level of kurtosis allows the researcher to judge how close a particular distribution is to what is considered normal from the perspective of *variability along the vertical axis.* A distribution that looked like a tall and narrow wizard's hat or like a flattened pancake with a small mound in the middle would each indicate an extreme (i.e., nonnormal) amount of kurtosis. Stated in another way, the amount of kurtosis of a distribution indicates whether those values are very narrowly clustering around the middle (i.e., the mean value) or are widely overstretched in both directions so that the tails of the distribution look flat on both sides. A distribution that looks like a thin, pointed hat is formally labeled as **leptokurtic,** while a distribution with a thick, squeezed-down, and compressed appearance is labeled as **platykurtic.** The values in a leptokurtic distribution unnaturally form at the center; the values in a platykurtic distribution, on the contrary, atypically spread out from the center.

Similar to skewness measurements, you can consider the amount of kurtosis to be within the normal range if it computes anywhere in the 0.0 to 1.00 range. Kurtosis scores between 1.00 and 2.00 should cause you to hesitate and reconsider your options regarding what statistical test would be appropriate for analysis. Specifically, the closer a kurtosis score approaches 2.00, the more likely you can assume that your distribution is nonnormal. Kurtosis, just like skewness, is rarely, if ever, reported in formal research or program evaluation reports, and you are similarly able to compute its level in the SPSS program. Any extreme kurtosis level also stands as an early warning indicator that the scale-level quantitative values you have collected may not be normally distributed, and thus a particular statistical test that requires a normal distribution may not be appropriate for your analysis.

Continuing with the same residential agency example as above, if there was an unnaturally large number of mental health symptoms evident during the third week, that would influence the numerical intensity of the middle week (in a span of 5 weeks) and produce a nonnormal leptokurtic distribution of numbers (see Figure 7.3). An image of a hypothetical normal distribution is overlaid for comparison purposes.

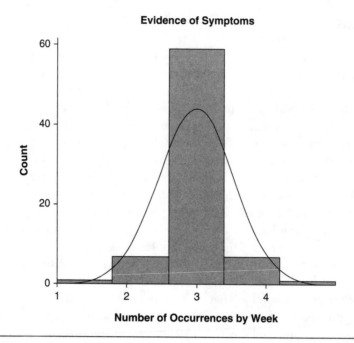

Figure 7.3   A Leptokurtic Distribution With Normal Curve Overlay

Finally, if the number of occurrences of the mental health symptoms happened to be spread out, more or less evenly, over the entire 5-week period, then you would have a flattened pattern of occurrences, also referred to as a platykurtic distribution, as seen in Figure 7.4. An image of a hypothetical normal distribution is again overlaid for comparison purposes.

The whole point behind this discussion about such strange topics as skewness and kurtosis is to demonstrate to you how close to a normal distribution are the particular set of values you are using for your analysis in a specific research project. Remember that no one expects you to have a perfectly normal distribution of values that absolutely and exactly reflect the requirements of a normal distribution. A close approximation to that ideal is sufficient.

Summary Points to Remember

- A frequency count is essentially the same as a sum.
- The valid percent is typically more useful because it does not include any missing values (i.e., missing data) in a variable.

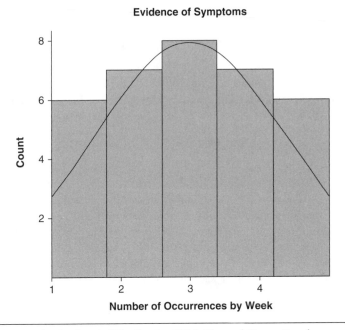

Figure 7.4   A Platykurtic Distribution With Normal Curve Overlay

- The cumulative percent is used only in situations where you wish to indicate the gradual increase in the percentage amount of a variable.

- Always include the percent whenever stating the frequency count or sum.

- Skewness measures how pitched left (negative) or right (positive) a distribution of values is from a central (mean) value.

- The direction of a distribution's skewness is determined by atypical distortion in the tail.

- Kurtosis measures how tall or flat a distribution of values is from a central (mean) value.

- As a general guide, a skewness or kurtosis value in the 0.00 to 1.00 range is considered normal.

- Skewness and kurtosis values are used only to estimate how normal any distribution is and are rarely, if ever, included in a formal report.

Case Illustration 7.1

Using a sample of 30 male sex offenders who were attending treatment groups, Gentry, Dulmus, and Theriot (2005) compared two distinct risk assessment instruments (the Static-99 and the Level of Service Inventory–Revised [LSI-R]) that are used to gauge the danger of further sexual offense. The researchers summarized the general results using the sum and percent statistics.

The authors noted that

> the LSI-R classified the majority of the sample as being at a low risk for reoffending (76.7%; $n = 23$). The remaining study respondents were classified as low-medium or moderate risk and none were identified as a medium or moderate-high risk for reoffending, Comparatively, the Static-99 classified 8 sex offenders (26.7%) as low risk, 18 (60.0%) low-medium or moderate risk, and 4 (13.3%) as medium or moderate-high risk. No sex offenders were labeled as high risk on either scale. (Gentry et al., 2005, p. 560)

Discussion. As is obvious, the sum and percent offer simple, straightforward summary calculations about values and value categories. The sum and percent are probably the most frequently reported statistical outcomes that you will encounter, not just in professional publications but in virtually all print media as well as on television, radio, or the Internet. This example demonstrates two ways in which you can actually cite sums and percentages as you compose the Presentation of Data section of a research report. The first way is to cite both together bracketed by parentheses: "(76.7%; $n = 23$)." An alternate format is to narrate one of the numbers followed by the second one bracketed by parentheses: "classified 8 sex offenders (26.7%) as low risk." A slight variation on this second format would be to reverse the two numbers and state the same information: "classified 26.7% sex offenders ($n = 23$) as low risk."

Case Illustration 7.2

In a study that explored the **validity** and **reliability** of a five-item neighborhood measurement scale, the researchers reported, in very general terms, total sum values in two separate places in their report. These sum values relate to different variables and, thus, are not comparable to each other.

Their final report documented that

> whether using averaged ($n = 178$) or independent ratings that included blocks with only one rater ($n = 325$), the neighborhood scores spanned the whole

scale. . . . A total of 319 rating scales were included in the final model examining interviewer effects, which involved observations from all interviewers on which complete data were available. (Andresen, Malmstrom, Miller, & Wolinsky, 2006, pp. 31–32)

Discussion. While it is certainly possible for a researcher to report just the sum procedure in a report, as in this example, the usual advice offered is to report *both* the sum and the percent at the same time for reasons of clarity and understanding. Numbers, in and of themselves, never tell the whole story. Is 178 a large number? It certainly is within a total of 200, but it is quite small within a total of 100,000. By providing the reader with both the sum and the percent, based on 100%, you will place that number within a context, a framework that is clearer and easier to comprehend than just the sum or the percent by itself.

Case Illustration 7.3

In a 2006 evaluation study of an intensive program designed to treat males convicted of abusing their spouses, Buttell and Carney (2006) describe the participants at the beginning of their report. This description is stated in terms of frequency counts, percentages, and sums.

They report that

the agency has been using the combination of assessment tools since August 1999. Since that time, 3,595 men have been referred to the 26-week program by the courts. Of this group of men, 1,941 men (54%) have dropped out or been terminated from the program, 899 men (25%) have graduated from the program and 755 men (21%) are still active in the program. The sample for this study included all 26-week treatment completers (*n* = 899). (Buttell & Carney, 2006, p. 123)

Discussion. This is a helpful example of how the use of both the sum and the percent of various categories can aid understanding, particularly when you need to report together a series of numbers that all relate to multiple categories. Also, the last sentence in this citation from Buttell and Carney (2006) serves as a practical reminder that the specific sample of participants for this study ("treatment completers") is the same group of 899 men who graduated from the treatment program and represent only 25% of the original group of 3,595 men referred at the beginning of the program.

Activities Involving Other Descriptive Statistics

1. Using Data Set 4 (Client Satisfaction Survey), compute the frequency and valid percent of the categories within the variables *gen* and *stat*. Narrate the results in a format appropriate for a formal research report.

2. Using Data Set 1 (Client Demographics and Treatment Results), compute the frequency, valid percent, and cumulative percent of the variables *age* and *faminc*. Narrate the results in a format appropriate for a formal research report.

3. Using Data Set 3 (Client Single-Case Evaluation), compute the skewness and kurtosis of the variables *base1*, *base2*, and *base3*. Explain to a colleague the meaning and relevance of the output.

4. Using Data Set 5 (Community Social Needs Survey), compute the skewness and kurtosis of the variable *age*. Explain to a colleague the meaning and relevance of the output.

SPSS Procedures

Frequency Counts, Percent, Valid Percent, and Cumulative Percent (for Nominal and Ordinal Data)

In either the *Data View* or *Variable View* window, do the following:

CLICK on the *Analyze* menu at the top of the window.

PLACE THE CURSOR over the *Descriptive Statistics* choice.

CLICK on *Frequencies*.

CLICK on the variable(s) you are interested in. Do not mix nominal and ordinal variables together.

CLICK on the right-pointing button in the middle of the window.

NOTE that, for this procedure, you do not have to engage the *Statistics* button at the bottom of the window because the production of *Frequency*, *Percent*, *Valid Percent*, and *Cumulative Percent* are the default outcomes.

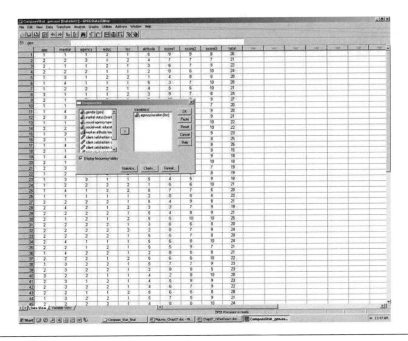

Figure 7.5   *Frequencies* Screen for a Nominal Variable in SPSS

CLICK on the *OK* button at the top right of the window. To return to the *Data View* or *Variable View*, CLICK on the close button [**X**] at the top right of the window.

Applying the SPSS Output

In the output box, do the following:

NOTICE that there are the four columns of numbers, labeled *Frequency*, *Percent*, *Valid Percent*, and *Cumulative Percent*. Consider whatever column(s) is relevant for your use.

REMEMBER that *Percent* includes missing values (i.e., data not available or not entered into the appropriate SPSS cell), and *Valid Percent* excludes missing values.

INCLUDE only the data you need for your formal report.

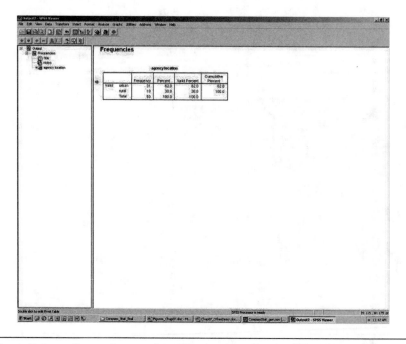

Figure 7.6   Output Screen of *Frequencies* for a Nominal Variable in SPSS

Sum (for Scale Data)

In either the *Data View* or *Variable View* window, do the following:

CLICK on the *Analyze* menu from the top of the window.

PLACE THE CURSOR over the *Descriptive Statistics* choice.

CLICK on *Frequencies*.

CLICK on the variable(s) you are interested in. List only scale-level variables.

CLICK on the right-pointing button in the middle of the window.

CLICK on the *Statistics* button at the bottom of the window.

CLICK on the *Sum* button.

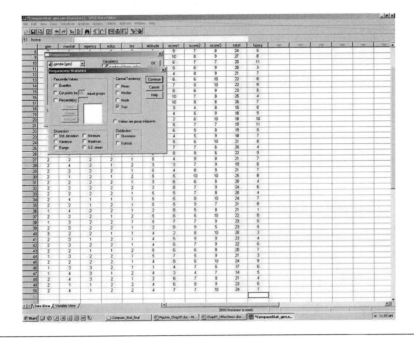

Figure 7.7   *Frequencies: Statistics* Screen in SPSS for a Scale Variable

CLICK on the *Continue* button.

CLICK on the *OK* button at the top right of the window. To return to the *Data View* or *Variable View*, CLICK on the close button [X] at the top right of the window.

Applying the SPSS Output

In the output box labeled *Statistics*, do the following:

NOTICE the number of valid cases (N) and the number (if any) of missing cases.

NOTICE the values listed for *Sum*.

INCLUDE only the data you need for your formal report.

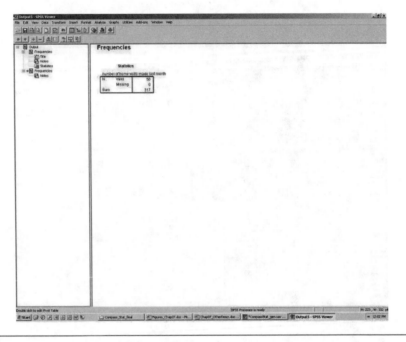

Figure 7.8   Output of *Sum* in SPSS

Skewness and Kurtosis (for Scale Data)

In either the *Data View* or *Variable View* window, do the following:

CLICK on the *Analyze* menu from the top of the window.

PLACE THE CURSOR over the *Descriptive Statistics* choice.

CLICK on *Frequencies*.

CLICK on the variable(s) you are interested in. List only scale-level variables.

CLICK on the right-pointing button in the middle of the window.

CLICK on the *Statistics* button at the bottom of the window.

CLICK on the *Skewness* and *Kurtosis* buttons at the bottom right of the window.

CLICK on the *Continue* button.

CLICK on the *OK* button at the top right of the window. To return to the *Data View* or *Variable View*, CLICK on the close button [**X**] at the top right of the window.

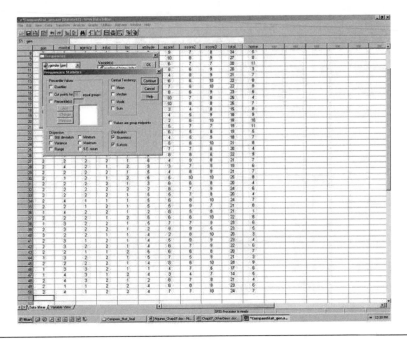

Figure 7.9   *Frequencies: Statistics* Screen for Skewness and Kurtosis in SPSS

Applying the SPSS Output

In the output box, do the following:

INCLUDE only the data you need for your formal report. Use the values to decide if your sample is normally distributed or not.

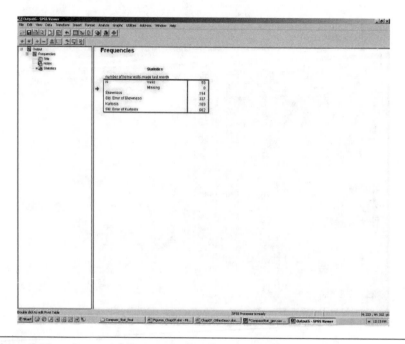

Figure 7.10   Output of *Frequencies* for Skewness and Kurtosis in SPSS

References

Andresen, E. M., Malmstrom, T. K., Miller, D. K., & Wolinsky, F. D. (2006). Reliability and validity of observer ratings of neighborhoods. *Journal of Aging and Health, 18*(1), 28–36.

Buttell, F. P., & Carney, M. M. (2006). A large sample evaluation of a court-mandated batterer intervention program: Investigating differential program effect for African American and Caucasian men. *Research on Social Work Practice, 16*(2), 121–131.

Gentry, A. L., Dulmus, C. N., & Theriot, M. T. (2005). Comparing sex offender risk classification using the Static-99 and LSI-R assessment instruments. *Research on Social Work Practice, 15*(6), 557–563.

Pettit, B., & Western, B. (2004). Mass imprisonment and the life course: Race and class inequality in U.S. incarceration. *American Sociological Review, 69*, 151–169.

8

Probability and Statistical Significance

The theory of probabilities is at bottom nothing but common sense reduced to calculus.

—Laplace, *Theorie Analitique des Probabilities*, 1820, cited on www.quotegarden.com/statistics

One of the most frustrating and confusing issues to explain in statistics is the concept of *probability*. Once you enter this smoky realm, you soon realize that common words we use every day, words such as *significant* or phrases such as *high probability* or *low probability,* all of a sudden assume some different and annoyingly rigid meanings. You will also come across this thing called **hypothesis testing**, which, at times, might make you feel like you have slipped into some weird alternative universe where everything is backward.

The assumption is that you are using this book because you have already completed an introductory research methods class, or perhaps you are taking that class right now. Either way, you have learned (or are learning) about what is called *the research process.* Typically, the steps in this research process involve

- deciding on some topic of interest;
- conducting a comprehensive literature review on that topic;

- proposing a hypothesis to be tested quantitatively or a research question to be answered qualitatively;
- choosing a research design and data collection method;
- collecting, sorting, and analyzing the data;
- developing a discussion of your findings; and
- offering conclusions and implications based on your data.

Or perhaps you did not launch your own individual research project but were part of a group project. Either way, the foundation of all of that research activity, if your research project is quantitative in nature, is called *probability theory.*

If you are ever moved to investigate further, there are, literally, whole chapters in many statistics textbooks devoted to just the quantitative theory that serves as the conceptual base for any discussion of probability. As it turns out, that base happens to be, once again, the famous bell-shaped curve. Then, too, there are usually additional chapters in traditional textbooks that delve into the importance of the term *probability* for understanding statistical analysis in general. This present chapter will not try to duplicate, or even synthesize, that important theoretical material but will instead attempt to move beyond it to a level of discussion immediately applicable to the needs of the social services practitioner. You are advised, however, to keep that background material on probability available for reference sake whenever you need it.

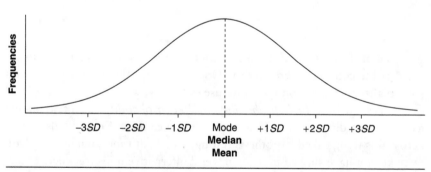

Figure 8.1   The Bell-Shaped Curve

Sample and Population

Before we begin the discussion on probability, you should be thoroughly familiar with the terms *sample* and *population,* as well as with the special type of sample known as a *random sample*. These subjects were previously discussed in Chapter 1 of this book, so what appears here is only a brief reminder of what you will find there.

Think of an enormous glass bowl filled with 1,500 colored marbles. Suppose that in the bowl, there are exactly 250 marbles each of the following six colors: red, blue, green, purple, brown, and yellow. After swirling the marbles around for a few minutes to make sure all the colors are evenly dispersed throughout the bowl, you take out, without looking, 150 marbles, which represents 10% of the total. That 10% of the marbles ($N = 150$) is a *sample* that you drew from the entire *population* of all the 1,500 marbles in the bowl.

Certainly, there exist many other marbles in the world that are not in your bowl at this point in time, but you are not concerned about them right now. You are focusing on only this particular bowl of 1,500 marbles, which can be referred to as your *study population*. By pulling out a sample of 150 marbles, you hope that they represent the whole batch of marbles in the bowl, at least on the variable of *color*.

One more thing about your sample of 150 marbles: Since you stirred them around in the bowl and did not look at the marbles when you drew them out, you can assume that each of the 1,500 marbles in the bowl had an equal **chance** of being selected. That means that your group of 150 marbles is a random sample drawn from the entire population of 1,500 marbles. On the other hand, if you had made some personal decision about which marbles to draw out (e.g., only those on the top layer because it will save time, or mostly the blue and yellow ones because those are your favorite colors), then your 10% sample will be considered a nonrandom sample.

What does this stuff about marbles have to do with probability? Well, technically speaking, or better yet, speaking as a statistical purist, you should be concerned about probability theory in only those situations in which you have drawn a clear random sample of respondents from a specifically identified study population, then gained information about them in some manner (e.g., through observation of their behavior or from their responses on a mailed survey), and now you want to *generalize* the results of your investigation back to all of the respondents in the population from which you drew your sample. Having said that, however, you will soon learn, if you do not know already, that this strict limitation of probability theory to random samples is, rightly or wrongly, often ignored in published social science research. Frequently, you will come across articles and reports that use statistical procedures described in the rest of this chapter in situations where the respondents are clearly drawn from populations in a nonrandom manner.

Univariate and Bivariate Analysis

As a second introductory point, you should note another piece of information that will save you a lot of grief: This discussion of probability relates only to *bivariate analysis* and not to *univariate analysis*. These are two other terms that also were presented in more detail in Chapter 1 of this book.

Remember that a univariate analysis is performed by those statistical methods that simplify, clarify, or summarize one variable at a time (e.g., the variable of *age*). Thus, if 159 respondents shared with you their age at their last birthday, you could conduct a univariate analysis of these data by presenting to the reader their average age, their median age, their modal age, or their range of ages. Other examples of univariate analysis could be the average age and standard deviation in years and months of children freed for adoption by a family court; the total number of female and male offenders incarcerated, by county, in the state prison system; or the range of the number of counseling sessions attended by clients in a community methadone maintenance program.

Bivariate analysis, on the other hand, will occur using those statistical methods that seek to determine whether a relationship exists between two variables at the same time (e.g., between gender and political party affiliation). Furthermore, if such a relationship is discovered, then a bivariate analysis also points out what *the probability is that the relationship exists only by a chance occurrence*. For example, if you discovered in a random sample of voters that women tended to vote Republican (rather than Democrat or Independent) statistically more so than did men in the same sample, then what is the likelihood that your results were due to a chance occurrence? In other words, how confident are you that you did not select a very unusual *sample* of voters that, for some unknown reason, just happened to contain a large amount of female Republican voters and, therefore, that sample does not accurately represent the whole *population* of female and male voters you are studying?

A second example may help clarify things. Suppose you plan to study whether there was a relationship between the variable *physical abuse of children* and the variable *excessive alcohol use in the home*. You draw a random sample of 50 families out of a population of 350 families who have an active case file with the Protective Services Division of the county Department of Children and Family Services. After obtaining the appropriate permissions, you read the case intake summaries and interview the caseworkers involved with the 50 families using a research instrument that quantifies the severity level of physical child abuse discovered in the home as well as the amount of alcohol use by the adults responsible for the care of the children. Following a statistical analysis of the data, you conclude that there exists a significant correlation between the amount of alcohol use by the adults and the severity of the physical abuse encountered in the home. Specifically, you discover that the more the adults used alcohol, the more severe the physical abuse of the children was. However, you also learn from your statistical analysis that the *probability factor* was higher than is typically accepted by social science researchers. This probability factor is an indicator of whether you, as the researcher, can assure your readers that whatever you discovered in your sample (i.e., the 50 families) can be safely generalized to the entire population from which you drew your sample (i.e., the 350 families). In this hypothetical example, you are not certain that your sample truly reflects your population regarding the amount of alcohol use and the severity of child abuse in those families. There is too much of a danger that the results gained from your sample (even though it is a random sample) relate to only them alone and not to the entire population of families. Stated another way, as a researcher, you do not have the confidence to state that there exists a distinct relationship between alcohol use and child physical abuse among all the 350 open protective services cases in your county. If you have not achieved *statistical significance* in your analysis, then you cannot generalize to the population from which you drew that sample precisely because that sample of families you have examined might provide you with erroneous information about the whole population.

All this still may sound terribly confusing and irrelevant to you at this point. As we keep going and delve further into this chapter, however, you will understand why this discussion about probability is so critical for you to know.

Multivariate Analysis

As an aside, the concept of probability is also considered in **multivariate analysis,** which is the study of the relationship among *three or more variables* at the same time (e.g., income, age, and years of work experience). But relax. The good news is that multivariate analysis is such a highly complex issue that any further discussion of it is beyond the scope of this book. For our purposes in this book and in this chapter, it is sufficient that you possess a clear understanding of the difference between univariate and bivariate analysis and, furthermore, that the use of probability procedures is only relevant in the context of bivariate analysis.

Probability

The straightforward definition of *probability* is disarmingly simple. It refers to the mathematical chance or possibility that something will happen in the future. Turn on your television or radio and you may hear your local newscaster announce that "there is a fifty-fifty chance of rain this weekend," which is a common way to state that there is a *50% probability* of rain.

Or, your savvy friends may advise you that there exists a "three-to-one odds in favor of the house" whenever you gamble, which is another way of saying that you have only a *25% probability of winning and a 75% probability of losing* if you travel to Las Vegas or Atlantic City for excitement.

If there is virtually very little possibility that some event will *not* take place because it is under your control (for example, you are quite certain you are going to eat a ham and cheese sandwich because it is in your right hand and you are moving it toward your mouth), then, for all practical purposes, you could say there is a *100% probability* that you will eat the sandwich.

Technically speaking, however, it is imprecise to talk about *absolute 100% probability* for any human activity because of the nature of free will and the influence of external forces. For instance, you might change your mind about that sandwich when you see up close that the bread is moldy, or your dog might distract you, causing you to drop the sandwich on the floor before you take your first bite.

Probability and Bivariate Analysis

This concept of probability is linked irrevocably with the process of bivariate analysis because your goal as a researcher who uses many statistical procedures is to establish that a relationship exists between two variables (or does not exist) at an acceptably high level of probability. Remember that in this context, probability means that the relationship you discovered in your sample will also be found in the population from which you drew that sample. On the other hand, you might uncover the opposite in another research project: You have, in fact, a very low level of probability that the sample truly represents the population. What researchers consider *high probability* and *low probability* will be discussed a little later in this chapter. Be prepared, however, for the unusual, and remember that comment at the beginning of this chapter about entering an alternative universe.

As an illustration, if you were interested in testing whether there exists a relationship between gender and political party affiliation, you could develop a conclusion about that issue by executing the following five steps.

- *Step 1.* You determine a population of eligible voters in a specific geographical area (e.g., a county) by obtaining a list of all registered voters from the office of the County Clerk.

- *Step 2.* Assuming the records indicate each registrant's gender and the political party selected, you draw a 25% random sample (i.e., one out of every four) from the list of all registered voters.
- *Step 3.* You enter data into a statistical program for each registered voter on the variable of gender (female, male) and the variable of political party affiliation (Democrat, Republican, Independent).
- *Step 4.* You run the appropriate statistical test to discover whether gender influenced in a significant manner the choice of a political party affiliation. In other words, did men tend to choose Democratic more than women did? Or did women tend to choose the Republican Party, or one of the other parties, more than men did? Or, was there no significant pattern visible, in the sense that men and women tended to choose the various political parties at about the same rate?
- *Step 5.* Whatever the conclusion is, the researcher can *generalize those results back to the entire population* from which the sample was drawn since a random sample was used. You are also able to indicate the probability level of that conclusion—that is, the likelihood that the results from the sample were due to a chance occurrence (also called *sampling error*) or not.

As mentioned at the beginning of this chapter, if the data were derived from a nonrandom sample, then the researcher should not, strictly speaking, generalize back to the population from which it was drawn. Having stated that, however, you should be aware of contrary common practice. In many social services research projects using nonrandom samples, you often find statements that report the level of statistical probability that the results were due merely to chance.

The ability to generalize results for a random sample (or nonrandom sample) is *not absolute,* however, for the same reasons that we could not say that there was an absolute 100% probability that you would eat that ham and cheese sandwich. Happily, for our purposes in social service research, we do not require absolute 100% probability. Social science researchers, in general, have agreed that a *95% level of probability* is acceptable to be able to generalize the results from a random sample back to the population from which it was drawn.

You should begin to think counterintuitively at this point. The flip side of that 95% probability level is to say that social science researchers accept a *5% level of improbability* (i.e., 100% − 95% = 5%) that the sample correctly reflects the population.

Stated otherwise: You can live with a 5% chance of committing a statistical error; or there is a 5% chance that the results based on the sample data are due to sampling error and thus do not reflect accurately back to the population.

Note that you will never encounter the word *improbability* in a statistics textbook, but you will come across it commonly expressed as some statistical output having a p **value** of .05 or less. In this context, the p stands for the probability that the results you are reporting (e.g., that women in X County were significantly more likely to register as Democrats than men) had only a 5% risk of being due to chance or to some bizarre coincidence in your sample than to what all women in that county really registered for. Such a chance occurrence or coincidental set of events would mean that the random sample of registered voters pulled from the population was not truly random after all—it was some strange fluke of nature that did not truly reflect the political party choices made by the whole population of all registered voters. But since the possibility of that happening is relatively low (i.e., only 5% or less), we can proceed with our research process and report the results as significant (for example, that women register Democratic more than men) with a p value at .05 or less.

One final point: Another way of thinking about the probability level (i.e., p level) is to consider it a measure of the probability that you are committing a Type I error. In other words, if a statistically significant relationship is found to exist following some statistical test, it indicates that the probability of committing a Type I error is acceptably low (usually at the .05 level or less). Remember that a Type I error occurs whenever you reject a null hypothesis in situations where a true relationship does not exist between the variables. Another way of defining a Type I error is to say that it occurs when you reject a null hypothesis in a situation where you should not do so.

Probability Level . . . a Sort of Tolerance Level?

Another way to think about a p value of .05 or less is to consider what engineers and building contractors call a *tolerance level,* by which they mean the amount of error or imprecision they will accept in their physical projects. This is not meant to presume any real similarity between the concepts of probability and tolerance level—it is just a pale resemblance that may help to clarify things a bit.

A NASA engineer working on a space probe traveling toward one of the distant planets in the universe must operate with only a tiny, infinitesimal amount of possible error in calculations. Otherwise, that probe could miss the planet by thousands of miles due to a very slight miscalculation.

Similarly, the carpenter building a stairway or the construction supervisor bolting together massive steel beams at a building site must constantly check if lines are straight and angles are as precise as dictated in the blueprints. In these situations, the tolerance level for error must also be extremely low to avoid serious problems in the future. No scientific team can accept missing its planetary landing site other than by the smallest amount of distance, and nobody wants a stairway to wobble or a building to start leaning to one side like the Tower of Pisa in Italy!

Since social science research projects do not typically involve such need for near-perfect precision in measurements, our tolerance level for inaccuracy is higher, with the result that researchers have agreed to accept up to, but not higher than, a 5% level of uncertainty regarding whether the results are truly generalizable. To say that another way: Social scientists can live with a 5% margin of error in their calculations. But what does that really mean? First of all, it does not mean that the calculations are 95% true, valid, or acceptable or any adjective like that. What it does mean is that there is only a 5% possibility out of a 100% possibility that the results reported were due to a chance or accidental occurrence rather than to the reality of the situation.

Putting that statement into social service practice language would be asserting something like, "The results of this survey of a random sample of social workers indicate, at a 95% probability level, that MSW social workers in X County are more knowledgeable regarding the causes of HIV/AIDS than are MSW social workers in Y County, as measured by the ABC survey instrument." A probability of 95% (or its equivalent statement: $p < .05$) in this context means that, statistically speaking, there exists only a 5% probability that the reported results were due to sampling error when the participants were drawn from the pool of all possible participants in the study. In other words, the probability of (or tolerance for?) committing a Type I error (i.e., rejecting the null hypothesis that there was no difference in the knowledge levels of social workers in X and Y Counties) was at or below the acceptable social science level of .05 out of a possible 1.00.

Probability, Sampling Error, and Null Hypothesis

Another way to discuss the danger that a sample does not really represent the population from which it was drawn is to call it simply *sampling error*. For all practical purposes, sampling error, chance occurrence, and the possibility of statistical error mean the same thing.

Sampling error is just another way to point out that using a sample, especially a small sample, can be risky because there always exists the possibility that the sample just happens to be so unusual in its composition that it does not reflect the true characteristics of the entire population. The bigger the sample (i.e., the larger the sample size), the better will be the possibility that the sample will serve as an accurate mirror of the population. For example, the correct ratio between females and males in your sample might not appear

w a sample of only 25 respondents out of a population of 500, but
d have a greater chance of reaching that accurate ratio if you
your sample to 100 respondents. You would gain an even higher
accuracy level if you increased your sample size to 150, 200, and so on.

Once you compute the appropriate statistical test, you can be assured that
the sample does accurately reflect the population as long as you stay within
the accepted level of probability that you might be committing sampling
error. As noted above, that minimum level of probability is 5% out of 100%,
which is always stated as $p < .05$.

Finally, you have encountered the phrase *null hypothesis* several times in
this book, along with the exhortation that you should *reject the null hypothesis* if you want to establish that a statistical relationship does indeed exist
between the two variables you are studying. You may have wondered why
on earth anyone in their right mind would first propose a hypothesis (called
the *research hypothesis*) and then immediately come up with an absolutely
opposite way of stating that hypothesis (called the *null hypothesis*). Well,
now you know the answer to that rhetorical question, because a null hypothesis is another way of stating that there might be a possibility that sampling
error is present in your research project. Thus, you can reject the null
hypothesis if (and only *if*) you possess the statistical evidence, gained from
SPSS or some other program, that the p level is at .05 or less.

One-Tailed or Two-Tailed Hypothesis

During your research and program evaluation activities, there is one more
decision you must engage in before you start collecting your data: In what
direction should your hypothesis be stated? Such a statement of direction is
a function of whether your hypothesis is *one-tailed* or *two-tailed*. The *tails*
in this metaphor relate to how specific you can be in stating your hypothesis. A **one-tailed hypothesis** is directional in the sense that you predict clearly
what the relationship will be between your two variables under study. *Women
are more sensitive than men as measured on the XYZ Social Sensitivity Scale* is
an example of a one-tailed hypothesis. A **two-tailed hypothesis** is less specific
and nondirectional. *Gender influences an individual's sensitivity as measured on the XYZ Social Sensitivity Scale* would be a two-tailed hypothesis
on the relationship between gender and sensitivity.

How you decide whether to state a one-tailed or two-tailed hypothesis is a
critical point. It is not a question of what you *think* the direction should be but,
rather, what direction the literature supports, based on prior empirical studies
and informed opinion. Once you have completed and digested the review of

the literature on your research topic, you will be able to make that decision much more efficiently and effectively. Just make sure that you have enough information that supports your decision before you choose a one-tailed hypothesis. If in doubt, it is wise to opt for the two-tailed choice of direction.

One final point: All of the statistical tests you will run in SPSS are programmed so that the two-tailed direction is the default value. Thus, if you ever want to compute your data with a one-tailed direction, you must manually change that default value by checking the appropriate box in the SPSS program window.

Summary Points to Remember

- Probability theory is the foundation of all quantitative research activity.

- The bell-shaped curve is one way to visualize the effects of probability theory.

- A random sample is a highly structured process of selecting research participants so that every respondent has an equal chance of being chosen.

- Because of probability theory, a random sample allows you to generalize the results from a sample to the entire population from which that sample was drawn.

- Univariate analysis focuses on one variable at a time; bivariate analysis explores the relationship between two variables at a time.

- The social science disciplines accept a 95% probability level, not an absolute 100% level, that the sample truly reflects the population.

- Probability (p) in social science statistics is stated as the amount of uncertainty that is acceptable regarding a sample's ability to truly reflect the population.

- Probability (p) in social science statistics is less than or equal to the .05 level of uncertainty ($< .05$).

- Probability level can be considered as the level of tolerance of uncertainty.

- The phrases *standard error, chance occurrence,* and *possibility of statistical error* can be used interchangeably.

- The research hypothesis assumes that there exists a relationship between the dependent and independent variables.

- The null hypothesis assumes that there exists no relationship between the dependent and independent variables.

- Social science research attempts to reject the null hypothesis at a $p < .05$ level.

Activities Involving Probability, Statistical Significance, and Hypothesis Testing

1. Review the chapter or chapters on probability and hypothesis testing in your research methods textbook, focusing particularly on the figures used and the examples provided. Discuss with a colleague the relative importance of probability theory to research and program evaluation in social services.

2. Using your local newspaper or weekly news magazine, read one edition quickly but thoroughly. How often do you find the word *probability* used? How often do you find the word *significant* used? Are these words used in the newspaper or news magazine the same way that they are used in statistics? Discuss your findings with a colleague.

3. Using the Internet, go to www.stat.sc.edu/rsrch/gasp. After scrolling down to *Educational Procedures,* click on the applet (interactive demonstration) labeled *Let's Make a Deal,* and follow the instructions to begin. Do the simple exercise 20 times; always switch the first 10 times and never switch the second 10 times. Compare the results. This exercise will give you a sense of how mysterious and counterintuitive the theory of probability is.

4. Staying at the same Web site, www.stat.sc.edu/rsrch/gasp, click on the applet labeled *The Central Limit Theorem,* and follow the instructions to begin. Experiment with different die combinations and with increasing numbers of rolls of the dice. This exercise will demonstrate to you that the bell-shaped curve is a phenomenon that appears spontaneously in nature without any human intervention.

SPSS Procedures

Since there are no specific SPSS procedures to demonstrate in this chapter, you might use this extra time to immerse yourself in the SPSS tutorial material that is available to you online. Simply open up a new SPSS window and CLICK on the button for *Tutorial* in the center of the screen. Choose any topic(s) that you want to learn more about or that you think might be useful to you as a researcher and program evaluator. This will be time well spent and will, without a doubt, improve your facility to use and understand SPSS procedures.

9

Chi-Square
Test of Independence

Do not put your faith in what statistics say until you have carefully considered what they do not say.

—William H. Watt, as cited on
www.quotegarden.com/statistics

Introductory Case Illustration

Kurz, Malcolm, and Cournoyer (2005) studied 194 women who were enrolled in the Women, Infant, and Child (WIC) nutritional program to ascertain the relationship between race, ethnicity, and acculturation on the prevalence of mental health symptoms. One part of their analysis focused on the difference between immigrants/migrants and nonimmigrants (i.e., those born in the United States). A series of chi-square analyses indicated a pattern of difference between the two groups.

The authors explain that "about two thirds of the immigrants/migrants did not speak English as their first language in comparison to almost none of the nonimmigrants, $\chi^2 (1, N = 187) = 84.2$, $p < .01$; proportionately fewer of the immigrants/migrants were in the younger age group (19.6% versus 54.7%), $\chi^2 (1, N = 194) = 17.4$, $p < .01$; and proportionately more of the immigrants/migrants did not have health insurance (15.2% vs. 2.7%), $\chi^2 (1, N = 192) = 10.1$, $p < .01$" (Kurz et al., 2005, p. 441).

Discussion. To understand the results of the three chi-square tests noted here, consider first how the variables and their interrelationships could be placed into the following three crosstabulation tables:

English Language and Migration Status		
	Immigrant	*Nonimmigrant*
English First Language		
English Not First Language		

Age and Migration Status		
	Immigrant	*Nonimmigrant*
Young		
Middle Aged		
Senior		

Health Insurance and Migration Status		
	Immigrant	*Nonimmigrant*
Health Insurance		
No Health Insurance		

In an actual chi-square output window in SPSS, each of the empty cells in these hypothetical crosstabulation tables would contain numbers and percentages corresponding to raw data you entered on each respondent in your study. For our general discussion here on how to interpret chi-square analyses, the presence of numbers and percentages in each cell is not required. The summary statements of the three chi-square values, as cited by Kurz et al. (2005), are sufficient.

You will discover in this chapter that a chi-square procedure reports whether there exists a statistical probability that the two nominal variables under consideration are independent of each other. This can be confusing because of the words *independent* and *relationship*. Here is a way to maintain your sense of reality whenever you encounter a chi-square analysis: (a) If you find that they *are independent* of each other, then that means (statistically speaking) that they have *no apparent relationship* to each other based on the data from your study, and (b) on the other hand, if you do discover that they are *not independent* of each other, then you can assume that your data suggest that they do indeed have a statistical relationship with each other.

As you discovered in the previous chapter, the key to knowing whether your variables are related to each other is the so-called p value, the measure of statistical significance. If you have a p value that is equal to or less than .05, you can assume that a relationship between the variables does exist (i.e., the variables are not independent of each other), and that relationship is probably not due simply to sampling error within the data you have collected.

Reviewing now what Kurz et al. (2005) reported in this example cited above, you should be able to understand three of their findings: (1) The variable *English language* is related to (i.e., not independent of) the variable *migration status* since the data show that more immigrants than nonimmigrants do not have English as their first language, (2) the variable *age* is related to (i.e., not independent of) the variable *migration status* since the data show that fewer immigrants than nonimmigrants are reported as young in age, and (3) the variable *health insurance* is related to (i.e., not independent of) the variable *migration status* since the data show that more immigrants than nonimmigrants do not have any health insurance.

This chapter will delve a lot deeper into the meaning and the usefulness of the chi-square test of independence.

The chi-square statistical test of independence, also referred to simply as χ^2, appears often in articles published in professional journals, especially journals that appeal to practitioners in the areas of human services or social services. The reason for the popularity of using the chi-square test is simple: It requires only nominal-level data, and social agency case records tend to contain a lot of demographic data at the nominal level (e.g., gender, race/ethnicity, religion, place of residence, marital status) as well as other identifying information measured at the nominal level (e.g., type of presenting problem, types of services needed, characteristics of professional staff providing those services). If a researcher is not depending on agency case records but is collecting data by sending out a survey or interviewing respondents, then at least some of the data collected are typically demographic and nominal in nature (e.g., in addition to the variables noted above, a researcher might want to know level of education, type of social agency, kinds of social services provided). These nominal-level variables are also referred to as *categorical* variables in many statistics texts.

The Strength of the Chi-Square Test

Within the hierarchy of statistical procedures, the **chi-square test** is not particularly strong or, in formal statistical terms, not particularly *robust*. This quality of robustness has to do with a test's ability to demonstrate if a significant relationship exists between two or more variables. In other words, how definite is a researcher able to declare that the variable *professional education* has an influence on the variable *client responsiveness*? For example, assume that you anonymously surveyed a group of clients in a large multiservice rehabilitation agency and asked them to indicate if each one's social worker, vocational counselor, and job coach was either responsive or unresponsive to their needs. You would be searching whether a relationship existed between the variable *professional title* and the variable *responsiveness*. Once you received and processed those data, you could then statistically determine if professional title did or did not have any influence on how the clients in this agency perceived the staff's responsiveness to their needs. In pragmatic terms, with a chi-square test of independence, you could compare the level of responsiveness, as reported by clients, for the categories of social worker, vocational counselor, and job coach in the agency.

The reason the chi-square test is not very robust has to do with the level of data (nominal) that it uses in its analysis. It is not a value judgment to note that the nominal level of measurement is inherently imprecise or inexact. Rather, that imprecision comes from the fact that nominal-level variables are simply *labels* without any firm boundaries between the categories of that variable. So the difference between whether one is judged as *responsive* or *unresponsive* tends to be vague and highly subjective since those are the only two choices offered, and the absolute dividing line between those two choices is unclear. Consider how much more precise the information would be collected from that client group if the researcher asked their opinions about their workers' responsiveness based on an 11-point dimension, which was divided by tenths and ranged from a high of 10 to a low of 0. In this case, you would no longer consider the **measurement level** as nominal because of the increased range of choices and the precision of measurements offered to the respondents. Technically speaking, such an 11-point measurement is ordinal in nature, but most researchers would treat it as scale for analysis purposes.

Furthermore, if you used an instrument that allowed your participants to rate their workers' responsiveness on a measurement that ranged from

0 through 100, you would be providing even more precision. In this final example, the measurement would be considered at the scale level, the highest level possible. If this discussion about levels of measurement is still a bit confusing, you might consider returning to the discussion of measurement levels in Chapter 1 of this book.

As noted above, despite the limitations of the chi-square test, it can serve a very useful function in human services research because of the availability of and accessibility to so much nominal-level data in day-to-day social agency operations.

Understanding the Process of a Chi-Square Test

Step 1. Picture in your mind a square or rectangular box with lines for columns running vertically and lines for rows running horizontally. Consider each of the enclosed areas as a *cell* that will eventually contain data. Technically speaking, this figure is called a *contingency table,* as illustrated in Figure 9.1.

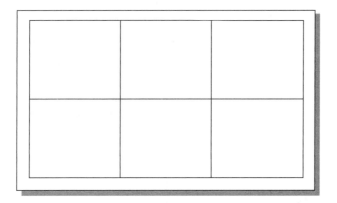

Figure 9.1   Blank Contingency Tables

Step 2. Consider which variable is the *active one* that possibly produces the influence and place that variable, with its categories, on the left side of the contingency table as the *rows.* Assume this is the independent variable.

Step 3. Place the other variable, the *passive* one that is being acted upon, at the top of the contingency table as the *columns.* Assume this is the dependent variable.

Figures 9.2 and 9.3 present the arrangement of the dependent and independent variables in a contingency table.

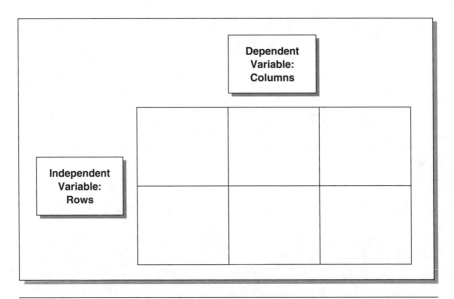

Figure 9.2   Contingency Table With Dependent and Independent Variables as Columns and Rows

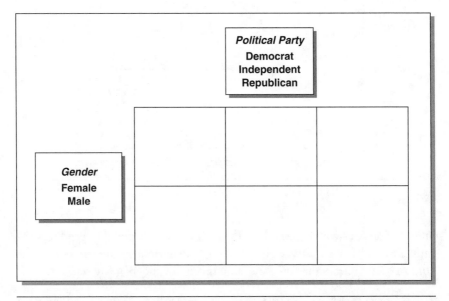

Figure 9.3   Contingency Table With Categories of Dependent and Independent Variables

Step 4. Once the data are entered into their respective cells and the chi-square test is computed, two different sets of frequencies are reported: The **observed frequency** is the actual number of respondents for each cell based on your data;

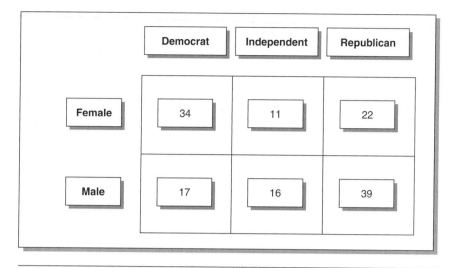

	Democrat	Independent	Republican
Female	34	11	22
Male	17	16	39

Figure 9.4   Contingency Table With Observed Frequencies Noted in Cells

the **expected frequency** is a hypothetical number derived from the execution of the chi-square formula. Figure 9.4 illustrates the placement of observed frequencies in the cells of a contingency table.

Step 5. Do not worry about the expected frequency. The SPSS program will compute the expected frequency automatically for you. This expected frequency is what you would expect to find if the two variables being analyzed were independent of (i.e., not related to) each other.

Step 6. Understand that the chi-square test formula compares the expected frequency against the observed frequency. The larger the gaps between what was expected and what you observed in the various cells, the greater the possibility that the independent variable (which is in the rows) has a significant influence on (i.e., is related to) the dependent variable (which is in the columns).

Step 7. In order for the chi-square test to perform adequately, certain requirements must be present: (a) For a 2-by-2 contingency table with four cells, no cell can contain an expected frequency of fewer than 5 subjects, and (b) in any larger contingency table (e.g., 2 by 3, 3 by 3), no more than 20% of the cells can contain an expected frequency of fewer than 5 subjects. This means that if one or both variables have a large number of categories (i.e., three or more), you will need to have a fairly large number of subjects in your sample (more than 100) or the chi-square test will not produce meaningful results. For example, if you plan to assess whether the variable *religion* (which could have categories such as *agnostic, atheist, Buddhist, Christian, Hindu, Jewish,*

Moslem, and *other*) is related statistically to the variable *level of education* (which has the categories of *elementary school, high school, some college, college, graduate school,* and *other*), that will produce an 8-by-6 contingency table, which will result in 48 cells. If more than 10 of these cells (i.e., 20%) have fewer than 5 subjects in them, any chi-square test results will be suspect. You can easily remedy this situation by *collapsing* the low-frequency variable categories into one. If only a few respondents checked the *agnostic, atheist,* and *other* categories, for example, you should collapse all those categories into a new category and label that new category *other.* Do this as often as you need to reach the 20% threshold, and then recompute the chi-square test.

Step 8. Note that you can report the existence of a statistically significant relationship between the independent and the dependent variables (i.e., that the independent variable is influencing the dependent variable) if the chi-square computation reveals a p value of .05 or less. Remember that $p < .01$, $p < .001$, and $p < .000$ are all less than $p < .05$. To state that $p < .05$ means that the probability that the revealed differences between the observed and expected frequencies (the gap) are due purely to a chance occurrence or to sampling error is less than 5% out of a possible 100%. Another way of reporting this is to note that there exists only a 1 in 20 possibility that the results are due to chance or to other unexplained factors. Thus, to uncover a statistically significant relationship in a chi-square test is to be able to assert that the variables are not independent of each other—they are related to each other in some fashion.

As an example, if your null hypothesis states that the variable *gender* is independent of the variable *political party,* that is the same as declaring that *gender* is not related to *political party.* If, upon computing a chi-square test on your real (i.e., observed) data, you discover that a statistically significant relationship exists, then you can reject your null hypothesis and assert that *gender* is indeed related to *political party.* By looking at the SPSS output and noticing where the gaps between the observed and expected values are, you can further assert which specific political party was chosen more or less by the females and males in your study.

Reporting the Results of a Chi-Square Test

There are only three basic pieces to include when you report the results of a chi-square test of independence:

1. The *absolute chi-square value* appearing as a whole number taken to two decimal places (e.g., 2.34, 4.67, 5.29)

2. The number of **degrees of freedom** appearing as a whole number (e.g., 3, 5, 8)

3. The *probability factor* appearing as a number less than 1.00 (e.g., .05, .001, .34), usually preceded by the symbol for less than (<) or more than (>)

There are two standard ways of writing up the results of a chi-square test: one traditional, the other a more modern alternative. You can choose either format as long as you are consistent throughout the entire research report.

$$\text{Traditional: } \chi^2 = 3.26, \, df = 2, \, p = < .01$$

$$\text{Modern: } \chi^2(2) = 3.26, \, p < .01$$

Measuring the Strength of the Relationship

Many researchers, after computing a chi-square analysis, will choose to stop at that point and go on to another analysis involving some other variables. However, if you want to learn just a bit more about the relationship you just discovered between the two variables in the chi-square analysis, you can take one more step and determine how strong that relationship is. This is also referred to as determining a statistical test's effect size. Reporting such an effect size is becoming increasingly common today in many books, monographs, and journals published throughout the field of social services.

Suppose you analyzed a sample of college students and discovered a statistically significant relationship between *gender* and *academic major,* as categorized into education, psychology, or social work. Furthermore, assume that your data suggest that males in your sample tended to choose social work over education or psychology, while females showed no particular preference for one over the other two choices of major. By computing the strength of that statistically significant chi-square relationship, you would possess important additional information, especially if you want to compare your results with other similar studies that may have used different statistical tests but did report the effect sizes of those tests.

There are a number of tests of the strength of the relationship between nominal-level variables (all easily computed for you in the SPSS program), but in this book, only two of the most popular will be discussed: the *phi* test and Cramer's *V* test. The only substantive difference between them is that *phi* is used when you have a 2-by-2 contingency table, and Cramer's *V* is used whenever you have any larger-size contingency table (2 by 3, 3 by 3, etc.).

The strength of the relationship is reported as a decimal number (e.g., .45) based on a perfect score of 1.00. To understand what this means, think of a dollar bill, with the *phi* or Cramer's *V* value as cents on the dollar. So, .45

would be equivalent to 45 cents out of a dollar, .70 would be 70 cents out of a dollar, and so on. A handy rule to remember is that any strength measured between 0.0 and .19 is considered to be *virtually nonexistent,* any strength measured between .20 and .40 is considered a *weak relationship,* any strength measured between .41 and .60 is considered a *moderate relationship,* and any strength measured between .61 and .100 is considered a *strong relationship.* You should include that characterization (i.e., weak, moderate, or strong) in any narrative you write to explain to your readers the meaning of the *phi* or Cramer's *V* values.

When used, the *phi* and Cramer's *V* value is typically reported at the end of the chi-square test statement in either of the following formats.

$$\chi^2 = 3.26, \, df = 2, \, p < .01, \, phi = .28$$

$$\chi^2 \, (2) = 3.26, \, p < .01, \, \text{Cramer's } V = .28$$

Interpreting the Meaning of a Chi-Square Test

Imagine that you are back in high school and you notice that two of your friends are walking together down the hallway away from you. Since you know both of them very well and you know that they are not dating each other, you would undoubtedly assume that they just happened to meet accidentally in the hallway. Furthermore, you could imagine that they were walking together in the same direction, probably talking about something as innocuous as the weather or as impersonal as some upcoming test or sports event. But what if they were secretly dating and were walking down the hallway alone, planning to meet someplace privately after school? In that case, you had been duped, and your assumption about your friends was wrong.

Think of that example whenever you have to interpret the meaning of a chi-square test. As you calculate the relationship between two nominal variables, start out with the assumption that *there exists no relationship.* In other words, assume that the variables are *independent* of each other. However, if the results of a chi-square test indicate that the p value is .05 or less (e.g., $\chi^2 = 3.26$, $df = 2$, $p < .01$), then you can report that there does indeed exist a relationship. In other words, they are *not independent* of each other. If the p value calculates at some higher level than .05 (e.g., .16), then you can conclude that the two variables are *truly independent* of each other and, as such, are not related to each other in any way. There is no right or wrong, or good or bad, answer here—it is simply a question of whether a relationship appears to exist statistically.

A *p* value of .05 or less allows you to add the word *significant* or the phrase *statistically significant* to your explanation because you know that a *p* value at that low level indicates that there is only a 5% out of a possible 100% probability that the results are due only to sampling error or to some chance occurrence. In essence, a chi-square test begins with the assumption that no association exists between two nominal-level variables and then proceeds to demonstrate if such an association is (or is not) so intense and forceful that mere sampling error or chance is the unlikely reason. Assuming you found statistical significance as evidenced by a low *p* value and went further to calculate a *phi* or Cramer's *V* value, you would then be able to report not only that a relationship exists but also how strong that relationship is in terms of whether it is virtually nonexistent, weak, moderate, or strong.

Summary Points to Remember

- This discussion concerns the most common type of the chi-square test, known as the *chi-square test of independence*. This is also called the *chi-square test of association*. Take your pick.

- Consider the chi-square test whenever you place nominal-level variables in a crosstabulation table.

- Nominal-level variables are sometimes noted as *categorical* variables.

- The assumption underlying the chi-square test is that there exists no relationship between the variables. In other words, the variables are independent of each other. By computing a chi-square test, the researcher will discover whether the variables are independent of (i.e., not related to) or dependent on (i.e., related to) each other.

- The chi-square test measures only if a relationship exists between two nominal-level variables.

- Each nominal variable must have at least two categories contained in it (e.g., the variable *gender* possesses the categories of *female* and *male;* the variable *place of residence* contains the categories of *urban, suburban,* and *rural*).

- A statistically significant relationship between two nominal-level variables calculated by the chi-square test indicates only *association,* not cause and effect.

- The subsequent calculation of either *phi* or Cramer's *V* provides an indication of the strength of a statistically significant relationship as weak, moderate, or strong.

Case Illustration 9.1

A university-based study that evaluated the risk factors associated with those who perpetrate sexual assault used two survey instruments administered at three points in time: a pretest at the start of the study, a 3-month follow-up, and a 7-month follow-up. The instruments, distributed to undergraduate male college students, analyzed adherence to traditional gender-role ideology and acceptance of the rape myth regarding victims. One set of results was reported using a chi-square test of independence.

The authors reported that

> men who withdrew from the current study during the 3-month follow-up were not significantly different from those who participated during that interim period in terms of history of perpetration, $\chi^2 (N = 324) = 1.41 \ p > .05$; however, men who reported engaging in sexually aggressive behavior that met the legal definition of rape prior to entering the study were more likely to withdraw from the study during the 7-month follow-up period than men without a history of perpetration or those with a moderate history of perpetration, $\chi^2 (N = 324) = 6.91 \ p < .05$. (Loh, Gidycz, Lobo, & Luthra, 2005, p. 1329)

Discussion. The use of the χ^2 symbol within the statistical notation serves as a shorthand statement that the researchers conducted a chi-square test of independence between the variable *level of participation* (i.e., stayed in or dropped out) and the variable *history of perpetration* (i.e., no history, low history, moderate history). Furthermore, because the p value was reported as *more than* .05 ($p > .05$), you know that the two groups of subjects (those who withdrew and those who stayed during the first 3 months) were *not* independent of each other—they were similar in regards to whether they had exhibited no history, low history, or moderate history of perpetration. That finding allows the researchers to say that there seems to be *no significant* difference between the two groups. Continuing on, the researchers note that at the 7-month follow-up time, those who revealed a low history of perpetration were, statistically speaking, more likely to drop out during that period when compared to those with no history or with a moderate history. In other words, that "low-history" group was independent of the two other groups. You know that because the p value was noted as less than .05 ($p < .05$). Finally, note that the different results were due solely to whether statistical significance was achieved at less than or more than the .05 level.

Case Illustration 9.2

Examining the extent of domestic violence on female victims, researchers have been particularly interested in its impact on the victims' social and psychological functioning. One study surveyed a sample of 398 women who reported experiencing violent behavior in a previous or current relationship within the past 5 years. For analytical purposes, the women were divided into three age cohorts—18 to 29 ($n = 157$), 30 to 44 ($n = 187$), and 45 and older ($n = 54$)—and studied across several indicators of physical domestic assault. One set of results was discussed using the results of chi-square tests. The researchers concluded that

> no differences among the cohorts were found in the type of perpetrator who committed the violence. About 94% of the respondents indicated that an intimate partner (a spouse or partner), rather than another family member (e.g., son or daughter), was the perpetrator. There were statistically significant differences among the cohorts in the rate of domestic violence in their current relationships ($\chi^2 = 6.452$, $df = 2$, $p = .04$), with 41% of the women aged 45 and older versus 36% of those aged 30–44 and 26% of those aged 18 to 29 reporting a current violent relationship. (Wilke & Vinton, 2005, p. 322)

Discussion. Unlike Case Illustration 9.1, Wilke and Vinton (2005) chose not to report the actual statistical output for tests that showed no statistical significance (i.e., type of perpetrator across the three age cohorts). This is an alternate approach in social services research. Even though they did not report the actual test numbers showing a *p* value of greater than .05, the authors did discuss the finding that a statistical relationship did not exist because that has meaning in and of itself. Remember that *not to find a statistical relationship* is a result that you should include in your written report. Not to find a statistical relationship between variables is not automatically a sign of research ineptitude or of corrupted data. On the contrary, assuming the test is conducted correctly using data from a valid and reliable instrument, a finding of no statistically significant relationship means something in the real world. It is your responsibility to take the facts as they are revealed statistically to you, incorporate those facts in your research report, and explain what you believe they mean to your readers.

   The researchers, in this example, then proceed to report that a statistically significant relationship does indeed appear to exist between the variable *age* and the variable *rate of domestic violence in current relationship*. According to the chi-square test results, women ages 45 and older experience statistically significant more domestic violence in their current relationships than do younger women in both the 30 to 44 and 18 to 29 age categories.

Case Illustration 9.3

In a recent longitudinal study of adult survivors of childhood sexual abuse (CSA), Liang, Williams, and Siegl (2006) documented the long-term affects of the abuse on the victims' later intimate and marital relationships. This follow-up study included 136 women, mostly African American, who had been sexually abused between 1973 and 1976. Part of the study's analysis included a chi-square test on the variables *maternal attachment* and *marital or cohabitating relationship*.

The final report noted that "unexpectedly, the chi-square analysis demonstrated that CSA survivors with strong maternal attachment were less likely to enter a marital or cohabiting relationship, whereas those who had poor maternal attachment were more likely to marry (χ^2 (1) = 5.84, $p < .05$)" (Liang et al., 2006, p. 50).

Discussion. To understand this case illustration, assume that the variable *maternal attachment* has two categories (strong/weak), and the variable *marital or cohabitating relationship* similarly has two categories (yes/no). The chi-square findings clearly propose that these two variables are not independent of each other but are, in fact, related to each other. The specifics of how they were related were unexpected, as the authors further noted. Those women in the study who were abused as children and who also had a strong maternal attachment tended not to marry or enter a cohabitating relationship as adults. As discussed above in the other case illustrations, the statistical significance of that relationship arises from the reported fact that the *p* value was less than or equal to .05.

Activities Involving the Chi-Square Test

1. Using Data Set 5 (Community Social Needs Survey), compute a chi-square analysis to test the relationship between the variables *gen* and *emp*. Narrate the results in a format appropriate for a formal research report. Remember to explain clearly what the results mean in reference to the two variables.

2. Using Data Set 2 (Agency Satellite Offices), compute a chi-square analysis to test the relationship between the variables *loc* and *adv*. Create a table in

Microsoft Word and place the statistical results under the table. Remember to explain clearly what the results mean in reference to the two variables.

3. Using Data Set 1 (Client Demographics and Treatment Results), compute a chi-square analysis to test the relationship between the variables *rel* and *mar*. Narrate the results in a format appropriate for a formal research report. Remember to explain clearly what the results mean in reference to the two variables.

4. Find an article in a recent issue of a professional journal in your library that contains an example of a chi-square analysis. Summarize the results and practical meaning of that example within the context of the entire article. Then, discuss your observations with a colleague.

SPSS Procedures

Chi-Square Test of Independence (for Two Nominal Variables That Contain Two or More Categories Each)

When Used

Used in situations to explore if one nominal-level variable is exerting any influence on (and therefore is not independent of) a second nominal-level variable. Examples could include what influence the following might have: *gender* (male/female) on *career choice* (counselor/psychologist/social worker), *staff education level* (bachelor's/master's degree) on *client achievement* (major/minor/none), or *social agency structure* (public/nonprofit) on *community attitude* (positive, neutral, negative).

The chi-square (χ^2) test indicates whether one variable is affecting the other. *Affecting* in this context does not mean *causing;* it simply implies "influencing" in some manner. If a statistically significant relationship is found to exist, it indicates that the probability of committing a Type I error is acceptably low (usually at the .05 level or less). Remember that a Type I error occurs *whenever you reject a null hypothesis in situations where a true relationship does not exist* between the variables. Another way of defining a Type I error is to say that it occurs *when you reject a null hypothesis but should not do so.*

If you do uncover a statistically significant relationship after computing a chi-square test, then the *phi* and Cramer's *V* tests further indicate the strength of that relationship based on the following patterns:

- A *phi* or Cramer's *V* value of .60 to 1.00 = a strong relationship.
- A *phi* or Cramer's *V* value of .40 to 59 = a moderate relationship.
- A *phi* or Cramer's *V* value of .20 to .39 = a weak relationship.
- A *phi* or Cramer's *V* value of .01 to .19 = a virtually nonexistent relationship.

If, on the other hand, a chi-square test does not report any significant relationship between the variables under study (i.e., $p > .05$), then you can ignore the *phi* and Cramer's *V* values because they are irrelevant for further analysis.

Process

In either the *Data View* or *Variable View* window, do the following:

CLICK on the *Analyze* menu from the top of the window.

PLACE CURSOR over the *Descriptive Statistics* choice.

CLICK on *Crosstabs*.

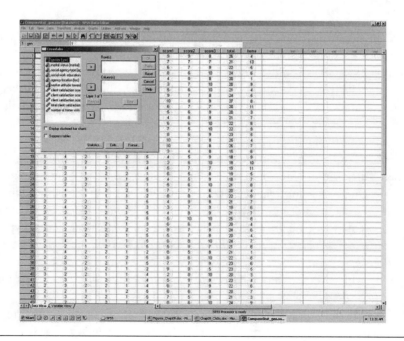

Figure 9.5   *Crosstabs* Screen in SPSS

CLICK on the first of two variables you are interested in. Include only nominal-level variables. Assume this is the variable that might be exerting the influence (i.e., the independent variable).

CLICK on the right-pointing button in the middle of the window to the left of the box labeled *Row(s)*.

CLICK on the second of the two variables you are interested in. Include only nominal-level variables. Assume this is the variable that is being influenced (i.e., the dependent variable).

CLICK on the right-pointing button in the middle of the window to the left of the box labeled *Column(s)*.

NOTE that the placement of the independent variable as the row and the placement of the dependent variable as the column is only a suggested procedure. The reverse placement of the dependent and independent variables will result in the same chi-square output, so that choice is ultimately your decision to make.

CLICK on the *Statistics* button at the bottom left of the window.

CLICK on *Chi-Square* at the top left of the window.

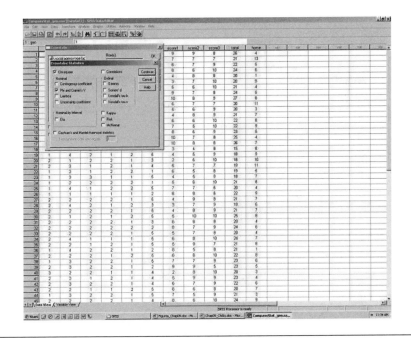

Figure 9.6   *Crosstabs: Statistics* Screen in SPSS

CLICK on *Phi and Cramer's V* near the middle left of the window.

CLICK on the *Continue* button.

CLICK on the *Cells* button at the bottom middle of the window.

LEAVE the *Observed* button clicked at the top left of the window.

CLICK on the *Expected* button directly underneath the *Observed* button.

CLICK on the *Row* button on the left column labeled *Percentages*.

CLICK on the *Continue* button at the top right of the window.

CLICK on the *OK* button at the top right of the window.

Applying the SPSS Output

From the table labeled Variable 1 * Variable 2 Crosstabulation, do the following:

REMEMBER that the chi-square test assumes that the two variables are independent of each other (i.e., one variable has no effect on the other variable). This assumption stands if no statistically significant relationship is found. This assumption is rejected if a statistically significant relationship is found. The *active* variable is considered the independent variable; the *passive variable* is considered the dependent variable.

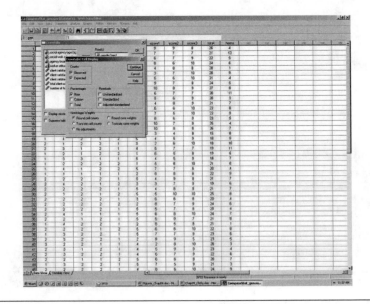

Figure 9.7   *Crosstabs: Cell Display* Screen in SPSS

NOTICE the difference in values between the *Count* and *Expected Count* for each category of the variables. Large gaps between these numbers will contribute to a result that might indicate that a statistically significant relationship exists.

NOTICE the *row percent* value from each cell. REPORT relevant percentages if a statistically significant relationship is discovered.

From the output box labeled *Chi-Square Tests,* do the following:

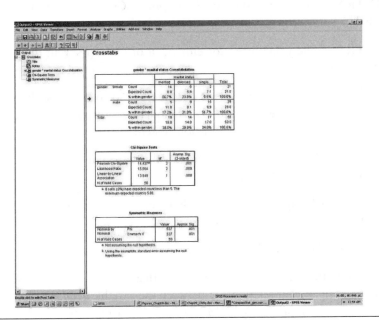

Figure 9.8   SPSS Output of *Crosstabs* Screen With Chi-Square, *Phi,* and Cramer's *V* Tests

EXTRACT the value listed for *Pearson Chi-Square.* REPORT this value as χ^2.

EXTRACT the value listed for *df* on the row labeled *Pearson Chi-Square.*

EXTRACT the *Asymp. Sig. (2-Tailed)* value on the row labeled *Pearson Chi-Square.* If this *Asymp. Sig. (2-Tailed)* value is .05 or less (e.g., .01, .000), you have found a statistically significant relationship between the two variables. REPORT this value as *p*.

PROCEED to the next table labeled *Symmetric Measures*. If, however, the *Asymp. Sig. (2-Tailed)* value is greater than .05 (e.g., .07, .215), you have not found a statistically significant relationship between the two variables.

DO NOT PROCEED to the next table since what is there is irrelevant for further analysis.

From the output box labeled *Symmetric Measures*, do the following:

EXTRACT the value listed for either *phi* or Cramer's *V* in the column labeled *Value*.

EXTRACT the value listed for either *phi* or Cramer's *V* in the column labeled *Approx. Sig.*

INTERPRET a *phi* or Cramer's *V* value of .60 to .99 as strong, a *phi* or Cramer's *V* value of .40 to .59 as moderate, and a *phi* or Cramer's *V* value of .01 to.39 as "weak" or nonexistent.

INTERPRET any *Approx. Sig.* with a value less than .05 (e.g., .01, .000) as statistically significant.

INTERPRET any *Approx. Sig.* with a value of more than .05 (e.g., .17, .56) as not statistically significant.

IGNORE the rest of the output.

NOTE in this example, Figure 9.8, that there does appear to exist a statistically significant relationship between the variable *gender* and the variable *marital status* ($\chi^2 = 14.437$, $p = .001$). In other words, those two variables are not independent of each other because there exists a significant difference between the observed values and the expected values in some of the cells. If no difference was observed, then you could assume that the variables are truly independent of each other. Upon examining the crosstabulation table further for more information, you can see that among this sample of participants, women tended to be single more often than did men. Scan the column labeled "Single" and notice the obvious gap between the "Count" and the "Expected Count" reported there. Since "Single" is pragmatically distinct from "Married," observe also that the column labeled "Married" correspondently reports a similar disparity between the "Count" and the "Expected Count." Furthermore, the strength of that relationship between *gender* and *marital status* appears to be moderate (i.e., *phi* and Cramer's $V = .557$, $p = .001$).

REMEMBER that discovering a statistically significant relationship between variables does not mean one "causes" the other—only that one variable "affects" or "influences" the other variable.

References

Kurz, B., Malcolm, B., & Cournoyer, D. (2005). In the shadow of race: Immigrant status and mental health. *Affilia, 20*(4), 434–447.

Liang, B., Williams, L. M., & Siegl, J. A. (2006). Relational outcomes of childhood sexual trauma in female survivors. *Journal of Interpersonal Violence, 21*(1), 42–57.

Loh, C., Gidycz, C. A., Lobo, T. R., & Luthra, R. (2005). A prospective analysis of sexual assault perpetration: Risk factors related to perpetrator characteristics. *Journal of Interpersonal Violence, 20*(10), 1325–1348.

Wilke, D. J., & Vinton, L. (2005). The nature and impact of domestic violence across age cohorts. *Affilia, 20*(3), 316–328.

10

Correlation

Scattergrams

Statistics may be defined as "a body of methods for making wise decisions in the face of uncertainty."

—W. A. Wallis, cited on
www.quotegarden.com/statistics

Introductory Case Illustration

Most voting-age Americans remember quite vividly the contentious presidential election when George W. Bush narrowly defeated Al Gore in 2000. Erickson (2001) tracked the rise of the Gore candidacy during the early fall of that year as well as its steady demise as election day approached in September. The statistical technique the author used, called a *scattergram* or *scatterplot*, demonstrates any changing pattern of data from two variables by visually spreading (i.e., scattering) out the various points on a two-dimensional plane. Erickson's use of the scattergram format in the following instance illustrates how clearly and simply a large amount of data can be presented.

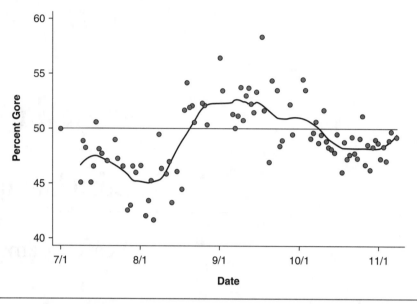

Figure 10.1   Daily Polls, July–November 2000

SOURCE: Erickson (2001).

After inserting the scattergram in his article, Erickson (2001) noted that

the wealth of poll data for 2000 makes it possible to trace the progress of the campaign on a virtually daily basis. Figure 3 [see Figure 10.1] presents a wide-angle view over a lengthy span of time, revealing the progress of the trial-heat polls from July 2000 to election day. Each point represents the two-party vote estimated from the one or more polls with the particular date as the center of its polling period. Because the polls fluctuate more because of random sampling error than real trends, it is necessary to summarize the trajectory of the polls by some sort of moving average. This is done by using the well-established LOWESS procedure (locally-weighted scatterplot smoothing). (pp. 38–39)

Discussion. You can plainly see how attractive and easy to understand a scatterplot is when you are trying to communicate the intersection points between two sets of quantitative data aligned with two distinct variables (i.e., percent of probable voters for Gore and the average number and the dates on which polls were taken). Think how more difficult it would be to derive some understanding of those numbers if they were presented in a table filled with columns and rows of numbers. As stated so simply by the author, a scatterplot provides a "wide-angle view" of a large amount of data. The use of a smoothing technique, such as a LOWESS line, is not essential for a scatterplot but is commonly introduced in reports produced for political science and economics audiences. What is important, however, is that you carefully label a scattergram as a figure with a consecutive number and provide some narrative commentary to ensure that your audience understands the meaning of your data.

As you will learn further in this chapter, a scattergram/scatterplot is simply a visual technique for representing data from two variables being combined in a correlation format.

---

*C*orrelation is one of those words commonly used in everyday speech that has a special meaning when used in a research or statistics context. When you hear someone say, "There's a definite correlation between how I'm feeling right now and whether I want to go to work today," it means simply that there exists a *connection* or a *relationship,* or some *link,* between personal health and the commitment to a job for this one point in time. When researchers talk about a **correlation** between variables, they are not referring to such a vague and imprecise association but rather to a strict mathematical relationship that can be demonstrated visually as well as quantitatively.

The word *correlation,* broken down to its Latin roots, means *co-relation* or *existing together* in a similar sense as the words *cohabitation, coconspirator,* and *cooperation* indicate joint activity. If you ever read in some formal report that there is a "correlation in the United States between family income and the education of the wage earners," that means that some researcher had access to numerical data that revealed both the level of income and the amount of formal education from a sample of people. Furthermore, that researcher conducted a formal statistical analysis of those data and discovered the existence of a clear, mathematical association between those two variables, *level of income* and *amount of formal education.* So, as a researcher or program evaluator, be careful how and when you use the word *correlation.* Employ it only when you have conducted one of the procedures that will be discussed in this chapter and in the next chapter, Chapter 11.

A Visual Image of Correlation

Imagine you are standing directly behind your friend but not touching him. As he starts to walk forward, you follow in lock-step fashion, exactly moving your left foot and your right foot in unison with your friend. You never touch him or influence his movement in any way; you simply shadow him, stopping when he stops, turning left when he turns left, and so on. Now, suppose you drop back 20 feet from your friend and continue to follow him, although no longer in absolute lock-step fashion. When he stops, you slowly come to a stop also, but the distance between you is no longer important. In other words, whether you are now 19 feet away from him or 21 feet away makes no difference at all. When he turns left, eventually you will also turn left, but not necessarily at the same spot he did. Again, you are not influencing his movements in any way. Finally, you act as if you are an undercover police officer trailing a suspected criminal and let your friend move 75 or 100 feet ahead of you. Your eyes are always locked on him and you keep pace with him, but you also weave and dodge among other pedestrians to stay hidden in case he turns around and sees you. Clearly, in this situation, you have no ability to influence his decisions as you are relegated to a passive role of observer and follower.

Now, think of the first scene as a symbol of a *strong* correlation. You have taken the same number of steps and have turned directions at precisely the same angle as has your friend. The second scene presents the image of a *moderate* correlation, a less precise but still rather substantial association between you and your friend. Finally, the third scene represents a *weak* correlation, in the sense that to a casual observer of the incident, you would be just another face in a crowd of people walking down a street, without any apparent relationship with your friend. You might even consider a fourth possibility, a *virtually nonexistent* correlation. In that unusual situation, the connection between you and your friend is even more feeble than what could be considered weak. In other words, you are following your friend from such a long distance that you eventually lose sight of him. So, for all practical purposes, any relationship you thought you had with him on this journey is no longer present. Remember these four possible levels of relationship when you interpret the meaning of the strength of a correlation value.

Positive and Negative Correlations

In addition to being virtually nonexistent, weak, moderate, or strong, you could also report correlations as either positive or negative, highlighting the direction in which the relationship flows. The words *positive* and *negative* carry with them no inherent implication about goodness or badness. Here, again, is another example of words that have a very unique and nontraditional meaning within a research environment.

A *positive correlation* indicates that the numbers (i.e., the values) contained within the two variables both *increase* at the same time or both *decrease* at the same time. If you were to track whether a correlation exists between a group of workers' annual income and the amount of formal education those workers had, you would probably discover a positive correlation since most people's salaries tend to increase as the amount of their formal education increases. In everyday terms, that means most college-educated workers tend to earn more than high school–educated workers do. Typically, however, you would not find a perfect (i.e., total) correlation in the sense that absolutely every college-educated worker earns more than a comparable group of high school–educated workers. This is due to the fact that some of the lower-income workers might have advanced graduate degrees but were underemployed (e.g., the person with a PhD in English who is working as a retail salesperson). On the other hand, there might be some high-income workers who have only a high school education but also possess a valuable skill (e.g., a construction trade supervisor or an international security specialist).

Using another example, if you collected from a particular auto insurance company the amount of damage claims paid in a single month for auto accidents and the odometer speed of the auto clocked at the time of those accidents, you would most likely discover a positive correlation between those two sets of numbers. Lining up the numbers in two columns, you would probably notice that as the recorded speed of the auto decreased, the amount of damages paid also lessened. Again, this would undoubtedly not be a perfect correlation since some accidents that led to high-damage claims might have occurred during a winter storm when autos were traveling slowly due to poor road conditions.

So, a positive correlation means that both sets of numbers either increase with each other or decrease with each other. If the patterns of the two sets of scores *pass each other,* so that as one increases the other one decreases, you would experience a *negative correlation,* also called an *inverse correlation.* Consider this example. After you register for a new course at a college or university, you typically experience some level of anxiety or nervousness as the first day of class approaches. You wonder what the professor will be like, how much work will be expected of you, and whether the content will engage your interest or put you to sleep. If there was some objective measurement of student anxiety (e.g., on a 100-point scale), and your professor was able to collect those data systematically for all the students in your class, you, as well as your professor, would expect (hope?) that the student anxiety level would decrease week by week as the semester progressed. You could predict that the more time you and your colleagues spent in the class, the less anxious you all would feel about the course. Analyzing all these data would probably produce a negative correlation between the variable *anxiety* and the variable *time spent in class* (i.e., as the amount time in class increased, the anxiety level decreased).

Figures 10.2 and 10.3 present the possible patterns for the direction of correlations.

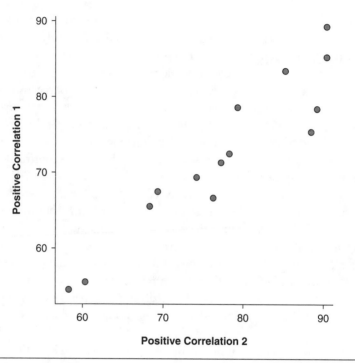

Figure 10.2   Pattern of a Positive Correlation

Correlations for Descriptive or Inferential Purposes

There are two common uses for correlations: first, to describe or summarize the numerical relationship between two variables and, second, to infer from a random sample of respondents the likelihood that the numerical relationship between the two variables can also be found in the entire population from which the sample was drawn.

A correlation used for descriptive purposes could be a simple table or figure that expresses, for example, the visual connection between the grade point average (GPA) of a sample of high school students and the average amount of hours per week those same students spend on homework. An

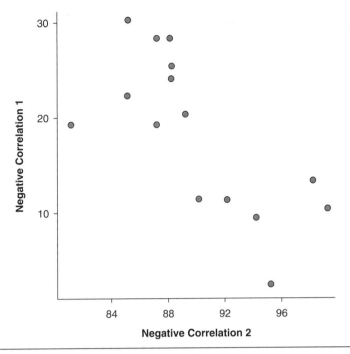

Figure 10.3   Pattern of a Negative Correlation

inferential correlation for the same two variables requires that the sample of students be randomly selected from the student population and an appropriate statistical test be conducted that allows the researcher to state the probability that the results of the sample's correlation pattern of GPA and hours of homework exist also throughout the entire high school.

The remainder of this chapter focuses on descriptive correlations. The following chapter, Chapter 11, will introduce correlations used for inferential purposes.

Scattergrams/Scatterplots

It would be perfectly legitimate to portray the existence of a numerical correlation between two variables in a standard table, as in Table 10.1.

Unfortunately, the true nature of this correlation is not easily apparent in a table format. Only partially revealed in Table 10.1 is the fact that the data indicate (surprisingly) that the longer clients stayed in treatment at this agency, the worse became their attitude about that agency's effectiveness. It is for this

Table 10.1 Table of the Length of Client Contact (in Weeks) and Client Attitude
Toward Agency Effectiveness (10 = *Very High*, 1 = *Very Low*)

Client #	Contact in Weeks	Attitude Toward Agency
01	2	10
02	4	8
03	7	2
04	6	3
05	4	6
06	2	10
07	7	2
08	10	1
09	5	5
10	7	3
11	3	8
12	2	8
13	8	3
14	9	1
15	4	10
16	8	2
17	4	10

reason that most researchers create scattergrams, rather than tables, to present correlations used solely for descriptive purposes.

A **scattergram,** also called a scatterplot, offers a clear visual image of the intersection of the values contained in the two variables. Scattergrams are conceptually based on the image of the X axis and Y axis. You are undoubtedly familiar with this image since it is commonly used as a template in economics and business administration classes to display economic trends and forecasts.

A scattergram literally pinpoints where individual cases (usually people) are placed on a grid bounded by the possible values of the two variables being analyzed, then *scatters* those points, thereby forming some variation of a pattern. These possible values start at an absolute zero point, where the X axis crosses the Y axis, and then continue to increase vertically and horizontally out from that zero point, as illustrated in Figure 10.4.

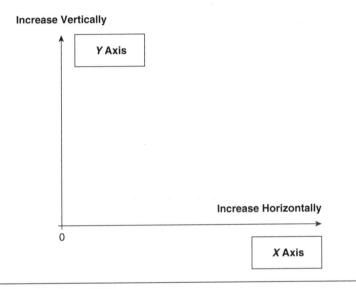

Figure 10.4   The X and Y Axes

By applying this X and Y Axes image to the example noted above, the negative correlation between the variable *length of client contact* and the variable *client attitude toward agency effectiveness* becomes much more evident. In Figure 10.5, the dots represent the intersecting values of the two variables.

Using the same two variables but assuming different sets of scores (values) reported by the clients, Figure 10.6 and Figure 10.7 demonstrate other possible patterns that could show up in a scattergram. Figure 10.6 visualizes a positive correlation, while Figure 10.7 indicates no correlation at all.

Naming the Variables

The **independent variable**, also referred to as the **predictor variable**, is traditionally placed on the Y axis running vertically, while the **dependent variable**, also called the **criterion** or **outcome variable**, is found on the X axis, running horizontally. This arrangement of data vertically or horizontally has little

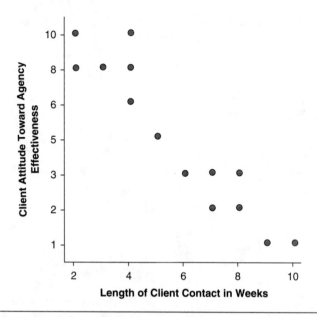

Figure 10.5   Scattergram of the Length of Client Contact (in Weeks) and Client Attitude Toward Agency Effectiveness (5 = *Very High*, 3 = *Not Sure*, 1 = *Very Low*)

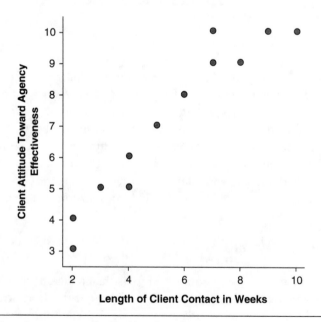

Figure 10.6   Scattergram of a Positive Correlation Between Client Contact and Client Attitude

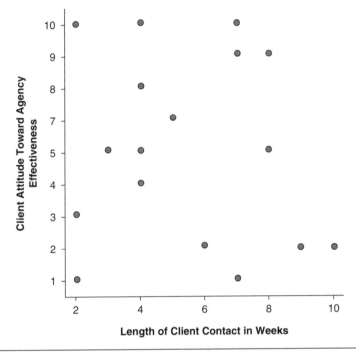

Figure 10.7   Scattergram of No Correlation Between Client Contact and Client Attitude

practical importance, however, because a completed scattergram will appear with the same basic pattern when viewed from either direction. What is important for the researcher, however, is to consider carefully and rationally which variable is the active one (independent/predictor) and which is the passive one (dependent/criterion/outcome). It might help to conceptualize the independent variable as the *pusher* and the dependent variable as the *one being pushed.*

When considering the construction of a scattergram, common sense should play a dominant role in your deliberations with yourself. For example, if you plan to create a scattergram identifying the correlation between the annual number of successfully completed adoption cases and the professional experience of adoption workers measured in years employed as an adoption worker, the independent variable should be *professional experience,* while the dependent variable is the *number of completed adoption cases.* Otherwise, you would be defying common sense by assuming that the number of cases closed was influencing in some substantive manner the amount of time someone was employed as an adoption worker. As noted above, if you did switch the placement of those variables vertically and horizontally, the resulting scatter-gram might look similar, but it would be unintelligible as well as irrational.

Correlation and Causality

Despite the temptation to consider a visibly strong correlation as evidence of **cause and effect** between the two variables, you must resist that temptation, no matter how interesting it might seem. Remember well the admonition that has passed down through the generations of statisticians: *Correlation does not equal causality.*

For instance, it is highly probable that you could demonstrate a strong positive correlation between the variable *average daily temperature* and the variable *number of juvenile offenses committed* in most communities throughout the United States. Having discovered such a strong positive correlation, however, does not mean that a high temperature *causes* the commission of juvenile offenses. In fact, we know from a broad array of sociological studies, as well as from research conducted in various human service professions, that many biopsychosocial factors influence deviant behavior. What undoubtedly could influence such a high positive correlation in this example is the obvious fact that most juvenile offenses occur in the summer when there is more free time and when parental supervision tends to be less strict. High temperatures, certainly common in the summer, are therefore not a cause of juvenile deviant behavior but, rather, a phenomenon that accompanies that season in most communities in the United States. Thus, there may exist a strong positive correlation between temperature and juvenile deviant behavior but certainly no causality.

Having said that, however, a strong positive or negative correlation *might* serve as an indication of possible causality in some situations. Assume, for example, that you discovered a strong negative correlation between the *length of time* spent in a prerelease community residential center for offenders and the *number of negative reports* filed by offenders' parole officers during the first 6 months of parole. In that situation, follow-up experimental research should be conducted, which builds upon your correlation data, to decide if a true cause/effect relationship does indeed exist, as one of several factors, between those two variables. Another way to look at this issue is to assert that every correlation does not lead to a cause/effect relationship, but every cause/effect relationship does assume that a prior correlation does exist. Think about that for a few minutes and let it sink in.

Summary Points to Remember

- Correlation shows a connection between two variables measured at either the ordinal or scale level.

- Scattergrams (scatterplots) are visual representations of correlations used primarily for descriptive purposes.

- The independent variable is also called the predictor variable.

- The dependent variable is also called the criterion or outcome variable.

- The independent (predictor) variable is typically placed on the X (horizontal) axis.

- The dependent (outcome) variable is typically placed on the Y (vertical) axis.

- Correlations can be used descriptively or inferentially.

- A scattergram is the most common format to display a descriptive correlation.

- Correlation is not the same as causality.

Case Illustration 10.1

One research measure of the intellectual abilities of elderly persons suffering with schizophrenia is the Cognitive Abilities Screening Instrument (CASI), which had been developed and pilot tested in the United States and Japan in 1994. The instrument consists of 25 questions grouped into nine domain areas (e.g., attention, language) that provide a total quantitative score ranging from 0 to 100. Researchers tested CASI on a sample of 77 chronically ill elderly patients in the metropolitan Chicago area and chose to represent some of the findings in a scattergram that highlighted age in years with composite CASI scores in three domain areas considered "most sensitive" (i.e., orientation, short-term memory, and fluency).

The authors noted that "the plot of age with the CASI 'most sensitive domain' score is presented in Figure 5 [see Figure 10.8]. . . . The scatterplot illustrating the relationship between age and cognitive status contains a line indicating the predicted CASI total score at each age which clearly shows a negative relationship" (Sherrell, Buckwalter, Bode, & Strozdas, 1999, pp. 551–552).

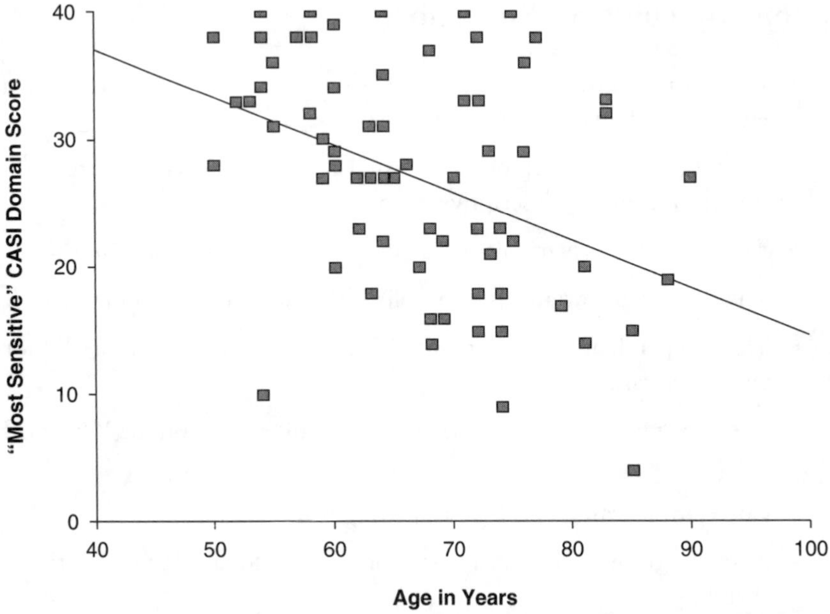

Figure 10.8   Relationship Between Age and Selected Domains

SOURCE: Sherrell, Buckwalter, Bode, and Strozdas (1999).

Discussion. In this example, the authors included a theoretical construct (called a *regression line*) that projects the string of average points in the actual scatterplot array that is presented. Although the whole topic of regression analysis is beyond the scope of this book, suffice it to say that a computed regression line can be hypothesized to predict the approximate point where quantitative values of the two variables being correlated would intersect in future data sets of a similar nature. Because of the downward slope of the data points and regression line in this example, you can clearly recognize that there exists a negative (inverse) relationship between age and total CASI scores on those selected domains (i.e., those total CASI scores correspondingly lower as respondents age). Note that you will be able to add the regression line to any scattergram/scatterplot you choose to create in SPSS.

Case Illustration 10.2

During the past few years, both the American College of Sports Medicine and the surgeon general of the United States have recommended attainable goals for healthy amounts of physical activity for adults. Using these goals, researchers have attempted to measure the intensity of leisure time physical activity (LTPA) by observing 619 healthy men and 497 healthy women ages 18 to 94 who participated in the Baltimore Longitudinal Study of Aging. The LTPA was a self-report of the amount of time in minutes spent engaged in 97 identified activities. A second measure, which was correlated to the LPTA score, was the highest amount of oxygen consumed (peak VO_2), expressed in milliliters per kilogram per minute, while respondents participated in a clinical treadmill exercise test. The authors presented part of their data through the use of a scattergram (Talbot, Fleg, & Meter, 2001, p. 317).

As part of the narrative discussion of their findings, the authors added that "the combination of high and moderate absolute intensity LTPA was directly related to peak VO_2 (Figure 1 [see Figure 10.9]) in both sexes ($r = 0.30$, $p < 0.0001$ for men; $r = 0.27$, $p < 0.0001$ for women)" (p. 315).

Discussion. This is a good example of a scattergram that also includes (in the upper-right corners) a statement of the values resulting from a statistical correlation test (Pearson's r). Although it is not required that they be stated along with the scattergram figure itself, the Pearson's r values, in this example, do add to the explanation by informing the reader about the actual quantitative strength and direction of the correlation, as well as if there appears to exist statistical significance. In this instance, you can visually see that there is a positive, increasing pattern between the two variables so that as the amount of LTPA in minutes increases, so does the peak oxygen expenditure in milliliters. Furthermore, and as you will discuss in greater detail in the next chapter, you know that the strength of those correlations is considered "weak" ($r = 0.30$ and $r = 0.27$), but you also know that there does seem to exist a statistically significant relationship in those patterns ($p < .0001$).

Case Illustration 10.3

In their study of gender bias and the prevalence of a reading disability (RD) in 11-year-old schoolchildren, Share and Silva (2003) used a scattergram to partially highlight the positive correlation between IQ scores as assessed by the Wechsler Intelligence Scale for Children—Revised and reading levels as reported by the Burt Word Reading Test. Separate scatterplots were produced for boys and girls. The authors also added two regression lines to reveal what they discuss as "1.5 standard error cutoffs," which identifies the points below which children are diagnosed with specific reading disabilities.

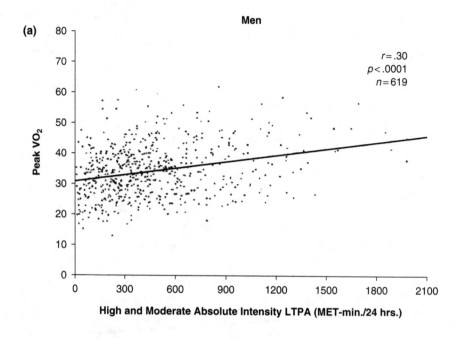

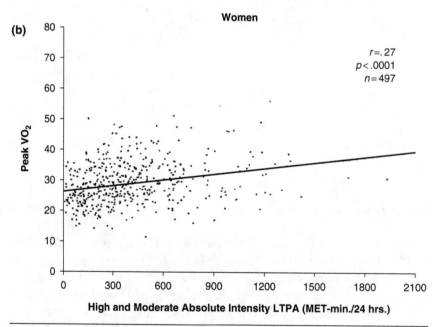

Figure 10.9   Scatterplot Showing the Combination of High and Moderate Absolute Intensity LTPA Energy Expenditure as a Function of Peak VO$_2$ in (a) Men and (b) Women

SOURCE: Talbot, Fleg, and Meter (2001).

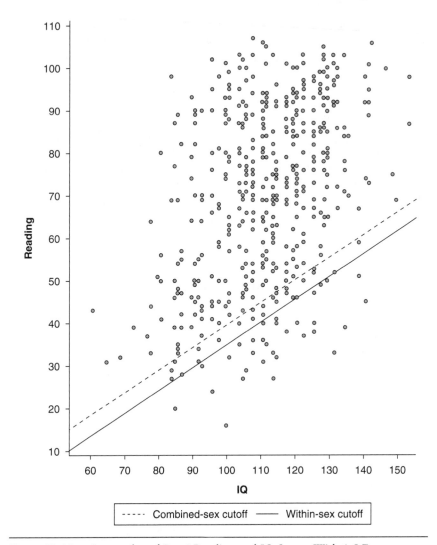

Figure 10.10   Scatterplot of Boys' Reading and IQ Scores With 1.5 Error
Cutoffs for Specific Reading Disability

SOURCE: Share and Silva (2003).

NOTE: Solid line indicates cutoff on within-gender regression equation; broken line indicates
cutoff based on combined-gender regression equation.

In their accompanying narrative, the authors remark that, "as is evident in Figure 1 [see Figure 10.10], the customary combined-gender cutoff classifies an additional 23 boys as having RD who would not otherwise be so identified" (p. 7).

Discussion. Leaving aside for this discussion the meaning of what the authors refer to as "regression equations" and "combined-sex and within-sex cutoffs," notice how vivid the representation is of the reading scores as correlates with the IQ scores. The title of their Figure 1 is uncommonly long, but it certainly does describe exactly what the reader is presented within the scatterplot itself. You are advised to create short but expressive titles for your scattergrams and leave any long descriptive remarks either as a footnote to the figure or in the narrative text that follows.

Activities Involving Scattergrams

1. Using Data Set 5 (Community Social Needs Survey), create a scattergram that visually describes the relationship between the variables *inf* and *sen.* Construct a second scattergram that visually describes the relationship between *inf* and *adol.* Are the patterns in these two displays different or similar? Discuss with a colleague your observations.

2. Using Data Set 2 (Agency Satellite Offices), create a scattergram that visually describes the relationship between the variables *adm* and *dirserv.* In your judgment, does a **positive relationship,** a **negative relationship,** or no relationship exist? What does the pattern mean in the context of these two variables? Discuss your observations with a colleague.

3. Using Data Set 3 (Client Single-Case Evaluation), create a scatterplot for the variables *withd1* and *withd2,* then a second scattergram for the variables *withd2* and *withd3.* Copy these two scattergrams into a Microsoft Word document. Underneath the scattergrams, narrate their meaning in a format appropriate for a formal research report. Remember to explain clearly what the scattergrams mean in reference to the two variables.

4. Find an article in a recent issue of a professional journal in your library, in a newspaper, or in a news magazine that contains a scattergram used for descriptive purposes. Is it clear and easy to understand? Summarize the results and practical meaning of that example within the context of the entire article. Then, discuss your observations with a colleague.

SPSS Procedures

Scattergram/Scatterplot (for Two Variables Measured at Ordinal or Scale Level)

When Used

This is used in situations when you want to visually represent the strength and direction of a correlation relationship between two ordinal-level variables (e.g., the *attitudes toward abortion* and *attitudes toward same-sex marriage* measured on a 5-point Likert scale) or scale-level variables (e.g., the amount of formal education *in years* and the amount of income earned *in dollars*).

Process

In either the *Data View* or *Variable View* window, do the following:

CLICK on the *Graphs* menu from the top of the window.

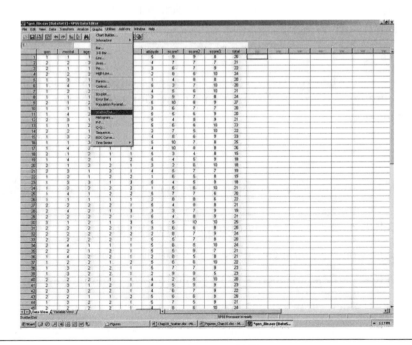

Figure 10.11   *Graphs: Scatter/Dot* Screen in SPSS

CLICK on *Scatter/Dot* choice.

CLICK on the *Simple* icon on the left of the window.

CLICK on the *Define* button on the upper right of the window.

CLICK on the first of the two variable(s) you are interested in. Include only ordinal- or scale-level variables.

CLICK on the right-pointing button in the middle of the window and place that variable into the *Y* axis slot. Consider that variable the dependent variable.

CLICK on the second of the two variable(s) you are interested in. Include only ordinal- or scale-level variables.

CLICK on the right-pointing button in the middle of the window and place that variable into the *X* axis slot. Consider that variable the independent variable.

CLICK on the *OK* button at the top right of the window.

Copying and Saving Scattergrams/Scatterplots in Microsoft Word

When Used

This is used when you want to copy any graph created in SPSS in order to paste it into a Microsoft Word document (e.g., for a final program evaluation report).

Process

With the scattergram/scatterplot displayed (one at a time), do the following:

CLICK on the scattergram/scatterplot in the center.

CLICK on the *Edit* menu at the top left of the window.

CLICK on *Copy* (or PRESS DOWN on *Control* + *c* on the keyboard).

OPEN a new or an existing Word document.

CLICK on the page where you want to place the scattergram/scatterplot.

CLICK on the *Edit* menu at the top left of the window.

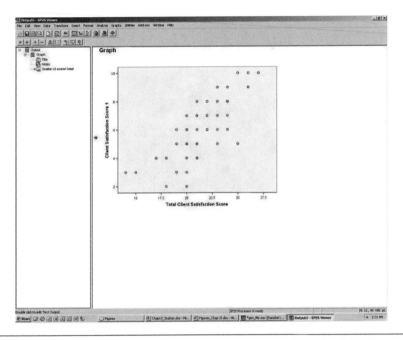

Figure 10.12   Output of *Graphs: Scatter/Dot* Screen in SPSS Available for
Copying Into Microsoft Word

CLICK on *Paste* (or PRESS DOWN on *Control + v* on the keyboard).

CLICK on the *File* menu at the top left of the window.

CLICK on *Save* (or PRESS DOWN on *Control + s* on the keyboard).

References

Erickson, R. S. (2001). The 2000 presidential election in historical perspective. *Political Science Quarterly, 116*(1), 29–52.

Share, D. L., & Silva, P. A. (2003). Gender bias in IQ-discrepancy and post-discrepancy definitions of reading disability. *Journal of Learning Disabilities, 36*(1), 4–14.

Sherrell, K., Buckwalter, K. C., Bode, R., & Strozdas, L. (1999). Use of the Cognitive Abilities Screening Instrument to assess elderly persons with schizophrenia in long-term care settings. *Issues in Mental Health Nursing, 20,* 541–558.

Talbot, L. A., Fleg, J. L., & Meter, E. J. (2001). Absolute versus relative intensity classification of physical activity: Implications for public health policy. *Educational Gerontology, 27,* 307–321.

11

Correlation

Spearman's *rho* and Pearson's *r*

While the individual man is an insoluble puzzle, in the aggregate he becomes a mathematical certainty. . . . Individuals vary, but percentages remain constant. So says the statistician.

—Arthur Conan Doyle, cited on
www.quotegarden.com/statistics

Introductory Case Illustration

Because of the prevalence of dating violence in current society, research is being conducted on this problem, especially on the severity of this problem's impact on adolescent victims. Using a combination of focus group discussions and survey questionnaires, Prospero (2006) explored the dating perceptions and behavioral expectations of 89 middle school students in the southwestern part of the United States and performed a correlation analysis on some of the results. In this study, the male student was identified as the protagonist.

The researcher notes, "A Spearman rank correlation was conducted to investigate the relationship between the perceptions and the behavioral expectations of the protagonist. All perceptions questions were aggregated to form a 5-point scale (0 to 4), where 0 = *not aggressive* responses to all four questions and 4 = *aggressive* responses to all four questions. The result of the correlation analysis was statistically significant with $r = .388$, $p < .000$" (Prospero, 2006, p. 476).

Discussion. A Spearman *rho* test for a correlation between two variables (in this example, the variable *male perceptions* and *male behavioral expectations*) captures whether there exists a relationship between variables measured at the ordinal level. A correlation at either the ordinal or scale level describes whether a quantitative association exists between variables, how strong that association is, and, finally, in what direction it flows. In other words, and using this case illustration, if respondents tended to answer low or high on a question involving *their own perception,* would they also tend to answer in a similar way on another question related to *behavioral* expectations? And, if such a pattern is observed, then three additional observations would emerge: What is the strength of that relationship, is the association in a positive or negative direction, and what is the level of probability that the observed relationship is not simply due to sampling error? Depending on the observed data, an alternate finding might indicate that no pattern seems to exist at all.

After aggregating all the responses for both variables (i.e., combining them, probably by averaging all the individual answers), the author reports that there seems to exist a positive correlation (since no negative sign appears) between the two variables of slightly less than moderate strength (i.e., .388 out of a possible 1.00), which is statistically significant (i.e., $p < .000$). Even though the author does not report the degrees of freedom (*df*), you know from prior information that the $df = 87$ (i.e., $89 - 2$) since there were 89 participants in the study, and degrees of freedom for correlations are always calculated as 2 minus the total number of participants.

Notice that the letter *r* is sometimes applied in place of the more exact Spearman *rho* notation, as in this example. Furthermore, a *p* value of less than .000 is an indication that the possibility for a chance occurrence due to sampling error is very much less than 5 out of 100. Since in SPSS, the *p* value is stated to only three decimal places, .000 means that the possibility of a chance occurrence is less than 1 out of 10,000 or even less than 1 out of 100,000.

This chapter will focus on correlation when used for inferential purposes.

A s mentioned in the previous chapter, you can also compute correlations for inferential purposes, as well as descriptive purposes. With correlations used for inferential purposes, you are able to generalize (i.e., infer) the results from the sample back to the entire population from which you drew the original sample. The only requirement, technically speaking, is that the sample has been randomly selected out of the study population in the first place.

Consider this example. You might be considering a career in the field of criminal justice and might logically assume that a probation and parole officer's age is directly related to an officer's salary. In other words, logic would suggest that older probation and parole officers make more money because they have more experience and have been on the job longer than younger probation and parole officers. That thought typically leads to the assumption that a strong positive correlation exists between the age and the salary level of all probation and parole workers in your state (i.e., as age increases, so does salary). You could test that assumption (hypothesis) by accomplishing the following steps:

- You compile an accurate list of all probation and parole workers in your state (the actual number, not just an approximate number or "guesstimate").
- You then systematically draw a random sample of those probation and parole officers from that list (which is technically called a *sampling frame*).
- After contacting that sample by mail, telephone, or Internet, or after reviewing their personnel records that you can ethically access, you know each one's age at their last birthday and salary level in whole dollars for this year.
- Then, you compute the appropriate analysis that indicates whether a statistically significant and strong positive correlation exists between age and salary in your sample.
- Following this process, you will be able to generalize or infer from this randomly drawn sample that the same basic relationship pattern between age and salary exists within *the entire population* (i.e., your original sampling frame) of probation and parole workers in your state.

What would it mean, however, if your analysis did not compute to indicate a statistically significant and strongly positive relationship? If your study showed that advanced age was not related to higher salary, then several possible explanations present themselves. Perhaps the population of probation and parole officers you sampled contained a large number of second-career individuals, who entered the field of probation and parole after many years in another profession or job. That might explain why their salaries were lower than much younger colleagues who have been working as probation and parole officers a longer period of time. Or perhaps your state has a career incentive program in probation and parole designed to attract graduate-level entrants with higher salaries or more lucrative promotion possibilities. In that situation, younger, graduate-educated probation and parole officers could earn more than their colleagues who were longer on the job but did not have an advanced degree.

Range, Strength, and Direction of a Correlation

Determining the strength of a correlation is easily known once you have output from the computation of either of the two common correlation tests, Spearman's *rho* and Pearson's *r*. Think of a one-dollar bill and how many cents are in a dollar and you will never make a mistake about the strength of a correlation. Presented below are the commonly accepted classifications of the possible correlation values in regards to their range, strength, and direction.

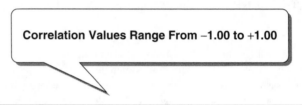

Correlation Values Range From –1.00 to +1.00

Figure 11.1   Range of Correlation Values

Correlation Values of ±.60 to ±1.00 Are Considered *Strong* **Correlations**

Correlation Values of ±.40 to ±.59 Are Considered *Moderate* **Correlations**

Correlation Values of ±.20 to ±.39 Are Considered *Weak* **Correlations**

Correlation Values of ±.01 to ±.19 Are Considered *Nonexistent* **Correlations**

Figure 11.2   Strength of Correlation Values

The point of this discussion is that a correlation between two variables, depending on whether it is *strong, moderate,* or *weak* and whether it is *positive* or *negative,* can provide the researcher with an interesting pattern of relationship between those variables. Furthermore, depending on whether the

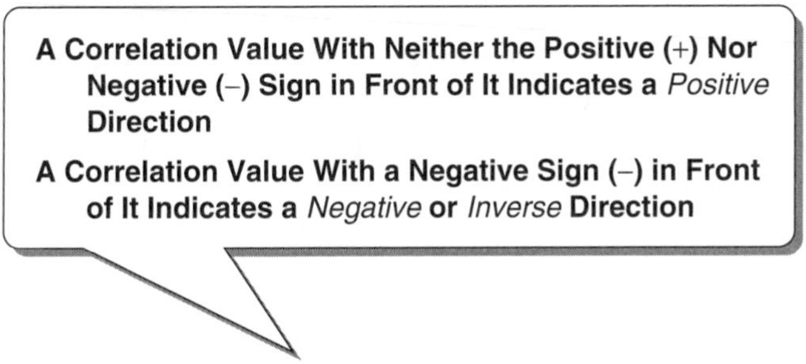

A Correlation Value With Neither the Positive (+) Nor Negative (–) Sign in Front of It Indicates a *Positive* Direction

A Correlation Value With a Negative Sign (–) in Front of It Indicates a *Negative* or *Inverse* Direction

Figure 11.3   Direction of Correlation Values

correlation is statistically significant, that relationship pattern might also be generalized back to the entire population from which the sample was drawn.

Correlation Is Not Causality

Before moving on to a more thorough discussion of the two most common statistical tests for correlations, it is important to remind you that finding a correlation is not the same as finding a cause/effect relationship. All a correlation indicates is that two variables are always connected to each other somehow, but it does not mean that one variable produces some effect in the other. If you studied a sample of 50 individuals and discovered a *strong negative relationship* between the individuals' body weight measured in pounds and height measured in feet/inches, it would mean that shorter individuals tended to be heavier than taller individuals within your sample. A correlation, in this example, would *not mean* that the individuals' height influenced or caused in any way their increased weight. This particular correlation simply means that these two variables—height and weight—tend to be related to each other in a negative (or inverse) pattern for this sample of individuals at this point in time.

Inferential Correlation for Ordinal Data: Spearman's *rho*

If you are working with data measured at the ordinal level, the appropriate statistical test to run is Spearman's *rho*. Ordinal data consist of any ranking of the categories contained within a variable. The most common example of ordinal data in social services are data produced by any 5-point scale that ranks responses from the value of 5 (meaning *always, very much,* or *most*) down through the value of 1 (usually meaning *never, very little,* or *none*).

Consider this example. You send a satisfaction survey to a 25% random sample of all clients whose cases were closed from your social agency and ask them a series of questions that could be answered by circling one answer on the following scale:

5 = Always	4 = Sometimes	3 = Not Sure	2 = Occasionally	1 = Never

Once you received your surveys back, you would have collected ordinal-level data. In addition to computing how the respondents answered each question individually, you could also examine whether a correlation existed between how the respondents answered—for example, Question 3 (How satisfied are you with the services you received from our agency?) and Question 8 (How responsive was your worker to your needs?). Since your data are measured at the ordinal level, you should run Spearman's *rho* procedure.

If the statistical output reported that Spearman's $rho = .55$, $df = 43$, $p = .226$, then you would know that the scores of 45 respondents were calculated ($df = 43$) and that there exists a moderate, positive correlation (i.e., if respondents scored high on Question 3, they tended to score high, although not absolutely so, also on Question 8). The probability score (*p* value) of .226 indicates that since it is higher than .05, there is an unacceptable danger that the sample responses do not represent the assumed responses of the entire population of former clients. Stated another way, since the correlation is not statistically significant ($p = .226$), the results could be due to chance and, therefore, could be quite different if you chose another sample and sent them the same survey.

Inferential Correlation for Scale Data: Pearson's *r*

In a very similar fashion, if you have access to scale-level data (e.g., age in years, height in inches, weight in pounds, time in minutes, income in dollars, number of children, number of home visits made, number of misdemeanor convictions) and are interested in discovering whether a correlation exists between any two variables, you would use Pearson's *r* procedure. A researcher working in a vocational rehabilitation agency, for example, might be interested in whether any correlation exists between the number of weeks of training completed by clients and the income they were receiving 6 months after they left the agency. In other words, did staying longer in training positively affect the amount of income earned after 6 months, negatively affect the amount of income, or have no effect at all?

Assuming that the researcher could extract those data from client files and/or from follow-up contacts with former clients, a computed Pearson's *r* score might appear as $r = .803$, $df = 106$, $p < .01$. This would indicate that for the 108 clients studied ($df = 106$), there existed a very strong positive correlation between the amount of time spent in training at the agency and the amount of income they were earning after 6 months. In other words, more training correlates with higher salaries after 6 months. Since the probability that these results were due solely to chance is acceptably low and, therefore, statistically significant ($p = .01$, which is less than .05), the researcher could generalize those results back to the population of all clients, if that researcher did, in fact, draw a random sample.

If, on the other hand, the sample was not drawn randomly but was simply the last 112 clients who left the agency, then the researcher, strictly speaking, should not generalize the results to anyone beyond that sample of 112 clients. The ability to generalize from a sample to a population is highly dependent on the clear identification of all possible members in a population under study (i.e., a sampling frame), followed by the precise selection of a random sample according to defined procedures. As discussed in other chapters of this book, however, the practice of generalizing from a nonrandom sample back to the population from which it was drawn is very frequently encountered in the popular media and even, unfortunately, in the social services literature. You, as a consumer of other people's research reports, should be aware of this regrettable practice should you come upon it in your reading or literature reviews. You would be advised to treat with skepticism any conclusions that derive from such reports that rely on generalizations from nonrandom sample data.

One final point concerning the use of a scattergram/scatterplot in conjunction with either Spearman's *rho* or Pearson's *r*. It is useful to run a scattergram/scatterplot along with Spearman's *rho* and Pearson's *r* in order to note if there exist any serious visual outliers within the data. Remember that statistical tests, such as Spearman's *rho* and Pearson's *r*, must necessarily combine and massage the data in order to produce their quantitative results. A scattergram, on the contrary, maintains the individuality of the intersecting values and provides you with a visual picture, not just of any pattern present but also any noticeable outlying values apart from the pattern. These outliers might, at times, serve as a distortion to the conclusions that seem to flow logically from the test results alone. Thus, as a researcher using both the scattergram and the correlation tests, you will receive a more comprehensive understanding of both the strength and the direction of the data under study.

Summary Points to Remember

- Correlations can be used for both descriptive and inferential purposes.

- Correlations can be strong, moderate, weak, or virtually nonexistent.

- You should note the direction of a statistically significant correlation as either positive or negative depending on the output.

- A correlation is only a measure of association between variables, not a statement of cause and effect.

- To uncover no correlation between variables can be useful in social services research and program evaluation.

- Use Spearman's *rho* test when you have ordinal data.

- Use Pearson's *r* test when you have scale (i.e., interval or ratio) data.

- Use a scattergram/scatterplot in conjunction with Spearman's *rho* or Pearson's *r* test to visualize if the distribution contains serious outliers.

Case Illustration 11.1

A study of how African American adolescents view the variable *respect,* particularly as it is experienced by them from others, was recently conducted in Oregon. The sample included 200 African American males between 14 and 18 years of age. Half the sample were incarcerated, while the other half were nonincarcerated and currently associated with a community youth development program. The researchers administered the 20-item African American Respect Scale (AARS) and a 45-item Scale of Racial Socialization–Adolescent Version to all participants. Four of the variables measured by these two instruments included *societal respect, family respect, peer respect,* and *racial socialization.* A correlation analysis was conducted among all four variables.

The researchers report that

> Pearson product-moment correlations were calculated for the three obtained subscales, [and for] the scale measuring racial socialization. . . . As expected, Societal Respect ($r = .216$, $p < .01$) and Family Respect ($r = .257$, $p < .001$) were positively and significantly associated with racial socialization—a scale that focuses on family and societal domains. Racial socialization was not correlated with peer respect; socialization regarding the peer domain is not a focus of the scale of racial socialization. (Leary, Brennan, & Briggs, 2005, p. 467)

Discussion. The Pearson *r* correlation in this case illustration supports the finding that the 200 African American adolescent respondents tended to score in a pattern that positively associated their perceptions of *societal respect* with *racial socialization,* as well as their perceptions of *family respect* with *racial socialization.* These correlations (i.e., associations between the variables) were statistically significant ($p < .01$ and $p < .001$) but are considered weak in terms of their strength ($r = .216$ and $r = .257$). However, the researchers discovered no apparent association between the variables *peer support* and *racial socialization.* As is typical in professional literature, you are simply informed of this nonassociation without being provided with the actual numerical outcomes of the statistical test.

Case Illustration 11.2

Tyson in 2006 tested the validity of a 24-item, self-administered instrument (RAP) that measured a person's beliefs and perceptions regarding both the effects and the content of rap music. A nonrandom sample of 605 college students was surveyed for this study. As part of the statistical analysis of the data, Pearson's *r* tests were used.

Tyson (2006) reports,

> Pearson's correlations were conducted to determine the level of association between the RAP and its three subscales and three criterion-related validity questions: (a) frequency of listening to rap (7-point scale, 0 = *never* to 6 = *everyday*), (b) number of rap CDs and tapes owned (7-point scale, 0 = *10 or less* to 6 = *more than 60*), and (c) level of agreement in favor of censorship of rap (5-point scale, 0 = *strongly agree* to 4 = *strongly disagree*). . . .
>
> The amount of time spent listening to rap music had a moderate, positive correlation with global RAP scores (i.e., $r = .44$, $p = .000$). In addition, global RAP scores were also moderately associated with the extent to which the participants owned rap music (i.e., $r = .33$, $p = .000$) and moderately, negatively associated with favoring censorship of rap music (i.e., $r = -.43$, $p = .000$). (p. 217)

Discussion. This is a clearly explained discussion of what this author discovered and what the results mean. Notice the following points in this case illustration:

1. While it may sound incorrect at first, a 0 to 6 ranked scale is actually a 7-point (not a 6-point) scale, and a 0 to 4 ranked scale is a 5-point scale since the 0 position counts as the first of seven or five rankings.

2. Since all the rankings proceed from a "low status" (i.e., 0) to a "higher status" (i.e., 5 or 7), you should be able to understand the basic premise of correlations (i.e., that quantitative scores on the first measurement tend to be related to the quantitative scores on the second instrument).

3. The author did not just supply you with the statistical output but also informed you in a narrative manner about both the direction of the correlation (i.e., "associated" = positive association and "negatively associated" = negative association) as well as the strength of the correlation (i.e., "moderately").

4. The author treated the responses to the 5-point and 7-point items as scale-level data and, therefore, used Pearson's r test rather than Spearman's rho test for ordinal-level data.

5. As discussed earlier in this chapter, this is an example of a technically incorrect use of inferential statistics since the sample was drawn nonrandomly from the population. Thus, the reporting of the p values could be misleading since the reader might unfortunately assume that the results could be generalized to the entire population from which the sample was drawn. In this instance, the Pearson's r test technically reports only descriptive information about the 605 college students.

In this context, a positive correlation means that high scores tended to relate to high scores on overall RAP scores against both *frequency of listening to rap* and *number of rap CDs and tapes owned*. A negative association translates as meaning that high scores on overall RAP scores tended to indicate corresponding low scores on *level of agreement in favor of censorship of rap*.

Case Illustration 11.3

In the mental health field, the Multnomah Community Ability Scale (MCAS) is considered a reliable measure of the ability of consumers with severe mental health issues to function in a community setting. Several researchers recently published a study during which they adapted the form, which is typically completed by a case manager, so that it could be self-administered by the consumers themselves (MCAS-SR). There were 338 study participants recruited from a pool of Medicaid recipients who had been diagnosed with severe and persistent mental illness. The consumers' self-reported scores were correlated by means of Spearman's *rho* test, with the scores recorded by the trained research staff who interviewed them.

The researchers reported that

> because the instruments were made up of Likert scales, nonparametric measures, such as Spearman's *rho* were used in the data analysis. . . . Self ratings and ratings by research interviewers were available for 50 urban and 288 rural Medicaid clients with severe mental illness. . . . The total score correlations were .57 for urban clients ($p < .01$, $df = 48$) and .31 for rural clients ($p < .001$, $df = 286$). No items had notably low correlations between self-report and research interviewer scores. (O'Malia, McFarkland, Barker, & Barron, 2002, p. 328)

Discussion. Comparing the self-perceptions of a sample of mental health clients with the perceptions of trained interviewers, there appears to be a statistically significant, moderately strong positive association between MCAS-SR scores for urban clients (.57) and a weaker positive association for rural clients (.31). Notice that these researchers did decide to report the degrees of freedom ($df = 48$ and $df = 286$), which reports the number of participants in each subsample minus 2. Furthermore, the authors also chose to use Spearman's *rho* correlation test since they correctly considered that the responses to the Likert scales are measured at the ordinal level.

Activities Involving Correlations for Inferential Purposes

1. Using Data Set 1 (Client Demographics and Treatment Results), compute a Spearman's *rho* test on the association between the variables *att1* and *att2*. Narrate the results in a format appropriate for a formal research report. Remember to explain clearly what the results mean in reference to the two variables.

2. Using Data Set 5 (Community Social Needs Survey), compute a Spearman's *rho* test on the association between the variables *reduce* and *pay*. Narrate the results in a format appropriate for a formal research report. Remember to explain clearly what the results mean in reference to the two variables.

3. Using Data Set 2 (Agency Satellite Offices), compute a Pearson's *r* test on the association between the variables *servu* (independent variable) and *satis* (dependent variable). Narrate the results in a format appropriate for a formal research report. Remember to explain clearly what the results mean in reference to the two variables.

4. Find an article in a recent issue of a professional journal in your library that contains an example of either a Spearman's *rho* or a Pearson's *r* test of association. Summarize the results and practical meaning of that example within the context of the entire article. Then, discuss your observations with a colleague.

SPSS Procedures

Spearman's *rho* Correlation
(for Two Variables Both Measured at the Ordinal Level)

When Used

This is used to report whether a statistically significant correlation exists between two ordinal-level variables (e.g., any two responses in survey questions that employ a 5-point Likert scale).

SPSS Process

In either the *Data View* or *Variable View* window, do the following:

CLICK on the *Analyze* menu from the top of the window.

PLACE THE CURSOR over *Correlate* choice.

CLICK on *Bivariates*.

CLICK on the first of two variable(s) you are interested in. Include only ordinal-level variables.

CLICK on the right-pointing button in the middle of the window.

CLICK on the second of the two variable(s) you are interested in. Include only ordinal-level variables.

UNCLICK the *Pearson* button toward the bottom left of the window.

CLICK on the *Spearman* button directly across from the *Pearson* button.

LEAVE UNTOUCHED the remaining buttons in the window.

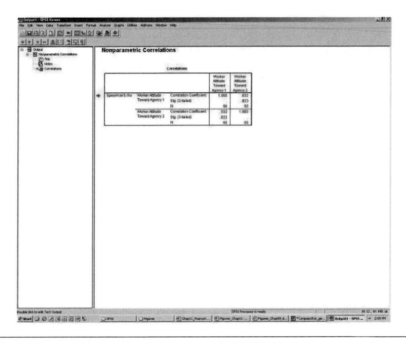

Figure 11.4   *Bivariate Correlations* Screen in SPSS With Spearman's *rho* Selected

CLICK on the *OK* button at the top right of the window.

Applying the SPSS Output

From the table labeled *Correlations,* do the following:

NOTICE that the table contains a mirror image of the values so that the values at the top right are repeated at the bottom left. In any cell where the variable is correlated with itself, the value of "1" appears.

EXTRACT the *Spearman's rho* value for each variable. REPORT this as the value for *rho.*

INTERPRET a *rho* value of .60 to 1.00 as "strong," a *rho* value of .40 to .59 as "moderate," a *rho* value of .20 to .39 as "weak," and a *rho* value of .01 to .19 as "virtually nonexistent."

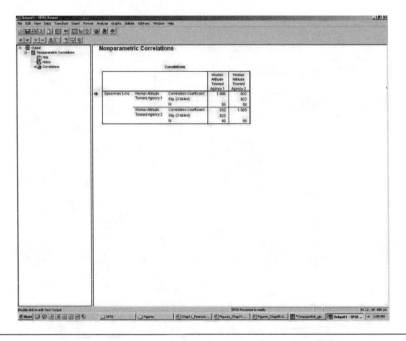

Figure 11.5   *Nonparametric Correlations* Output Screen in SPSS

INTERPRET a *rho* value that is a positive number (e.g., .45) as an indication that both variables are related in the same (i.e., a positive) direction from each other and a *rho* value that is a negative number (e.g., −.45) as an indication that both variables are related in the opposite (i.e., negative) direction from each other.

EXTRACT the value listed for *N*. That number, minus 2, equals the degrees of freedom for each variable. REPORT this as the *df* value.

EXTRACT the *Sig. (2-tailed)* value for each variable. If the *Sig.* value is .05 or less (e.g., .01, .000), you have found a statistically significant correlation between the two variables. If, however, the *Sig.* value is greater than .05 (e.g., .07, .215), you have not found a statistically significant correlation between the two variables.

NOTICE which Spearman's *rho* value is followed by a double asterisk (**). This notation indicates that the *Sig. (2-tailed)* value is statistically significant at the .01 level or less.

NOTICE that in this example, the positive correlation between *worker attitude toward agency 1* and *worker attitude toward agency 2* is virtually nonexistent (*rho* = .031), and there is no statistical significance present (*p* = .823). Thus, you are not able to reject the null hypothesis, which states that the two variables are not correlated with each other, because the probability of committing a Type I error is higher than .05. Stated otherwise, you cannot dismiss the probability that any relationship between the two variables is due simply to sampling error. Thus, based on the analysis of your present data, you should proceed in your discussion and conclusions as if the null hypothesis is true.

Pearson's *r* Correlation (for Two Variables Both Measured at the Scale Level)

When Used

This is used to report whether a statistically significant correlation exists between two scale-level variables (e.g., height measured in inches and weight measured in pounds).

SPSS Process

In either the *Data View* or *Variable View* window, do the following:

CLICK on the *Analyze* menu from the top of the window.

PLACE THE CURSOR over the *Correlate* choice.

CLICK on *Bivariates*.

CLICK on the first of two variable(s) you are interested in. Include only scale-level variables.

CLICK on the right-pointing button in the middle of the window.

CLICK on the second of the two variable(s) you are interested in. Include only scale-level variables.

CLICK on the right-pointing button in the middle of the window.

LEAVE CLICKED the *Pearson* button toward the bottom left of the window.

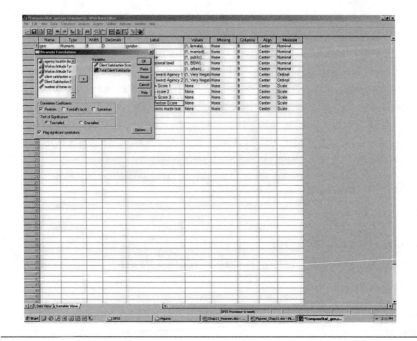

Figure 11.6   *Bivariate Correlations* Screen in SPSS With Pearson's *r* Selected

LEAVE UNTOUCHED the remaining buttons in the window.

CLICK on the *OK* button at the top right of the window.

Applying the SPSS Output

From the table labeled *Correlations*, do the following:

NOTICE that the table contains a mirror image of the values so that the values at the top right are repeated at the bottom left. In any cell where the variable is correlated with itself, the value of "1" appears.

EXTRACT the *Pearson Correlation* value for each variable. REPORT this as the value for *r*.

INTERPRET an *r* value of .60 to 1.00 as "strong," an *r* value of .40 to .59 as "moderate," an *r* value of .20 to .39 as "weak," and an *r* value of .01 to .19 as "virtually nonexistent."

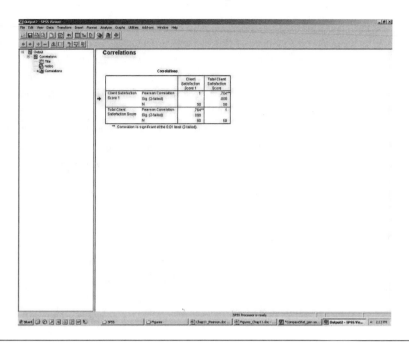

Figure 11.7   *Correlations* Output Screen in SPSS

INTERPRET an *r* value that is a positive number (e.g., .65) as an indication that both variables are related in the same (i.e., a positive) direction from each other and an *r* value that is a negative number (e.g., –.65) as an indication that both variables are related in the opposite (i.e., negative) direction from each other.

EXTRACT the value listed for *N* for each variable. That number, minus 2, equals the degrees of freedom for each variable. REPORT this as the *df* value.

EXTRACT the *Sig. (2-tailed)* value for each variable. If the *Sig.* value is .05 or less (e.g., .01, .000), you have found a statistically significant correlation between the two variables. If, however, the *Sig.* value is greater than .05 (e.g., .07, .215), you have not found a statistically significant correlation between the two variables.

NOTICE which *Pearson Correlation* value (if any) is followed by a double asterisk (**). This notation indicates that the *Sig. (2-tailed)* value is statistically significant at the .01 level or less.

NOTICE in Figure 11.7 that there does appear to exist a strong positive correlation between the variables *client satisfaction score 1* and *total client satisfaction score* (r = .764). Furthermore, statistical significance (p = .000, and a double asterisk appears next to the r value) is present. Statistical significance indicates that you can reject the null hypothesis within the acceptable level of probability of committing a Type I error. Stated otherwise, the strong positive correlation noted between the two variables probably does not exist because of sampling error, and you can be confident of generalizing your results back the population from which you drew your original random sample.

References

Leary, J. D., Brennan, E. M., & Briggs, H. E. (2005). The African American adolescent respect scale: A measure of a prosocial attitude. *Research on Social Work Practice, 15*(6), 462–469.

O'Malia, L., McFarkland, B. H., Barker, S., & Barron, N. M. (2002). A level-of-functioning self-report measure for consumers with severe mental illness. *Psychiatric Services, 53*, 326–331.

Prospero, M. (2006). The role of perceptions in dating violence among young Americans. *Journal of Interpersonal Violence, 21*(4), 470–484.

Tyson, E. H. (2006). Rap-music attitude and perception scale: A validation study. *Research on Social Work Practice, 16*(2), 211–223.

12

t-Test for Paired Samples

The death of one man is a tragedy. The death of millions is a statistic.

—Joseph Stalin, comment to
Winston Churchill at Potsdam, 1945,
cited on www.quotegarden.com/statistics

Introductory Case Illustration

Researchers in Illinois explored the risk factors surrounding sexual assault perpetrators by surveying male undergraduate college students with two instruments, the Illinois Rape-Myth Acceptance Scale (IRMA) and the Reactions to Offensive Language and Behavior Scale (ROLB). Both instruments were administered at three points in time: during pretest at the beginning of the study, then at a 3-month follow-up, and finally at a 7-month follow-up. The students were asked to compare their responses to what they assumed would be the responses of the typical male college student. Thus, two sets of responses were produced for each question: their own and what they believed would be the response of other male students.

The findings indicate that "paired sample *t*-tests were used to assess differences between perceived norms and personal responses on the IRMA, ROLB-behavior and ROLB-comfort scales. Compared to themselves, participants believed that the average college man demonstrated more rape-myth acceptance, $t(277) = -12.84$, $p < .001$, was less likely to intervene in situations where a woman was being mistreated, $t(288) = -9.52$, $p < .001$, and was more comfortable in situations where women are being mistreated, $t(288) = -6.45$, $p < .001$" (Loh, Gidycz, Lobo, & Luthra, 2005, p. 1334).

Discussion. The paired samples *t*-test is one of a group of inferential statistical tests that uses the average scores of values obtained on a scale-level measurement instrument. Two sets of scale-level scores are compared, and when a large enough distance (in the sense of a gap or space) is found between the averages of those two sets of scores, you can assume that there exists a statistically significant difference between them. In other words, whenever you find a p value that is less than or equal to .05, you can presume that the two sets of scores are significantly distinct from each other.

The fact that there exists a significant difference should be first stated in the Presentation of Findings section of the research report and then later discussed in terms of its implications for the study's objectives in the Discussion or Conclusion section of the report. Remember that a statistically significant finding does not "prove" anything in the formal sense of that word. It simply means that there is a small enough probability that the differences observed do not exist because of sampling error, which is the expected inaccuracy that occurs when you generalize about the study population based on what you know from a random sample of participants drawn from that population.

In this case illustration, the quantitative scores being compared are the self-perceptions of a sample of male college students against their own assumptions about what a "typical" college student would say in response to questions concerning sexual assault. These researchers discovered significant differences between the two sets of scores, as noted in the citation included above.

For the rest of this chapter, you will discuss in greater detail the importance of *t*-tests in general and when you would use paired samples *t*-tests during your research and program evaluation projects.

A very powerful statistical procedure for the social services researcher is the **t-test,** which is a calculation of the differences between two average (mean) scores when those scores are measured at a scale level. Remember that, in SPSS language, *scale* is the same level as what are commonly referred to as **interval** and **ratio levels of measurement.**

There are actually three different types of *t*-tests, the two most common of which are discussed in this book. This chapter covers the situation when the same sample of respondents is measured at two different times or when two carefully matched samples are measured against each other (the **paired samples** *t*-test), while the next chapter discusses the situation where the two samples of respondents are unmatched, distinct, and separate from each other (the **independent samples *t*-test**).

The third type of *t*-test that is presented in many statistics textbooks (the **one-sample *t*-test**) is rarely encountered in social services research because, as its name implies, it uses only one sample of respondents whose quantitative scores are compared to some known national or local norm. For example, you would use the one-sample *t*-test if you work in an extended-care facility for senior citizens and want to compare the average age of your clients to the average age of all senior citizens in other similar facilities in your state or in the entire country. The obvious problem is that it is *not always easy or even possible* to gain access to the state or national statistics that you would need for this type of *t*-test. Thus, in the interest of brevity and to make your life a bit less complex, the one-sample *t*-test is not presented in this book. Having said that, however, the general principles of presenting and understanding the meaning of a one-sample *t*-test are the same for all types of *t*-tests. You should be aware of this in the unlikely event that you would ever come across a one-sample *t*-test as either a consumer or a producer of your own social service research.

Understanding the Paired Samples *t*-Test

Without delving into a long and complicated discussion of the theoretical basis of the *t*-test, suffice it to say that it is a potent tool to discover if there is an important difference between two samples of scores, all the while factoring in both the sample size and the standard deviation of the scores. You do not have to worry about how the sample size and standard deviation fit into the calculations since the statistical formula of the *t*-test does that for you.

The paired samples *t*-test compares the first mean score with the second mean score and determines if there is a statistically large enough *gap* between the two scores.

This gap can consist of either an increase or a decrease in mean scores. In a typical program evaluation situation, you might test the following null hypothesis: Case managers at Agency X will not score differently on a cultural diversity test after participating in a 4-week diversity seminar by comparing test scores before and after the seminar. Your research hypothesis would then state that there is a difference between the mean scores (two-tailed) or (if you had information from other sources) that the specific difference is at least 10 points higher after the seminar (one-tailed). In this situation, a paired samples *t*-test would be appropriate because it would compare the mean of the two samples and let you know whether there exists a statistically significant difference for you to reject the null hypothesis and accept either the one-tailed or two-tailed hypothesis.

The most common use of the paired samples *t*-test is in situations where the same group is measured twice, such as under pretest/posttest experimental conditions or according to Time Period 1/Time Period 2 measurements. However, the paired samples *t*-test can also be employed, quite effectively, when you have two *carefully matched* pairs of respondents and you want to compare them on some scale-level measurement. In this latter situation, you, the researcher, must determine what variables you should use to match the groups across. Typically, two samples of respondents are matched on variables such as age, gender, race, education level, and so on. The process of *matching* means that you literally assign respondents to be in Group A or Group B in a very conscious and deliberate manner. In this situation, you should clearly identify in your report that you are using *matched* samples of respondents, and you should then state the specific basis (i.e., the variables chosen) upon which the matching is based.

Assume you work in a residential treatment center for adolescents with severe behavioral problems and you are conducting a series of intensive group sessions designed to improve the residents' in-house behavior patterns. By using the residential logbook in which staff record all serious acting-out behaviors of all the residents on a daily basis, you could accumulate the average number of negative incidents recorded before the group sessions begin. Following up perhaps 8 weeks later, you could then collect a second set of data from the logbook, after the group sessions stopped. In this illustration, you would hope for a significant decrease in negative behaviors at the end of the 8 weeks of intensive group therapy. On the other hand, if you worked in a psychiatric facility for residents who were chronically depressed, your intensive group therapy sessions might focus on improving your clients' self-image, communication skills, social activities, and so on. In this second treatment situation, assuming you also possessed data from the residential daily logbook, you would look for an increase in the number of positive behaviors after the 8-week period. In both contexts, a paired samples *t*-test would reveal whether a statistically significant difference (i.e., decrease or increase) in behaviors occurred after the 8-week period.

Rules for Use of the Paired Samples *t*-Test

Statisticians generally agree on the following set of requirements or rules for the appropriate use of the paired samples *t*-test:

- The researcher is trying to compare the mean values of two samples that contain either the same participants measured twice or are two samples of individuals matched on relevant demographic variables.
- The data are at the scale level (i.e., interval or ratio). In current practice, however, many researchers often use paired samples *t*-tests with ordinal-level data that contain at least five rank orderings (e.g., 5 = *always* to 1 = *never*).
- The samples have been randomly selected from the study population.
- The mean values under study across the samples are normally distributed. Refer back to Chapter 7 in this book for a fuller explanation of how to determine if you have a normally distributed set of values.
- The samples are large enough. A minimum sample size of 30 is typically cited by many statisticians. Refer to Chapter 15 in this book for a more comprehensive discussion of what constitutes an appropriate sample size for parametric tests such as the paired samples *t*-test.

Interpreting the Results of a Paired Samples *t*-Test

Since all *t*-tests compare average values drawn from samples, you should include the following elements from the SPSS output when reporting the results of a paired samples *t*-test:

- The mean score (*M*) and standard deviation (*SD*) of the sample at both times or for both matched samples
- The *t*-test value as either a positive or negative whole number to three decimal points
- The degrees of freedom (*df*)
- The **significance level** (*p*) at a two- or three-point decimal level

All of this information will be present in the SPSS output along with other data that are not essential to include in a report. Figure 12.1 represents an example of a typical SPSS output after a paired samples *t*-test was calculated. For this example, consider that the variable, *client attitude toward agency,* has been measured at two points: first, at the beginning of the project during a *pretest* phase, and a second time, following the introduction of some experimental variable, at the end of a *posttest* period.

You should recall that in any paired samples *t*-test for **experiments**, you are observing whether any change occurs between the average values collected at two different points from the same sample of respondents. Thus, for your written report, the only data you will need to extract from this particular SPSS output are the following: the mean values (4.84 for pretest and 6.04 for posttest) and standard deviations (2.41 for pretest and 2.42 for

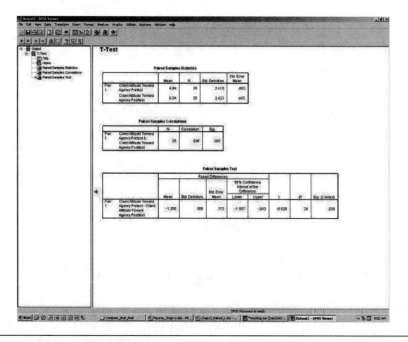

Figure 12.1   Output of a Paired Samples *t*-Test in SPSS

posttest) at both measurement times, the *t*-test value (−6.928), the degrees of freedom (24), and the level of statistical significance (*p* = .000 or *p* < .001). To keep your research report as consumer friendly as possible, you *should not include* any other data contained in the SPSS output.

You are particularly advised *not to simply copy and paste* the entire SPSS output screen into your written report. Such a procedure would undoubtedly cause an unfortunate level of confusion in your audience. Keep your data presentation comprehensive but simple. Just remember that most SPSS output screens contain much more information than you will ever need to share with your audience.

This particular set of paired samples *t*-test statistics reveals that there exists apparently an increase in the average values noted at the posttest (mean = 6.04) when compared to the pretest (mean = 4.84). Furthermore, upon computing a paired samples *t*-test, you can observe that there also exists a statistically significant difference between the two sample mean values, so you can conclude that the probability that those differences are present due to sampling error is acceptably low (*p* < .001), which allows you to reject the null hypothesis.

Summary Points to Remember

- In social services research and evaluation studies, the paired samples *t*-test is a familiar and rigorous tool for bivariate analysis when you have scale data.

- It is used most effectively for inferential analysis situations but can also be used for descriptive analysis when the samples are not drawn randomly.

- Two scale-level measurements are required from either the same group of respondents, as in pretest/posttest or before/after situations, or a matched pair of groups containing similar, but not the same, respondents.

- With the paired samples *t*-test, the two groups must be of equal size since they are the same group measured twice or the same number of participants matched from two groups.

- With the independent samples *t*-test (to be discussed in the next chapter), the two groups do not have to be of equal size since they are different groups, and average scores are used for comparisons.

- Finding a statistically significant difference between the mean values allows you to reject the null hypothesis.

Case Illustration 12.1

To examine whether patients at a major teaching hospital were satisfied as consumers of health services, Bendall-Lyon and Powers (2002) surveyed 150 women and 133 men at two points: immediately after each was discharged from the hospital and again, 2 years later. The respondents were compared by gender in order to learn if there existed any differences in their feelings of satisfaction over time. In the published report, T1 refers to the *time at hospital discharge,* and T2 refers to the *time 2 years later.*

The researchers note that

> patients completed a 60-item questionnaire containing satisfaction measures on a five-point Likert scale related to various aspects of the hospital stay. . . . Overall satisfaction was assessed using a global measure of satisfaction that measured an individual's overall perception of the hospital stay. . . . Based on results from the paired-samples *t*-test . . . men reported a significant decline in overall satisfaction (4.53 at T1 vs. 4.40 at T2, $p < .10$), intention to return (4.70 at T1 vs. 4.41 at T2, $p < .001$), and intention to recommend (4.77 at T1 vs. 4.52 at T2, $p < .001$). Similarly, women reported a significant decline in overall satisfaction (4.51 at T1 vs. 4.37 at T2, $p < .001$), intention to return

(4.62 at T1 vs. 4.42 at T2, $p < .01$), and intention to recommend (4.69 at T1 vs. 4.52 at T2, $p < .05$). (Bendall-Lyon & Powers, 2002, pp. 15–17)

Discussion. This is a good example of the appropriate use of the paired samples *t*-test. Two scores were compared from data collected from the same respondents at two different time periods. The same survey instrument was used on both occasions so the responses were comparable. Notice that these researchers treated the Likert scale data, which are technically ordinal in nature, as scale level for purposes of statistical analysis. As mentioned earlier in this chapter, this practice occurs frequently in social science research, especially if the researchers collect the ordinal data on an instrument that has 5 or more points of measurement (e.g., 5 = *very satisfied*, 1 = *very unsatisfied*). Furthermore, note that the authors here accept a *p* level of higher than .05 for two of their tests ("men reported a significant decline in overall satisfaction [4.53 at T1 vs. 4.40 at T2, $p < .10$]"). This is less commonly found in social service practice. To avoid confusion, the authors should have mentioned in the text that a level of probability higher than usual (i.e., < .05) was considered acceptable for statistical significance in this study. The authors also chose to report the paired samples *t*-test scores without noting the degrees of freedom (*df*), which, again, is not the recommended format for a published final report.

Case Illustration 12.2

Making Choices is a skills-training program designed to assist older elementary school children in the acquisition of effective problem-solving skills. The immediate target of the program is to increase their ability to process social information, to set realistic goals for themselves, and to engage in positive problem-solving activities. Researchers piloted the Making Choices program with 70 sixth-grade students in the same school by delivering it as part of the curriculum taught to five subgroups by individual homeroom teachers. Students were pretested before Making Choices was introduced, then posttested at the end of the program on a newly developed measurement tool, the Skill Level Activity (SLA). The variables measured in this study included *understanding social cues* (identified as Unit 2 on the SLA instrument), *interpreting social cues* (identified as Unit 3 on the SLA instrument), and *social goal formation* (identified as Unit 4 on the SLA instrument). Differences between the pretests and posttests were computed by means of paired samples *t*-tests.

The authors report that

> for all students, the results of the SLA score were significantly higher at posttest relative to pretest for two of the three units delivered in this study. For Unit 2, students had higher cue-encoding skills on completing the unit, relative to their skills prior to the unit, $t(47) = 4.52$, $p < .01$. . . . Similarly, results indicated an increased level of skill in distinguishing prosocial goals on completing Unit 4, $t(44) = 3.17$, $p < .01$. . . . However, SLS scores at posttest were not significantly different from pretest scores for Unit 3 (Interpreting Cues, $p > .05$). (Nash, Fraser, Galinsky, & Kupper, 2003, p. 440)

Discussion. In this study, the researchers compared two sets of scores from the same respondents in a classic "before-and-after" situation found in most experiments and quasi experiments. Note that the authors did report the paired samples *t*-test using the suggested format, which includes the *t* notation and value, the degrees of freedom, and the probability level (e.g., $t(47) = 4.52$, $p < .01$). Thus, you can see easily how there did exist a statistically significant difference between pretest and posttest values for two of the variables (*understanding social cues* and *social goal formation*) but not the third variable (*interpreting social cues*). A more complete and customary format, however, would have included the actual mean values for both the pretests and posttests, as you can see in Case Illustration 12.1.

Case Illustration 12.3

Examining the health behaviors of two groups of adolescent females, those who had an abortion and those who were never pregnant, researchers Felton, Parsons, and Hassell (1998) surveyed 52 respondents attending family planning clinics in the southern part of the United States. Their measurement instruments included the Health Promoting Lifestyle Profile (HPLP), a 48-item, 4-point Likert scale; the Problem-Solving Inventory (PSI), a 32-item, 6-point Likert scale; and the Offer Self Image Questionnaire (OSIQ), a 130-item, 6-point Likert scale. These instruments measured the variables of *overall health-promoting behavior, self-actualization, health responsibility, exercise, nutrition, interpersonal support, stress management,* and *global self-image.* The researchers carefully matched the two groups on the variables of age, race, grade level, and Medicaid status. For this study, paired samples *t*-tests were used to analyze much of the data.

The findings of this study indicate that

> the total HPLP scores and the six subscales for the matched pairs are shown. . . . Dependent *t*-tests showed that the two groups had similar overall health-promoting behavior scores (*t* (25) = 1.31, *p* = .20) and similar scores on the six subscale measures of Self-actualization, Health Responsibility, Exercise, Nutrition, Interpersonal Support, and Stress Management, and . . . Matched pairs also had similar global self-image, *t* (25) = 0.17, *p* = .86, and subscale scores on the 12 dimensions of self image. (Felton et al., 1998, pp. 41–42)

Discussion. This is a clear example of using the paired samples *t*-test (noted here as "dependent *t*-tests," which is synonymous with "paired samples *t*-tests") when two groups of respondents are not, literally, the same respondents but are two different sets of respondents who have been, however, consciously and carefully matched by the researchers across some relevant variables. In this study, those matching variables included age, race, grade level, and Medicaid status. Note that these were matching variables that the researchers used in conjunction with another set of measurement variables (*overall health-promoting behavior,* etc.). In the published report, all of the individual mean scores and standard deviations are included but were not reproduced here for the sake of brevity. The results of the paired samples *t*-test included here, however, do support the conclusion that the two matched groups studied (i.e., those who had an abortion and those who were never pregnant) did not significantly differ on the set of eight measurement variables. Thus, the authors can express such statements as "the two groups had similar overall health-promoting behavior scores."

Note that the researchers chose to report the actual *p* values (e.g., *p* = .20). They could also have presented those finding as *p* = *ns,* or simply narrated that no statistically significant difference between the samples was discovered. Within certain generally accepted guidelines, you, as the researcher, can decide on the format of your presentation of data and analysis.

Activities Involving the Paired Samples *t*-Test

1. Using Data Set 1 (Client Demographics and Treatment Results), compute a paired samples *t*-test for the variables *pre* and *mid*. Then, compute a second paired samples *t*-test for the variables *mid* and *post*. Narrate the results in a format appropriate for a formal research report. Remember to explain clearly what the results mean in reference to the two variables.

2. Using Data Set 2 (Agency Satellite Offices), compute a paired samples *t*-test for the variables *staff1* and *staff2*. Narrate the results in a format appropriate for a formal research report. Remember to explain clearly what the results mean in reference to the two variables.

3. Using Data Set 3 (Client Single-Case Evaluation), compute a paired samples *t*-test for the variables *reint1* and *reint2*. Then, compute a second paired samples *t*-test for the variables *reint2* and *reint3*. Narrate the results in a format appropriate for a formal research report. Remember to explain clearly what the results mean in reference to the two variables.

4. Find an article in a recent issue of a professional journal in your library that contains an example of a paired samples *t*-test. Summarize the results and practical meaning of that example within the context of the entire article. Then, discuss your observations with a colleague. Or, find an article in your local newspaper or weekly news magazine that describes a situation that could be tested empirically and, furthermore, could be analyzed statistically by the introduction of one or more paired samples *t*-tests. Discuss with a colleague how you would approach that situation as a formal research project and what your comparison variables would be for a paired samples *t*-test.

SPSS Procedures

Paired Samples *t*-Test (for Two Variables, Both Measured at the Scale Level)

When Used

This is used in situations such as a pretest/posttest of an experimental intervention, before/after the introduction of a new agency policy or procedure, outcome results measured at Time Period 1 and then again at Time Period 2, or a comparison of two samples of research participants strictly matched across meaningful demographic variables.

SPSS Process

In either the *Data View* or *Variable View* window, do the following:

CLICK on the *Analyze* menu from the top of the window.

PLACE your cursor over the *Compare Means* choice.

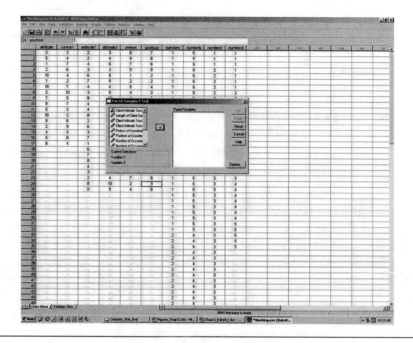

Figure 12.2   *Paired-Samples T Test* Screen in SPSS

CLICK on *Paired-Samples T Test.*

CLICK on the two variable(s) you are interested in, one at a time. These sample values will appear as two separate variables in your data set (e.g., pretest/posttest, time1/time2, or group1/group2 for matched groups). Include only scale-level variables.

NOTE that as you click on a variable, it automatically appears in the box titled *Current Selections* at the bottom-left corner of the window.

CLICK on the right-pointing button in the middle of the window.

CLICK on the OK button at the top right of the window.

Applying the SPSS Output

From the table labeled *Paired Samples Statistics,* do the following:

EXTRACT the mean value for each paired sample from the column labeled *Mean.*

EXTRACT the standard deviation value for each paired sample from the column labeled *Std. Deviation.*

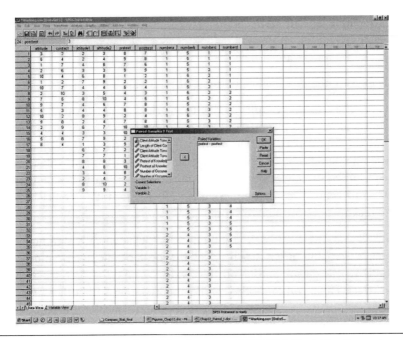

Figure 12.3   *Paired-Samples T Test* Screen in SPSS With Variables Entered

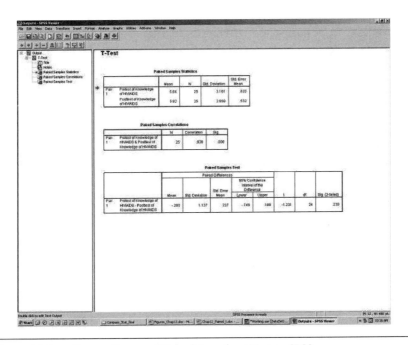

Figure 12.4   Output Screen of Paired Samples *t*-Test in SPSS

From the table labeled *Paired Samples Test,* do the following:

EXTRACT the *t* value on the right side of the table.

EXTRACT the *df* value to the right of the *t* value.

EXTRACT the *Sig. (2-tailed)* value to the right of the *df* value. If the *Sig.* value is .05 or less (e.g., .01, .000), you have found a statistically significant difference between the mean values from the two samples. This difference should be obvious when you compare the mean values of the two samples. If, however, the *Sig. (2-tailed)* value is greater than .05 (e.g., .07, .215), you have not found a statistically significant difference between the mean values of the two samples.

NOTE that in Figure 12.4, you do not have a statistically significant difference ($p = .230$ or $p > .05$) between the mean of the pretest values compared to the mean of the posttest values (5.64 for pretest, 5.92 for posttest). Thus, you cannot reject the null hypothesis (that there exists no difference between pretest and posttest values) since you are in evident danger of committing a Type I error.

References

Bendall-Lyon, D., & Powers, T. L. (2002). The impact of gender differences on change in satisfaction over time. *Journal of Consumer Marketing, 19*(1), 12–23.

Felton, G. M., Parsons, M. A., & Hassell, J. S. (1998). Health behavior and related factors in adolescents with a history of abortion and never-pregnant adolescents. *Health Care for Women International, 19,* 37–47.

Loh, C., Gidycz, C. A., Lobo, T. R., & Luthra, R. (2005). A prospective analysis of sexual assault perpetration: Risk factors related to perpetrator characteristics. *Journal of Interpersonal Violence, 20*(10), 1325–1348.

Nash, J. K., Fraser, M. W., Galinsky, M. J., & Kupper, L. L. (2003). Early development and pilot testing of a problem-solving skills-training program for children. *Research on Social Work Practice, 13*(4), 432–450.

13

t-Test for Independent Samples

Statistics: The only science that enables different experts using the same figures to draw different conclusions.

> —E. Esar, *Esar's Comic Dictionary*, cited on www.quotationspage.com/subjects/statistics

Introductory Case Illustration

Researcher Mano-Negrin in 1998–1999 compared two groups of public and private social service agencies in Israel on the variables of organizational effectiveness and managerial empowerment. Data were collected from a representative sample of 60 independent/voluntary nonprofit asocial agencies, identified in the study as independent service organizations (IPOs), and from 60 public social agencies, identified as public service organizations (PSOs). Some of the specific variables examined included *organizational size, organizational age,* and number of *administrative positions* in excess of 30% of all positions in the agency. The survey instruments measured responses by means of 7-point and 5-point Likert scales.

The author explained that

the analysis was conducted in four stages. First, a *t*-test analysis was estimated to see the mean differences in effectiveness gaps and empowerment between PSOs and ISOs . . .

Organizational Size IPO ($M = 8.48$) PSO ($M = 7.21$), $t = 2.329$, $p < .05$,

Organizational Age IPO ($M = 3.18$) PSO ($M = 2.66$), $t = 2.527$, $p < .05$.

Administrative Positions (more than 30%) IPO ($M = 0.231$) PSO
($M = 0.896$), $t = -1.22$, $p < .01$. (Mano-Negrin, 2003, Table 1, p. 35)

Discussion. The independent sample *t*-test compares the average scores of two groups of respondents who are autonomous of each other and were both analyzed according to the same set of variables. In other words, the two groups were drawn separately from the same population of possible respondents for a research project, and both samples were administered the same research instrument. A finding of significant difference between the two groups (i.e., the *p* is equal to or less than .05) means that they share no relationship to each other regarding that variable (e.g., a response on a survey that indicates one's attitude about some social issue).

Remember that a finding of statistical significance allows you to reject the null hypothesis (which assumes that the groups are not different from each other). A finding of no significant difference (i.e., the *p* is greater than .05) means that they do share a relationship in the sense that their responses were similar regarding some variable being investigated. Finding no significant difference means that your null hypothesis is correct in the sense that the two groups are not different from each other.

In this example, the particular sample of IPOs and PSOs in Israel appears, indeed, to be significantly different regarding the variables of organizational size, organizational age, and the number of administrative positions exceeding 30% of all staff. You can judge how "different" they are from each other by examining the differences in the mean values reported with the *t* values. For example, the average organizational size for all the IPOs is reported as being 8.48, which is higher than the mean of 7.21 for all the PSOs in the sample. If you are interested in understanding the explicit meaning of an average value of 8.48 or 7.21 for organizational size or understanding the other mean differences reported, you are advised to read the entire research report cited here.

Continuing the discussion of *t*-tests, this chapter explores the second most commonly used type, the independent samples *t*-test.

As discussed in the previous chapter, the **dependent samples *t*-test** requires the researcher to have access to two sets of data from the same respondents as in pretest/posttest or Time 1/Time 2–type situations or from two different sets of respondents who have been carefully matched on several relevant variables. Due to this fact, the use of the dependent samples *t*-test is somewhat limited since most social agency records and research activities do not routinely contain data on the same individuals collected at two distinct periods, nor are many agency-based researchers readily able to match two groups of respondents.

The opposite is true, however, for the independent samples *t*-test. As its name implies, the independent samples *t*-test measures the differences between two groups that have been separately drawn from the population under study. They are two different samples of participants, not consciously matched with each other across some demographic variables. If the independent samples *t*-test reports the existence of a large enough difference between the groups on some scale-level measurement, then we can say that there is a *statistically significant* difference between those two groups. The independent samples *t*-test is especially useful in experimental and quasi-experimental research situations where the researcher is trying to prove the effectiveness of some experimental intervention (i.e., independent variable) by measuring its influence on a predetermined measurement (i.e., the dependent variable). This "proof" (not in the technical sense of that word) can be assumed if the researcher is able to reject the null hypothesis at the generally agreed-upon level of probability (i.e., a *p* level that is equal to or less than .05) and accept the research hypothesis as stated.

Requirements for the Independent Samples *t*-Test

The *dependent variable*, which is the variable you use to measure your respondents, must be at the **scale level of measurement.** In the SPSS language for this test, the dependent variable is called the **test variable.** Typical examples of scale-level measurements for a dependent variable could be the number of times a client kept (or missed) an appointment; a client's weight or height or score on a standardized test; the length of time in hours, days, weeks, or months that a patient received treatment; the amount of income earned in dollars; the number of arrests, convictions, or negative reports filed; and so on. As noted in previous chapters, many social service researchers accept data from 5-point (or higher) Likert scales in lieu of scale-level data in order to use the independent samples *t*-test for analysis.

The *independent variable* for this statistical test is the variable used to form or to divide the respondents into two groups so as to make them independent of each other. In the SPSS language for this test, the independent variable is called the **grouping variable.** This independent variable must be at the nominal level that has at least two categories within it. Typical nominal-level variables used in an independent samples *t*-test include gender (male/female), education level of human service professionals (bachelor's degree/master's degree/ doctoral degree), professional identity of the service provider (case manager/ counselor/psychologist/social worker), organizational structure of the agency (public/nonprofit/for-profit), type of service delivered (inpatient/outpatient), and so forth.

You should note that if the nominal-level independent variable has more than two categories within it (e.g., urban/rural/suburban), the independent samples *t*-test could measure the statistical differences *between only two categories at any one time*. Thus, the independent samples *t*-test would allow you to report if there exists a statistically significant difference between the incomes earned by a sample of your clients separated by their urban/rural, urban/suburban, or rural/suburban status but not according to all three geographic categories together.

Using the Independent Samples *t*-Test

Assume you are the executive director of a large community mental health agency that has a main office in a downtown urban area as well as a satellite office in a suburban location 30 miles away. For the past 6 months, you have consistently received a number of complaints from clients at both locations regarding the professional staff who provide direct services treatment to the clients. This particular group of treatment staff generally reflects the local community and is well diversified at both locations along the lines of age, gender, sexual orientation, and race/ethnicity. According to many clients, however, the treatment staff, as a group, is not sufficiently sensitive to poor, minority clients of color and to gay and lesbian clients.

After consulting with your executive management team, you decide to set up a 6-hour mandatory sensitivity training session, at one central location, for all treatment staff. The evaluation tool used at the end of this session consists of a 50-item questionnaire that measures the attainment of specific information presented in the training session. Each question assumes that there is either a *correct* or an *incorrect* answer. Leaving aside, for this discussion, the legitimate research question as to whether such an instrument (or any instrument) could adequately measure true sensitivity in the staff, this situation does provide a clear example of how an independent samples *t*-test can be used in social service practice.

You would hope, as the executive director, that all treatment staff would pass the sensitivity test with a high enough score, but you would also be able to judge whether there existed a statistically significant *difference* between the staff in the urban office compared to the staff in the suburban office. As an aside, if such a difference did emerge as evidenced by the independent samples *t*-test results, you should pursue further research investigations since the independent samples *t*-test tells you only *if a difference exists* and not *why* it exists.

As another illustration, this time within a client context, assume you are a counselor working with at-risk adolescent students in an alternative public high school. After receiving approval from the Human Subjects Review Committee of the school district, you conducted a 6-month-long quasi experiment focused on school attendance. The **control group** of 15 students received only the normal range of services available to all students (e.g., academic classes, school-based social activities, individual academic counseling). The 15 students in the **experimental group** received, in addition to these regular services, a planned set of additional services from the school (e.g., weekly group counseling, community-based recreational and social activities, individual tutoring for academic deficiencies).

Since this was a quasi-experimental design (and, therefore, not a pure experiment), you did not randomly assign the students to the experimental and control groups, but you took their existing presence in one of two learning cohorts (i.e., classes) as the basis of your decision. You then flipped a coin to decide which class of students was to be the experimental group and which was to be the control group.

During the 6-month research period, the daily attendance record and the quarterly academic achievement scores of the experimental and control group students were monitored, and the total number of absences and academic achievement scores for each student was calculated. You, as the school counselor or social worker, did not provide any of the experimental services yourself, but you did serve as the general coordinator of the entire research project.

In this situation, the independent samples *t*-test would provide you, as the person responsible to present the results of the project, with the appropriate mechanism for interpreting those results. Here, you would obviously hope that the average difference would be significantly *higher* on both academic achievement and school attendance for the experimental group as compared to the control group. If, on the other hand, the results indicated that there exists no statistically significant difference between the groups, then several reasons might explain this. Perhaps the intervention chosen was not appropriate or robust enough, the groups were not comparable enough regarding the potential for school attendance and academic achievement (always an inherent danger in quasi-experimental research), or the measurements chosen did not adequately capture the effects of the intervention.

Whatever the outcome of this quasi experiment, you would be well advised to pursue further research (i.e., either replication of the original or a second attempt with a revised protocol). The main point here is that the independent samples *t*-test could serve as a powerful analytical tool you can use to understand the outcome so you can present the results of the project in a meaningful manner.

Rules for Use of the Independent Samples *t*-Test

The rules for use of the independent samples *t*-test are essentially the same as noted previously for the paired samples *t*-test:

- The researcher is trying to compare the mean values of two samples that have been separately selected from the study population.
- The data are at the scale level (i.e., interval or ratio). In current practice, many researchers often use independent samples *t*-tests with ordinal-level data that contain at least five rank orderings (e.g., 5 = *always* to 1 = *never*).
- The samples have been randomly selected.
- The mean values under study across the samples are normally distributed. Refer back to Chapter 7 in this book for a fuller explanation of how to determine if you have a normally distributed set of values.
- The samples are large enough. A minimum sample size of 30 is typically cited by many statisticians. Refer to Chapter 15 in this book for a more comprehensive discussion of what constitutes an appropriate sample size for parametric tests such as the paired samples *t*-test.

Interpreting the Results of an Independent Samples *t*-Test

When reporting the results of an independent samples *t*-test, you should include the following elements from the SPSS output:

- The mean score (*M*) and standard deviation (*SD*) of Group 1
- The mean score (*M*) and standard deviation (*SD*) of Group 2
- The *t*-test value as either a positive or negative whole number to three decimal points
- The degrees of freedom (*df*)
- The significance level (*p*) at a two- or three-point decimal level

All of this information will be present in the SPSS output along with other data that are not essential to include in a report. Figure 13.1 represents an example of a typical SPSS output screen after an independent samples *t*-test was calculated. For this example, consider that the dependent variable is *number of*

home visits last month, as measured in whole numbers, and the independent
variable is *agency location,* with the two categories of urban and rural.

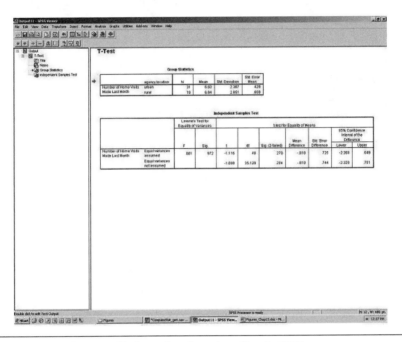

Figure 13.1   Output of Independent Samples *t*-Test in SPSS

Remember that in an independent samples *t*-test, you are observing whether
any change occurs between the average values on some measurement collected
between two different (i.e., independent) samples of participants. For your
written report, the only data you will need to extract from this particular SPSS
output is the following: the mean value (6.03) and standard deviation (2.387)
of the urban-based workers, the mean value (6.84) and standard deviation
(2.651) of the rural-based workers, the *t*-test value (–1.116), the degrees of
freedom (48), and the level of statistical significance (.270).

To keep your research report as consumer friendly as possible, you *should
not include* any other data contained in the SPSS output. You are particularly
advised *not to simply copy and paste* the entire SPSS output screen into your
written report. Such a procedure would undoubtedly cause an understandable level of confusion in your audience. Keep your data presentation comprehensive but simple. Just remember that most SPSS output screens contain
much more information than you will ever need to share with your audience.

It is clear from the data reported in Figure 13.1 that there exists no statistically significant difference ($p = .270$) in the average number of home visits completed last month by workers in the urban office as compared to workers in the rural office. Thus, you should not reject your null hypothesis that agency location has no influence on the average number of home visits completed last month by workers.

Summary Points to Remember

- The *t*-test for independent samples is an appropriate statistical tool for bivariate analysis whenever you have the dependent variable at the scale level and the independent variable at the nominal level with at least two categories.

- It is used most effectively for inferential analysis situations, but you can also use this test for descriptive analysis when the samples are not drawn randomly.

- Two scale-level measurements are required from two different groups of respondents who are independent of each other.

- With the independent samples *t*-test, the two groups do not have to be of equal size since the mean (average) scores are used.

Case Illustration 13.1

In a study on acculturation among 129 women of Mexican descent living in the United States, researchers sought to identify the strengths and resources necessary to cope with symptoms of depression. A nonrandom sample of women using one of three family health community clinics associated with a language school (Spanish/English) was surveyed. The entire sample was of childbearing age. Researchers measured symptoms of depression in the women on a 20-item scale (CES-D, which is a self-report measuring the presence of depression in the general population) and then determined an approximate level of their acculturation to mainstream society in the United States. One area explored was a comparison of the level of depression between those childbearing women who were exposed in their childhood to the United States and those who were raised in Mexico.

The authors note that

> data were entered and analyzed using Statistical Package for the Social Sciences (SPSS) version 10.0. We used *t*-tests to compare CES-D scores by childbearing status and by demographic acculturation parameters (birthplace, language

preferred, and exposure to United States in childhood). . . . When the child-bearing women were compared by childhood exposure to the United States, there were no group differences in intrinsic strength factors with the exception of life satisfaction. Women who were exposed to the United States in childhood reported significantly ($t = -2.16$, $p = .03$) lower life satisfaction (5.2 ± 1.54) than those who spent their childhood in Mexico (5.8 ± 1.48). There were no significant differences in resources such as income or adequacy of income, marital or partner status, employment, years of education, or number of adults in the household. (Heilemann, Frutos, Lee, & Kury, 2004, pp. 96–97)

Discussion. In this example, the authors discovered a statistically significant difference between those women exposed to the United Stated in childhood and those raised in Mexico across the dependent variable of *life satisfaction,* as measured by the CES-D instrument. The respondents raised in the United States appeared to have a significantly lower level of life satisfaction than those raised in Mexico, as indicated by the difference in mean scores (5.2 for U.S.-exposed women compared to 5.8 for those raised in Mexico). Since the probability level (p) is stated as < .03, you can assume that the noted differences between these two groups of women are probably not due simply to sampling error. Notice in this excerpt from the published article that the mean score is not directly identified as such (only the number is provided), and the symbol ± is used to indicate the standard deviation (*SD*) from the mean.

As discussed previously in other chapters, this is another unfortunate example of the technically incorrect use of inferential statistics since the sample in this case illustration was drawn nonrandomly from the population. Thus, the reporting of the *p* values could be misleading since the reader might incorrectly assume that the results could be generalized to the entire population from which the sample was drawn. To be more precise, the authors could have indicated that the results of the independent samples *t*-tests are being reported as descriptive, not inferential, statistics.

Case Illustration 13.2

Attempting to determine how individuals cope successfully with their dual roles as employee and parent, Drago (2001) compared parent teachers and nonparent teachers on their use of time in a 24-hour period. The researcher accessed a nonrandom sample of 310 public elementary school teachers in 46 schools throughout four school districts in the United States. Data were collected by means of time diaries and a telephone survey.

The author discussed the use and meaning of *t*-tests at two points in the final report. "*T*-tests are used later to test for statistically significant sources of parenting time, comparing parents and non parents on their allocation of time according to ten mutually exclusive categories of time use" (Drago, 2001, p. 13).

> Starting with the largest and moving to the smallest differences, we find parents [compared to the nonparents] spending an average of over 90 minutes more per day on *Child care,* exhibiting approximately 45 minutes less per day in *Working time* for the employer, engaging in around 20 minutes less of *Personal time* (including sleep), spending around 16 minutes on *Passive time* (including television), spending 13 minutes less on *Exercise,* spending an additional 10 minutes on *Housework,* and devoting approximately 9 minutes less to *Errands.* Other differences are well under 10 minutes and hence ignored. Note also that all of these differences except for *Housework* are statistically significant. (Drago, 2001, p. 17)

Discussion. This author chose to simply tell the reader what the independent samples *t*-tests indicated without providing the actual numerical data. This is unusual in social science research literature, and you are encouraged not to follow this author's example when you are reporting statistically significant outcomes. Although the findings are clearly stated in a narrative format, the author has the additional responsibility to produce the actual statistical output to support any conclusions that may flow from those quantitative findings. Furthermore, this author is inaccurately implying that the statistically significant results can be generalized to the entire population from which the sample was drawn, even though a nonrandom sample was used. See the final comments under Case Illustration 13.1.

Case Illustration 13.3

A 5-year federally funded research project examined the coping strategies exhibited by parents after the death of an adolescent or young adult child due to accident, suicide, or homicide. Data were collected five times during the study using a 53-item standardized questionnaire that contained 13 distinct subscales. One set of data indicating both the marital status and the age of the fathers (as independent variables) and the amount of mental distress experienced (as the dependent variable, measured on a scale specified as "GSI") was analyzed by an independent samples *t*-test. Other data were reported in a number of comprehensive tables showing means, standard deviations, and *t*-test scores.

The authors noted, "More married than single fathers were willing to participate in the study. However, married and single fathers did not differ significantly on age . . . nor on symptoms of mental distress studied (GSI).

Age (t =1.0, DF = 89, p = .32) . . . GSI (t = 1.2, DF = 89, p = .22)" (Murphy, Johnson, & Weber, 2002, p. 105).

Discussion. The independent samples *t*-test results point out that the married and single fathers did not significantly differ on the variable of age (p = .32) or on the presence of mental distress symptoms (p = .32). In other words, within the samples of fathers chosen for this study, there exists no evidence that those two groups differed from each other across the variables of age and symptoms of mental distress. Note that since no statistical significance was found, the author did not report the individual mean scores for the two groups of respondents. This is quite common under these circumstances when statistical significance is not discovered.

Activities Involving the Independent Samples *t*-Test

1. Using Data Set 2 (Agency Satellite Offices), compute an independent samples *t*-test for the variables *post* as the dependent or test variable and *gen* as the independent or grouping variable. Narrate the results in a format appropriate for a formal research report. Remember to explain clearly what the results mean in reference to the two variables.

2. Using Data Set 4 (Client Satisfaction Survey), compute an independent samples *t*-test for the variables *over* as the dependent or test variable and *stat* as the independent or grouping variable. Narrate the results in a format appropriate for a formal research report. Remember to explain clearly what the results mean in reference to the two variables.

3. Using Data Set 2 (Agency Satellite Offices), compute an independent samples *t*-test for the variables *satis* as the dependent or test variable and *adv* as the independent or grouping variable. Narrate the results in a format appropriate for a formal research report. Remember to explain clearly what the results mean in reference to the two variables.

4. Find an article in a recent issue of a professional journal in your library that contains an example of an independent samples *t*-test. Summarize the results and practical meaning of that example within the context of the entire article. Then, discuss your observations with a colleague. Or, find an article in your local newspaper or weekly news magazine that describes a situation that could be tested empirically and, furthermore, could be analyzed statistically by the introduction of one or more independent samples *t*-tests. Discuss with a colleague how you would approach that situation as a formal research project and what your dependent and independent variables would be.

SPSS Procedures

Independent Samples *t*-Test (for One Dependent Variable Measured at the Scale Level and One Independent Variable That Has Only Two Categories Measured at the Nominal Level)

When Used

This is used in situations such as comparing treatment outcomes of female and male clients or comparing attitudes of clients who live in urban and rural areas on a satisfaction survey that measures responses on a 10-point scale.

SPSS Process

In either the *Data View* or *Variable View* window, do the following:

CLICK on the *Analyze* menu from the top of the window.

CLICK on the *Compare Means* choice.

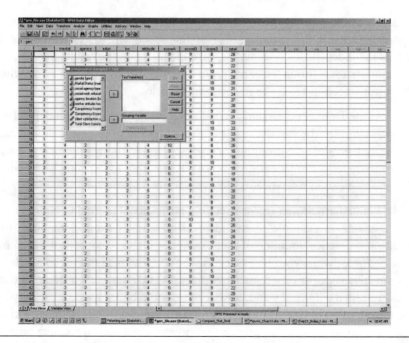

Figure 13.2   *Independent-Samples T Test* Screen in SPSS

CLICK on *Independent-Samples T Test*.

CLICK on the scale-level variable (dependent) in the box on the left.

CLICK on the right-pointing button in the middle of the window and move that variable to the box labeled *Test Variable*.

CLICK on the nominal-level variable (independent) that has only two possible categories in the box on the left.

CLICK on the right-pointing button in the middle of the window and move that variable to the box labeled *Grouping Variable*.

CLICK on the *Define Groups* button immediately below the *Grouping Variable* box.

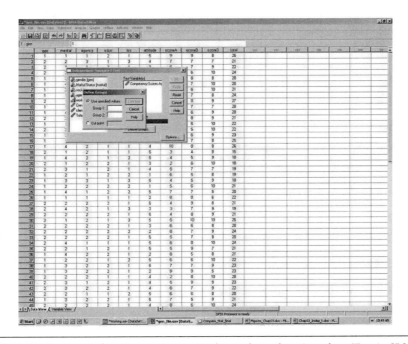

Figure 13.3   *Define Groups* Screen Within Independent Samples *t*-Test in SPSS

ENTER, in the box labeled *Group 1*, the same number you used in the *Variable View* window for the first category of the variable under the column labeled *Values* (e.g., female = 1 under the variable *gender*, BSW = 1 under the variable *social work education level*).

ENTER, in the box labeled *Group 2,* the same number you used in the *Variable View* window for the second category of the variable under the column labeled *Values* (e.g., male = 2 under the variable *gender,* MSW = 2 under the variable *social work education level*).

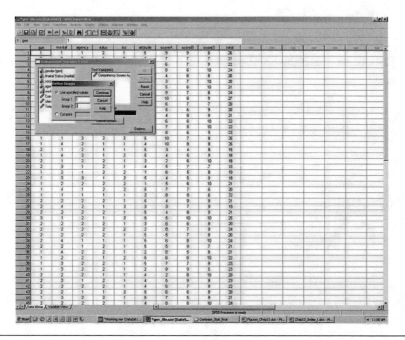

Figure 13.4   *Define Groups* Screen Within Independent Samples *t*-Test in SPSS With Groups Defined

CLICK on the *Continue* button.

CLICK on the *OK* button at the top right of the window.

Applying the SPSS Output

From the table labeled *Group Statistics,* do the following:

EXTRACT the mean value for each category (i.e., Group 1 and Group 2) of the variable from the column labeled *Mean.*

EXTRACT the standard deviation value for each category (i.e., Group 1 and Group 2) of the variable from the column labeled *Std. Deviation.*

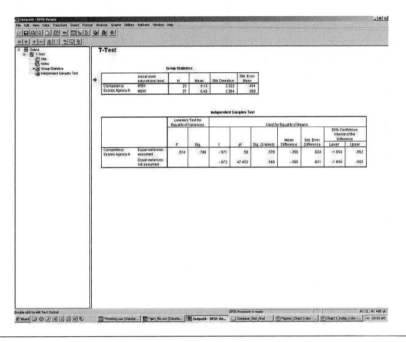

Figure 13.5   Output of *t*-Test Screen in SPSS for Variables *Competency Scores Agency A* and *Social Work Educational Level*

From the table labeled *Independent Samples Test,* do the following:

USE only the values listed on the first row labeled *Equal variances assumed.*

EXTRACT the *t* value in the middle of the table.

EXTRACT the *df* value to the right of the *t* value.

EXTRACT the *Sig. (2-tailed)* value to the right of the *df* value. If the *Sig. (2-tailed)* value is .05 or less (e.g., .01, .000), you have found a statistically significant difference between the two categories (i.e., between Group 1 and Group 2). This difference should be obvious when you compare the mean values of the two categories. If, however, the *Sig. (2-tailed)* value is greater than .05 (e.g., .07, .215), you have not found a statistically significant difference between the two categories (i.e., between Group 1 and Group 2).

NOTE that this set of statistics in Figure 13.5 indicates that while there is a slightly higher difference in the mean scores of the MSW workers over the BSW workers (5.49 compared to 5.13), the difference between the two scores is not statistically significant since the computed significance (two-tailed) is much higher than .05 ($p = .570$ or $> .05$). Thus, you cannot, in this situation, reject the null hypothesis that there is no difference in the competency scores between the BSW and MSW workers in Agency A.

References

Drago, R. (2001). Time on the job and time with their kids: Cultures of teaching and parenthood in the US. *Feminist Economics, 7*(3), 1–31.

Heilemann, M. V., Frutos, L., Lee, K. A., & Kury, F. S. (2004). Protective strength factors, resources, and risks in relation to depressive symptoms among childbearing women of Mexican descent. *Health Care for Women International, 25,* 88–106.

Mano-Negrin, R. (2003). Spanning the boundaries: A stakeholder approach to effectiveness gaps and empowerment in public and independent human service organizations. *Administration in Social Work, 27*(3), 25–45.

Murphy, S. A., Johnson, L. C., & Weber, N. A. (2002). Coping strategies following a child's violent death: How parents differ in their responses. *Omega: The Journal of Death and Dying, 45*(2), 99–118.

14

One-Way Analysis of Variance (ANOVA) With Post Hoc Tests

Statistics are human beings with the tears wiped off.

—P. Brodeur, *Outrageous Misconduct,* cited on
www.quotegarden.com/statistics

Introductory Case Illustration

In a recent study of child welfare workers in Florida, Perry (2006) examined if their educational background exerted any influence on the performance evaluations of their work by their supervisors. The researcher used the supervisor-based and peer-based performance evaluations of a random stratified sample of 457 child protective investigators. The evaluations were based on a 5-point Likert scale across 20 measures of performance. The seven categories of the independent variable (*university degree*) included the following: social work, psychology, sociology, criminology, education, business, and all other majors. The dependent variable examined was *performance evaluation* as measured over 20 items on a 5-point Likert scale by an agency-developed instrument. Each individual item was analyzed as well as the general, overall average score of all the 20 items. Since there were more than two categories in the independent variable, the researcher used the ANOVA test and two common post hoc tests for statistical analysis.

In the data presentation section of the final report, the researcher noted that

ANOVA procedures suggest that statistically significant differences in the ratings of workers' performance and skills apply to only one class of performance
expectations, professional training and development issues. Here, an ANOVA
test ($F = 2.395$, $p = .03$) and follow-up Bonferroni and Tukey's-B tests suggest
that those with degrees in education score significantly higher ($M = 4.25$, $SD = .75$) than those with degrees in sociology ($M = 3.48$, $SD = .75$) and criminology
($M = 3.53$, $SD = .75$) on their performance on tasks associated with *professional
training* and *development* issues. There was no significant difference in the *average performance scores* observed between workers with education degrees and
those with degrees in social work ($M = 3.67$, $SD = .75$), psychology ($M = 3.82$,
$SD = .68$), and business ($M = 3.94$, $SD = .86$). (Perry, 2006, p. 399)

Discussion. As you will explore further in this chapter, the **analysis of
variance** (commonly referred to simply as **ANOVA**) test is an expansion of
the independent samples *t*-test and is employed whenever your independent
variable has *more than two* categories in it and you want to compare all
those categories at the same time. The ANOVA test compares mean averages
and indicates only that there either is or is not present a significant difference
between more than two categories of the independent variable. One of a
number of follow-up tests (called a post hoc test) then identifies exactly
where (i.e., between which categories) the significant difference lies.

In this example, you are informed that there did seem to exist a higher,
statistically significant difference in performance on 2 of the 20 items on the
instrument ("tasks associated with *professional training* and *development*
issues") by those with education degrees as compared to those with degrees
in sociology and criminology. However, when the researcher analyzed the
overall average scores of all 20 items, there did not appear to be any significant difference in performance between those with education degrees and
those with degrees in social work, psychology, or business.

As is customary, the researcher did report the mean scores (M) of the various groups (i.e., categories of the independent variable), the standard deviation (SD), the ANOVA value (represented as F, the **F value**), and the level
of probability (p) that the differences noted are due simply to sampling error.

You will delve into further intricacies of the ANOVA test throughout the
rest of this chapter.

D espite the dreary and even mind-numbing title of this chapter, the
"One-Way Analysis of Variance (ANOVA) With Post Hoc Tests,"
these statistical procedures are extremely valuable in social services research

because they literally pick up where the independent samples *t*-test leaves off. The ANOVA is really nothing more than a series of independent samples *t*-tests computed for a nominal-level independent variable that has *three or more categories,* rather than simply two. Thus, in those situations where you would use an independent samples *t*-test for data analysis, you are no longer limited to only two categories of your nominal-level variable at any one time.

But . . . there is a slight complication. The ANOVA test will indicate only the fact that there exists a statistically significant difference among three, four, five, and so on categories of a variable. Specifically where that difference exists, however, is not revealed in the ANOVA test output. In other words, if data on infant birth weight from four separate child health clinics indicated, following an ANOVA test, that two of the clinic sites were significantly different, you would not know solely from the ANOVA values which individual sites reported that difference.

Enter the **post hoc test.** After computing one or more of the commonly used post hoc tests (a Latin phrase meaning *after the fact*), you will then know exactly where the differences take place—in other words, between what two or more categories is there a large enough difference in the reported mean values so that you can indicate there is a statistically significant difference? For this reason, you should always compute one of the post hoc tests whenever you analyze data by means of the ANOVA test.

One final introductory point: You will explore in this book only the simple form of the ANOVA, also called a *one-way* ANOVA. This test deals with one independent variable and one dependent variable at the same time, and it enjoys wide recognition within the research and evaluation community. There are more elaborate types of ANOVAs that compute the calculations for multiple independent variables and multiple dependent variables, but their discussion is beyond the scope of this book. So continue to relax . . . your life remains (relatively) uncomplicated.

Requirements

To compute an ANOVA test, you must have a nominal-level independent variable containing three or more categories within it. Examples could include variables such as *location* (north, south, east, and west), *type of agency* (public-nonprofit and private-for-profit), *professional title* (counselor, psychologist, psychiatrist, social worker, and teacher), *marital status* (married, divorced, single, and other), and *client presenting problem* (cutting class, truancy, verbal aggression, physical assaults, etc.). In the SPSS language used during this test, the independent variable is called the *grouping variable,* or simply the *factor.*

In addition, the dependent variable must be measured at the scale level. Some examples of scale-level measurements you might find in a social agency setting include *academic tests* graded on a 100-point scale; *attitude surveys* in which respondents responded on 11-point scales (i.e., 0–10); *income* reported in dollars; *length of time* measured in days, weeks, or months; *number* of home visits or office appointments required; *size* of caseload measured in absolute numbers; and so on.

From these introductory comments, you should be able to grasp how functional the ANOVA test can be in many social service contexts. The ANOVA test is especially practical for program evaluation projects that analyze outcome measurements of social agency operations. Consider how helpful it would be if you could learn the similarities or differences in effectiveness within a comprehensive mental health agency that operates six distinct satellite centers throughout a community, compare the practice outcomes among the various disciplines providing professional service in a medical facility, or gauge the difference in client satisfaction surveys from respondents who exhibit different cultural, social, or personal characteristics.

Using the One-Way ANOVA and a Post Hoc Test

Consider this possible social agency illustration. You are a regional supervisor of case managers in a statewide agency that provides physical protection and counseling services to women and children who are victims of domestic violence. One of the counseling services your agency provides is a series of daily group counseling sessions for the entire time that the women are in residence. At the point of leaving your agency, each woman is asked to complete an anonymous survey, which measures her attitudes about the daily group sessions, particularly whether these daily sessions met her physical, psychological, and social needs. These attitudes are measured by seven separate questions on an 11-point scale (10 = *very much*, 5 = *about average*, 0 = *not at all*).

All counseling staff have been thoroughly trained in the dynamics of small-group leadership, and all are actively involved in their own weekly peer group supervision. In addition, the format of these daily group support sessions is carefully outlined in an agency manual. As a result, you assume that the same general approach to and the procedures during the daily group sessions are being followed at each residence. You are responsible for five different residences located throughout your region, and for the past calendar year, the census count indicates that between 35 and 45 women have completed the program and left each of these residences voluntarily.

Assuming for this discussion that using the clients' perspectives can provide one measure (but not the only measure) of a program's effectiveness, you could discover valuable information by computing a one-way ANOVA on the data extracted from the attitude surveys completed by the women as they left the program. What, specifically, could you learn?

- First, since the scores are based on the value of 10, the average scores reported for each residence will indicate how effective the women believed each set of group discussions was in meeting their physical, psychological, and social needs. Were the average scores in the high range (7 to 10)? The moderate range (4 to 6)? Or the low range (1 to 3)? You would have this information readily available because the one-way ANOVA process will report the average scores for each residence.
- Second, you would know whether a statistically significant difference in attitude, as measured by the 10-point t scales, existed between two or more of the residences. Not finding a statistically significant difference would indicate either that the daily group sessions in all of the five residences were providing about the same level of effectiveness, at least as viewed by the women themselves, or the reported differences between locations could be simply due to chance.
- Third, if a statistically significant difference did exist somewhere among the mix of the five residences, then by computing one of the post hoc tests (e.g., the Tukey or the Sheffé test), you could pinpoint exactly where that difference at existed. In other words, which specific residences were significantly different from each other? And which residences were not significantly different from each other?

Remember, however, that if you did find a significant difference between one or more residences, then you know that the probability that the differences were due to chance or sampling error was acceptably low (i.e., below .05). Furthermore, if you used a random sample of all the women who left the program last year, rather than the entire population of them, then you could generalize (infer) the results from that sample back to the entire population of clients for that year.

Depending on what you discovered in your findings, you, as the regional supervisor, have at your option several possible courses of action. Whether the results were significantly different or not, you could reinforce group leaders for their competency and effectiveness, initiate critically needed staff development training, introduce targeted policy/program adjustments, or even institute selected personnel changes at specific sites.

The obvious point here is that the one-way ANOVA test, used with one of the post hoc tests, is another valuable set of statistical tools to gauge various aspects of program effectiveness and efficiency in every type of social service agency.

Interpreting the Results of a
One-Way ANOVA and Post Hoc Test

When reporting the results of a one-way ANOVA, you should include the following elements from the SPSS output:

- The mean score (*M*) and standard deviation (*SD*) for each category of the independent variable
- The *F* value as either a positive or negative whole number to three decimal points
- The degrees of freedom (*df*) for both *between groups* and *within groups*
- The significance level (*p*) at a two- or three-point decimal level
- If statistical significance of the *F* value is discovered, the results of the Tukey or Sheffé post hoc test, in a narrative format that indicates between what specific categories the differences were found

Keep in mind that in any ANOVA test, you are observing whether any difference in mean values exists between the three or more categories of the independent variable. The subsequent post hoc test detects specifically where (i.e., between what categories) any difference exists. All of this information will be present in the SPSS output along with other data that are not essential to include in a report.

Figure 14.1 represents an example of a typical SPSS output after the one-way ANOVA and Sheffé tests were calculated. In this example, the dependent variable was *total client satisfaction,* as measured by several instruments, which totaled a possible score (value) of 30; the independent variable was *agency type* with the following categories: public, not-for-profit, and private-for-profit.

For your written report, the only data you will need to extract from this actual SPSS output is the following: the mean score and standard deviation for each category of the independent variable (public: *M* = 21.67, *SD* = 2.0; not-for-profit: *M* = 21.58, *SD* = 2.6; and private-for-profit: *M* = 19.33, *SD* = 3.8), the *F* value (2.06), the degrees of freedom for both *between groups* and *within groups* (2, 47), the significance level (*p* = .138), and finally, if statistical significance is discovered, the results of the individual post hoc test described in a narrative format.

To keep your research report as consumer-friendly as possible, you *should not include* any other data contained in the SPSS output. Again, you are strongly advised *not to simply copy and paste* the entire SPSS output screen into your written report. Such a procedure would undoubtedly cause a level of confusion in your audience. Keep your data presentation comprehensive but simple. Just recall that most SPSS output screens contain much more information than you will ever need to share with your audience.

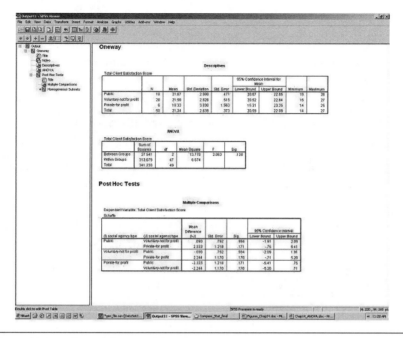

Figure 14.1   Output Screen of ANOVA in SPSS

This set of statistics reveals that you do not have any statistically significant difference between the mean values of the three categories of the independent variable ($p = .138$). Thus, the probability that the observed differences are simply due to sampling error and not to real differences is unacceptably high ($> .05$). As a result of this information, you should not reject the null hypothesis, which states that there exists no difference between the average scores of total client satisfaction, as recorded for each of the three types of social agencies studied.

Summary Points to Remember

- The ANOVA is simply a series of independent samples t-tests conducted for an independent variable that has three or more categories.

- The dependent variable must be at a *scale* level, and the independent variable must be at the *nominal* level or at the ordinal level but treated as the nominal level.

- In the SPSS procedure, the independent variable is referred to as the *factor*.

- The ANOVA test produces an *F* score.

- If a statistical significance is discovered, make note of the post hoc test output so you can learn the location of the differences. Specifically, you need to know between what categories of the independent variable the significant difference exists.

- If a statistical significance is not discovered, disregard the post hoc test output.

- The ANOVA test is particularly important in social service practice because it allows you to evaluate the effectiveness and efficiency of social agency programs and services.

- When reporting the results of an ANOVA, always include the mean and standard deviation values of all the categories of the independent variable.

Case Illustration 14.1

Research has suggested that during periods of unemployment, a person's perspective toward time can change. In a study involving 317 individuals who had suffered a spinal cord injury, Martz (2003) investigated whether there existed any differences regarding their time orientation for the future. The independent variable (i.e., grouping variable) was *work status* containing six categories (full-time employee, part-time employee, student, volunteer, retired, and unemployed). This variable was also collapsed into a new variable named *community role* with only two categories (active and nonactive). The active category contained the former categories of full-time employee, part-time employee, student, and volunteer, while the nonactive category contained the former categories of retired and unemployed. The dependent variable of *time orientation* was measured on the Future Time Orientation Scale (FTOS), which was a 14-item scale. Higher scores on the FTOS scale suggested the individual's greater personal orientation toward the future.

The author reported that

> a univariate analysis of variance (ANOVA) was conducted on future time orientation with work status as the grouping variable. Two steps were taken in order to examine the best grouping of the categorical variable of work status, due to the lower cell numbers of some of the categories. The first step involved an analysis of 6 categories of work status: full time ($N = 34$), part-time ($N = 13$), volunteer ($N = 9$), student ($N = 12$), retired ($N = 91$) and unemployed ($N = 125$). . . . There were no significant differences on future time orientation among the six categories, $F (5, 278) = 1.33$, $p = 0.25$, ns.

Because of the low cell numbers for some of the work status categories and the non-significant ANOVA, the data were collapsed in the second step into two categories: (1) unemployed and retired and (2) full-time, part-time, volunteer, or academic work. The means of future time orientation were then compared between these two groups: those with an active community role (full-time or part-time work, student or volunteer; $N = 68$) versus a non-active community role (retired or employed; $N = 216$). . . . . The results of the ANOVA indicate that there was a significant difference between these two groups on future time orientation, $F(1, 282) = 5.67$, $p = 0.018$. (Martz, 2003, p. 260)

Discussion. In this somewhat complicated example, the researcher first reported no statistically significant difference between the participants in the six categories of work status. Since no significance was discovered, no supplementary post hoc test was necessary. After collapsing the six categories into two categories, the researcher did discover a significant difference ($p = .018$), which is certainly less than a p value of .05 or less. Although the author did conduct a second ANOVA test on those two collapsed categories and did find, in that process, a significant difference between the two categories (active and nonactive community role), the author was, in fact, conducting an independent samples t-test (rather than an ANOVA) on the data since there were only two categories in the independent (grouping) variable.

As discussed in this chapter, the ANOVA statistical test functions by computing a series of several independent samples t-tests on independent variables with more than two categories. Thus, the choice of the ANOVA at the second step, though unusual, was not technically incorrect. Finally, the fact that the author chose not to include the actual mean scores with the ANOVA value is also somewhat atypical.

Case Illustration 14.2

Within the field of social services, research has been conducted on whether the type of social agency (i.e., public, not-for-profit, and proprietary) exerts any influence on workers' commitment to their organization and to their profession. In a study of 207 social service employees who were employed by one of three types of agencies, Giffords (2003) surveyed the participants at their work site. The researcher measured the dependent variable *organizational commitment* on the 15-item Organizational Commitment Questionnaire (OCQ) and professional commitment on the 15-item Professional Commitment Questionnaire (PCQ). Both instruments used 7-point Likert-type scales, and data were analyzed using ANOVA tests.

The author reports that

> a oneway analysis of variance was performed which compared the commitment of workers in the three types of auspices. The mean for *organizational commitment* of public employees ($n = 84$, $[M] = 4.09$, $S.D. = 1.14$) is significantly lower than the means of the not-for-profit ($n = 99$, $[M] = 4.84$, $S.D. = 1.10$), and proprietary ($n = 19$, $[M] = 5.30$, $S.D. = .93$) employees ($p < .05$). No significant differences ($p > .05$) appear between the not-for-profit and proprietary employees. The results of the analysis suggest that public employees are less committed to their organizations than the other two groups . . . the F test ($F = 15.16$, $df = (2, 199)$, $p < .05$) [and] pair-wise, multiple comparison tests were computed among the public, not-for-profit and proprietary organizations and indicate that workers are less organizationally committed in public organizations. (Giffords, 2003, pp. 15–16)

Discussion. This is a straightforward example of how an ANOVA test can be presented in detail and then its meaning explained in a relatively simple manner. From data retrieved from two instruments, it appears that those public agency participants in the study exhibited a statistically significant lower level of organizational commitment when compared to not-for-profit and proprietary agency participants. The mention in the citation of "pair-wise, multiple comparison tests" refers to one or more possible post hoc tests that are employed once you determine that an ANOVA test shows statistical significance. There are 18 different post hoc tests available for use within the SPSS program, but the author did not mention specifically which ones were used in this analysis. In reporting significant ANOVA results from your own research and program evaluation projects, you are advised to name any post hoc test you use.

Case Illustration 14.3

A research project in Israel investigated whether adolescents who were in recovery from alcohol and other drug dependence exhibited varying levels of moral judgment related to their recovery process. The researchers studied 114 male adolescents who were involved in five different types of treatment facilities: therapeutic communities emphasizing sociomoral issues ($n = 33$), day care units ($n = 56$), a day care unit solely for alcoholics ($n = 9$), methadone maintenance unit ($n = 14$), and unknown affiliation ($n = 2$).

The dependent variable *moral judgment* was measured by the Defining Issues Test (DIT), which yielded a *P*-score as an indicator of the percentage of statements chosen that reflect principled thinking. An internal check within the

DIT (the *M*-score) ensured consistency and meaningfulness of the responses. During the analysis phase of the project, the participants were placed in two subgroups according to their *M*-score, that is, strict ($M < 4$) or flexible ($M < 8$). The ANOVA test was then conducted twice, once each for the strict *M*-score group and for the flexible *M*-score group.

The researchers report that

> the *M*-score is the number of meaningless items that were chosen by any participant. These items are really meaningless and were included in the DIT to serve as an internal reliability check. . . . For the strict *M*-check sample ($M < 4$) the mean *P*-score of all participants remaining in the sample is 23.19 ($n = 49$, *s.d.* = 15.58). A one-way ANOVA of the *P*-scores by the treatment units failed to show significant differences . . . $F(5, 34) = 0.45$, $p = .811$ (n.s.). . . . For the flexible *M*-check sample ($M < 8$) the mean *P*-score of all participants remaining in the sample is 23.50 ($n = 270$, *s.d.* = 15.42). A one-way ANOVA of the *P*-scores by treatment units . . . also failed to show significant differences . . . $F(5,43) = .51$, $p = .767$ (n.s.). (Ronel & Teichman, 2003, pp. 53–54)

Discussion. This is somewhat atypical in that the authors chose to provide all the intricate details of the ANOVA tests even though no statistically significant differences were discovered between the various treatment units. A simple statement that ANOVA tests were conducted and that no significant differences were detected would normally suffice. Remember that how you explain your findings is ultimately your own responsibility.

Activities Involving the One-Way ANOVA and Post Hoc Tests

1. Using Data Set 1 (Client Demographics and Treatment Results), compute an ANOVA with the variables *pre* as the dependent variable and *eth* as the independent variable or factor. Narrate the results in a format appropriate for a formal research report. Remember to explain clearly what the results mean in reference to the two variables.

2. Using Data Set 3 (Client Single-Case Evaluation), compute an ANOVA with the variables *reint3* as the dependent variable and *type* as the independent variable or factor. Narrate the results in a format appropriate for a formal research report. Remember to explain clearly what the results mean in reference to the two variables.

3. Using Data Set 4 (Client Satisfaction Survey), compute an ANOVA with the variables *time* as the dependent variable and *marital* as the independent

variable or factor. Narrate the results in a format appropriate for a formal research report. Remember to explain clearly what the results mean in reference to the two variables.

4. Using Data Set 5 (Community Social Needs Survey) and treating a 5-point ordinal measurement as scale level, compute an ANOVA with the variables *pov* as the dependent variable and *emp* as the independent variable or factor. Narrate the results in a format appropriate for a formal research report. Remember to explain clearly what the results mean in reference to the two variables.

SPSS Procedures

ANOVA With Post Hoc Tests (for One Dependent Variable Measured at the Scale Level and One Independent Variable That Has More Than Two Categories Measured at the Nominal Level)

When Used

This is used in situations such as comparing treatment outcomes of employed, unemployed, and retired clients; comparing attitudes of rehabilitation counselors, psychologists, social workers, and teachers on a satisfaction survey; or contrasting the ethnic/racial sensitivity scores of employees tested at five different agency locations.

SPSS Process

In either the *Data View* or *Variable View* window, do the following:

CLICK on the *Analyze* menu from the top of the window.

CLICK on *Compare Means* choice.

CLICK on *One-Way ANOVA*.

CLICK on the scale-level variable (dependent) in the left box.

CLICK on the right-pointing button in the middle of the window and move that variable to the box labeled *Dependent List*.

CLICK on the nominal-level variable that has more than two possible categories (independent) in the left box.

CLICK on the right-pointing button in the middle of the window and move that variable to the box labeled *Factor*.

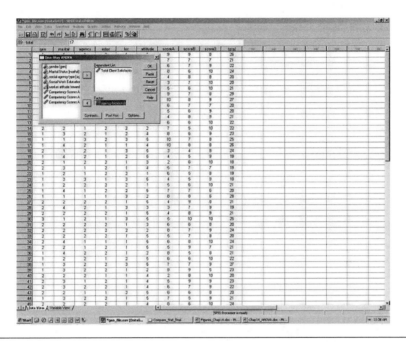

Figure 14.2   *One-Way ANOVA* Screen in SPSS With Variables *Total Client Satisfaction Scores* and *Agency Location* Selected

CLICK on the *Options* button at the bottom right of the *Factor* box.

CLICK on *Descriptive* at the top of the list on the left.

CLICK on the *Continue* button.

CLICK on the *Post Hoc* button in the middle below the *Factor* box.

CLICK on *Tukey* near the top of the second column on the left.

CLICK on the *Continue* button at the bottom on the left.

CLICK on the *OK* button at the top right of the window.

Applying the SPSS Output

From the table labeled *Descriptives*, do the following:

EXTRACT the *Mean* value for each of the categories of the independent variable (i.e., the *Factor*).

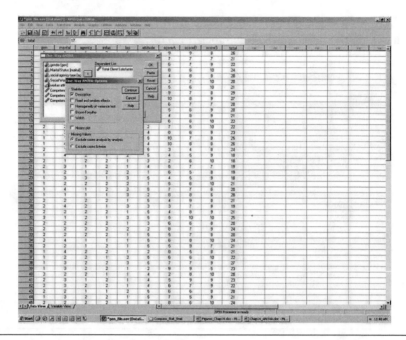

Figure 14.3   One-Way ANOVA: *Options* Screen in SPSS

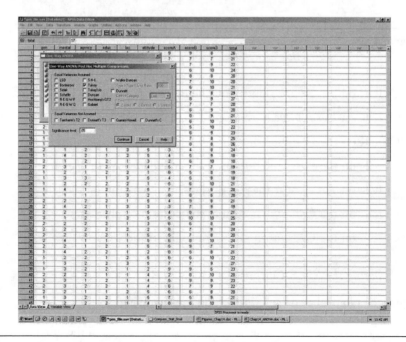

Figure 14.4   One-Way ANOVA: *Post Hoc Multiple Comparisons* Screen in SPSS

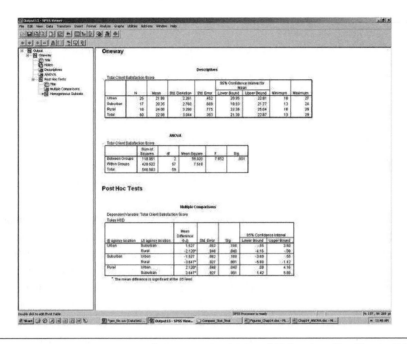

Figure 14.5   *Output* Screen of One-Way ANOVA and Tukey Post Hoc Test in SPSS

EXTRACT the *Std. Deviation* value for each of the categories of the independent variable (i.e., the *Factor*).

From the table labeled *ANOVA*, do the following:

EXTRACT the *df* value under the column labeled *df* for both rows labeled *Between Groups* and *Within Groups.*

EXTRACT the *F* value on the row labeled *Between Groups.*

EXTRACT the *Sig.* value on the row labeled *Between Groups.* If the *Sig.* value is .05 or less (e.g., .01, .000), you have found a statistically significant difference between the categories of the independent variable. PROCEED to the next step below, *Multiple Comparisons.* If, however, the *Sig.* value is greater than .05 (e.g., .07, .215), you have not found a statistically significant difference between the categories of the independent variable. DO NOT PROCEED further.

From the table labeled *Multiple Comparisons,* do the following:

> NOTICE which value(s) under the *Mean Difference* column is (are) followed by an asterisk (*).

> EXTRACT the value(s) and NOTE which categories of the independent variable under columns *(I)* and *(J)* are being compared.

> NOTE also that each *Mean Difference* value is repeated twice since all possible combinations are reported.

> NOTE that in this example, Figure 14.5, you can observe that the rural agencies received a higher average total client satisfaction score (20.00) as compared to the urban agencies (21.88) and the suburban agencies (20.35). The ANOVA test then confirms that you also have statistically significant scores at an acceptably low level of probability (*Sig.* or $p = .001$) of committing a Type I error. Then, once you examine the output from the Tukey multiple comparisons test, you also know that the statistically significant differences in total mean scores exist between the rural agencies and both the urban and suburban agencies (*Sig.* or $p = .040$ between rural and urban, and *Sig.* or $p = .001$ between rural and suburban). As you complete your written final report, you are advised to note these two items: (1) You are able to reject your null hypothesis based on the ANOVA test, and (2) you can discuss and interpret specifically where those differences lie based on the results of the Tukey post hoc test.

References

Giffords, E. D. (2003). An examination of organizational and professional commitment among public, not-for-profit and proprietary social service employees. *Administration in Social Work, 27*(3), 5–23.

Martz, E. (2003). Future time orientation and employment of individuals with a spinal cord injury: Does current work status reflect a greater orientation toward the future? *Work, 21,* 257–263.

Perry, R. E. (2006). Do social workers make better child welfare workers than non-social workers? *Research on Social Work Practice, 16*(4), 393–405.

Ronel, N., & Teichman, M. (2003). Moral judgment among alcohol-other drug dependent persons. *Alcohol Treatment Quarterly, 21*(1), 49–61.

15

Nonparametric Alternatives to Common Parametric Tests

Facts are stubborn things, but statistics are more pliable.

—Author unknown, cited on
www.quotegarden.com/statistics

Introductory Case Illustration

Between 1997 and 1998, researchers Pinquart and Sorensen surveyed a large number of older adults in Germany and the United States on their preferences for future care arrangements, both in the short term and in the long term. The participants were randomly selected from the geographic locations where they lived in their respective countries (Germany, $N = 812$; United States, $N = 565$). The two samples were generally matched on the variables of age, gender, percentage of married respondents, and normal activities of daily living. For this study, the researchers identified three types of possible future senior assistance: *informal* (provided by family, friends, neighbors, etc.), *formal* (provided by home health agencies, nursing homes, etc.), or *mixed* (some combination of informal and formal). The authors used several instruments that measured their preferences on both nominal and ordinal scales. The authors analyzed their data by the use of the Wilcoxon test, which is the nonparametric alternative to the paired samples *t*-test. The Wilcoxon test produces a *Z* value in its output.

In their published report, the researchers note that

the first research question asked whether older adults' preferences for informal, formal and mixed assistance would differ for short- and long-term care needs. The percentage of respondents indicating a preference for exclusive informal, exclusive formal, mixed, or no assistance is depicted. . . . Using Wilcoxon-Tests we found that the exclusive informal was preferred more often for short-term care needs than for long-term care needs (total sample: $Z = 5.10$, $p < .001$; U.S.: $Z = 2.29$, $p < .05$; Germany: $Z = 4.90$, $p < .001$). The exclusive use of formal assistance was more often preferred for long-term care needs than for short-term care (total sample: $Z = -12.54$, $p < .001$; U.S.: $Z = -7.78$, $p < .05$; Germany: $Z = -9.30$, $p < .001$). Whereas both results are in concordance with our expectations, we found a surprising result with regard to mixed assistance. Mixed assistance was more likely to be preferred for short-term than long-term care needs (total sample: $Z = 8.82$, $p < .001$; U.S.: $Z = 6.10$, $p < .05$; Germany: $Z = 6.37$, $p < .001$). (Pinquart & Sorensen, 2002, p. 300)

Discussion. As should be readily apparent, the only visible difference in this example from a situation in which you would use a paired samples *t*-test is the fact that the data collected are at the ordinal level of measurement. Other than that important fact, the meaning of the output from a Wilcoxon test is essentially the same as the meaning derived from the output of a paired samples *t*-test.

In this study, which compared the preferences of the German and American samples for future personal care of three different types (*informal, formal,* and *mixed*) in two distinct need situations (*short term* and *long term*), it appears from the statistical analysis that *informal* care was preferred for *short-term* needs for the total sample ($p < .001$) and for each country subsample (United States, $p < .05$; Germany, $p < .001$). For *long-term* care needs, however, the data suggest that the total sample preferred more *formal* care ($p < .001$), which was also apparent in each subsample (United States, $p < .05$; Germany, $p < .001$). With similar levels of p, the respondents chose the *mixed* option for *short-term* care needs rather than for *long-term* care needs.

This final chapter covers the various situations in which you will use nonparametric tests, such as the Wilcoxon test, to analyze your project data.

At the very beginning of this book, in Chapter 1, you had the opportunity to read a number of definitions, with examples, of a long list of technical terms used in statistics. The terms *parametric* and *nonparametric* are found at the end of Chapter 1 under the section Some Useful Nondefinitions, so you might want to go back there now and read the brief section on those two terms found there.

Welcome back! To reinforce and apply what you just read, note that there are a number of requirements before you should use any parametric test in your research and program evaluation projects. Now might be a good time to delve a bit deeper into those requirements since the differences between parametric and nonparametric statistical tests are rather important in the overall scheme of things.

Scale-Level Data

Parametric statistical tests, such as the *t*-tests and ANOVA, all require that you have scale- (i.e., interval or ratio) level data in your dependent variable. Furthermore, with Pearson's *r*, another parametric test, you must have scale-level data in *both* your dependent and independent variables. Since parametric tests are generally accepted as *robust* operations, in the sense that they are forceful tools, it is logical that they have at their disposal very precise measurement data.

Think of it this way. If you had a very expensive, specialized, ultra-powerful microscope in a laboratory, you would undoubtedly want to use it only on some slide with a highly complex cell structure and not squander it on some simple specimen that could be easily analyzed using one of the ordinary microscopes. In a similar manner, parametric statistical tests need to process very precise data so that the full force of the test can be unleashed. Only scale-level data, not ordinal-level or nominal-level data, can provide that required level of precision. So you might say that parametric tests are like those specialized microscopes, while nonparametric tests are closer to any ordinary microscope.

Normal Distribution

Having scale-level data is the first requirement for using parametric statistical tests. The second requirement is that the samples of data you are using were drawn from a population that is *normally distributed*. What is a normal distribution? One way to visualize it is to consider the following activity. Suppose you laid out all the values (numbers) in a population in groups of same numbers along a horizontal axis, so that repeating numbers appeared on top of each other. If the population were normally distributed, then the vertical distribution pattern would approximate the image of a bell-shaped curve. The mean, median, and modal values would be represented at the same (or approximately the same) point, and the outliers (very high and very low values) would be more or less evenly distributed at both ends.

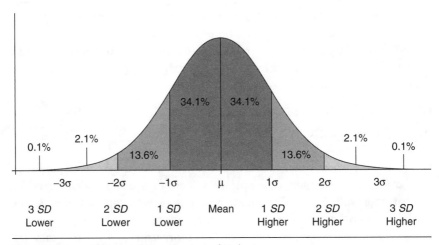

Figure 15.1   A Normal Distribution of Values

In literal terms, if you were measuring 976 human service staff on the variable of *length of professional service in years* and that population of 976 staff was normally distributed, you could visually represent the *average* number of years worked by the highest point in a bell-shaped curve, while the outlying numbers (i.e., those staff who just started working and those nearing retirement age) would appear at the fringes of both ends of the bell-shaped curve. In between those outliers and the mean value would be placed varying values that "flow away" from the mean point generally in an even pattern onto both sides. This near-perfect bell-shaped curve is hypothetical in nature and represents an idealized normal distribution of values. Life is rarely, if ever, so exact, so do not expect to find perfectly normal distributions in the samples you use for your research and program evaluation projects.

Since you are working only with samples and not the entire population, how do you ever know if your population is normally distributed? There is no exact way to tell since you usually do not have access to the shape of the full population. However, since you do have direct access to the samples themselves, a very practical way to make a judgment about the normality of the distribution is to *analyze the shape of those samples*. Assuming the samples were randomly drawn from the entire population and the samples appear to be normally distributed, you can then proceed on the assumption that they generally reflect the characteristics of the population. Thus, the population should also be normally distributed in most situations.

You can easily envision the shape of your sample by creating a *histogram figure* in SPSS and include an overlay of a normal curve over it. By comparing the normal curve with the distribution of your sample, you can judge how close your sample is to the ideal. Do not look for perfection—a close approximation is all you need to achieve.

Another way to know if your sample is normally distributed is to compute the level of *kurtosis* (i.e., the height of the distribution) and the level of *skewness* (i.e., the width of the distribution). A normally distributed sample will have a kurtosis of less than 1.00 and a skewness of also less than 1.00. So, if a sample reported a kurtosis of .49, you can assume it was normally distributed *vertically* (i.e., from the perspective of its height). On the other hand, a kurtosis of 1.95 would indicate an unnaturally elongated distribution whose values were squeezed together producing a tall, narrow shape rather than the shorter, more symmetrical bell shape. Likewise, a skewness of .68 would indicate that the sample was normally distributed *horizontally* (i.e., regarding its width or breadth), while a skewness of 1.86 would portray the distribution of values as stretching out in a very flat, pancakelike fashion, quite different from a bell shape.

In Figure 15.1, you can picture the image of normal, bell-shaped distribution of values. Contrary to that, Figure 15.2 symbolizes a distribution of values with an abnormal kurtosis. The values in this distribution are unnaturally crowded at the center or mean point.

Distinct in an alternate direction, Figure 15.3 conveys a distribution of values with an abnormal skewness. The values in this distribution demonstrate a negative distortion as the tail (i.e., the lower values) slants off unnaturally toward the left, thereby warping the normal shape you would expect.

The closer the values for kurtosis and skewness approach the level of 2.00, the more abnormal is the distribution and, thus, the less likely does your sample approximate a normal curve. You can easily visualize both the skewness and the kurtosis of any distribution by creating a histogram and computing the kurtosis and skewness values of that distribution. The necessary steps to produce a histogram are outlined in the SPSS Procedures at the end of this chapter.

Sample Size

The third requirement for using parametric statistical tests is that the samples are *large enough*. Again, there is no exact or universally agreed-upon definition of what is considered large enough, so it may come down to some combination of common sense and typical practice among researchers.

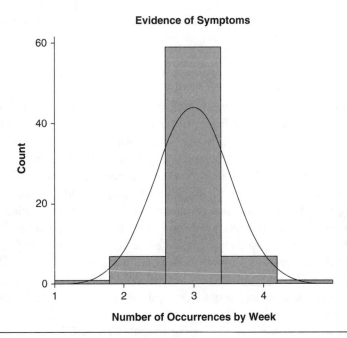

Figure 15.2   Distribution With Abnormal Kurtosis and a Normal Curve Overlay

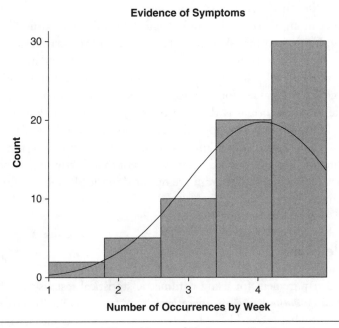

Figure 15.3   Distribution With an Abnormal Skewness and a Normal Curve Overlay

Unquestionably, numbers as small as 5 or 10 are generally recognized as small in virtually all situations, while numbers over 100 would reasonably be considered as large in most social service agency contexts. However, when your population total reaches into the thousands, as it could if you wanted to survey all the residents of an urban neighborhood or a suburban county, then a large enough sample might include several hundreds.

Some researchers recommend that the sample size should be *10 times* the number of variables under study. Under this assumption, then, if you focused on 17 different variables in your research project, you should have a minimum of 170 respondents in your sample. Other researchers follow a simpler, and equally unscientific, guide for action when deciding on sample size: For a meaningful quantitative analysis, you must have a *minimum of 30* cases; ideally, any number *over 100* would be better; and, finally, you would need *no more than 10%* of the total if your population is in the *thousands*. Think of the phrase *30, 100, 10%*, if you opt for this latter piece of practical advice.

Another way to look at sample size is to consider your total population to be a beautiful, flaky, 14-inch cherry pie that is staring at you, uncut, on a buffet table. One of your secret vices in life is that you have an unquenchable love for cherries, especially sweet cherries baked in a pie. You are next in line for the food so you skip the main dishes and head right for the pie. Your hostess has left the pie uncut on the table but thoughtfully has placed there a pie knife for guests to use. What should you do if you wanted to get as many cherries on your plate as humanly possible? Obviously, you would cut yourself the biggest piece that would fit on your plate! The bigger the piece, the more cherries for you. That is the very same principle to use when deciding on sample size. *The bigger the sample, the more chance you have of obtaining a true representation of the population you are studying.*

As if the situation was not complex enough, two additional issues should be factored in whenever you consider whether you have an adequately large sample. One issue has to do with how *diverse* your population is, especially in terms of typical demographic characteristics such as gender, race/ethnicity, religion, age, and so on. The general principle is this: The more diverse your population, the larger your sample should be in order to represent those different demographics. The second issue concerns the resources available to you, the researcher. Resources in this context mean three things: money, time, and effort. You should ask yourself three very pragmatic questions. How much financial resources do you have access to for items such as postage, office supplies, photocopying, and telephone calls? How much time do you have to complete the project, including preparation, data collection, data analysis, and final drafting of the written report? Finally, will you be working alone on this research project, or will support staff and/or colleagues assist you as part of a team? How you answer these and similar questions will help you determine how large your sample of respondents should be.

To summarize the discussion so far, parametric statistical tests have three general requirements. The absence of any one of these would create an obstacle that argues against your use of a parametric test.

- The dependent variable is measured at the scale level.
- The population is normally distributed.
- The sample is large enough.

Approaching this discussion from the opposite direction, you can conclude that you should use nonparametric statistical tests whenever any one of the following conditions is present:

- The dependent variable is measured at the nominal level.
- The dependent variable is measured at the ordinal level, and the independent variable is measured at the nominal level.
- The dependent variable is measured at the ordinal level, and the independent variable is measured at the ordinal level.
- The population is not normally distributed.
- The samples are small.

Nonparametric Alternatives to
t-Tests and One-Way ANOVA

As noted previously in Chapter 9 of this book, the chi-square test of independence is the most common example of nonparametric statistical tests used in social service research and evaluation projects. Furthermore, it will always be nonparametric in nature simply because it is designed to test whether there exists a relationship between two variables measured only at the nominal level. You also have seen in Chapter 11 that Spearman's *rho* test is the nonparametric option for correlations when you have ordinal data rather than scale data.

What follows below is a brief listing of other nonparametric tests that, admittedly, are not found very often in social science research literature. They can, nonetheless, serve a very pragmatic purpose, especially for social agency–based projects whose results are designed primarily for internal or local community consumption.

These nonparametric tests are alternatives to the more rigorous parametric tests that you have been examining so far. You can employ these tests in the same case situations as their parametric counterparts, the only difference being that one or more of the requirements for parametric tests is absent (i.e., either the dependent variable is not at the scale level, the population is not normally distributed, or the sample is small). The specific SPSS procedures for each of these nonparametric tests are presented at the end of this chapter.

- The **Wilcoxon signed-ranks test** is the alternative for the paired samples *t*-test. This test is used to compare two variables, both measured at the ordinal level. The assumption is that the two measurements are from the same respondents at two different times (such as in pretest and posttest situations or in Period 1 and Period 2 conditions) or between matched samples of two different groups. In the SPSS output, the Wilcoxon signed-ranks test produces a *Z* value.

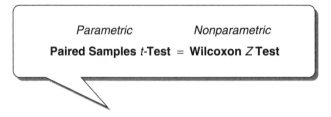

Figure 15.4   Wilcoxon *Z* Test

- The **Mann-Whitney *U* test** is the alternative for the independent samples *t*-test. This test compares the dependent variable measured at the ordinal level against the independent variable measured at either the ordinal level or nominal level. In this situation, that ordinal level of the independent variable is treated as a nominal-level variable. Like the *t*-test for independent samples, only two categories of the independent variable, whether it is ordinal or nominal, can be factored into the statistical analysis at any one time. In the SPSS output, the Mann-Whitney test produces a *U* value.

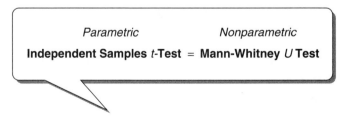

Figure 15.5   Mann-Whitney *U* Test

- The **Kruskal-Wallis *H* test** is the nonparametric alternative for the one-way ANOVA test. This test also compares the dependent variable measured at the ordinal level against the independent variable measured at either the ordinal level or nominal level. That ordinal level of the independent variable is also treated as a nominal-level variable. Like the one-way ANOVA, this test is used when the independent variable contains more than two categories and all of those categories are factored into the statistical analysis. You should note, however, that unlike the one-way ANOVA, there are no post hoc test options with the Kruskal-Wallis test. Thus, you must interpret where the differences lie between the categories of the independent variable by visually scanning the mean values of those categories as reported in the output of this test. In the SPSS output, the Kruskal-Wallis test produces an *H* value.

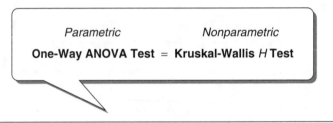

Parametric   *Nonparametric*

One-Way ANOVA Test = **Kruskal-Wallis *H* Test**

Figure 15.6   Kruskal-Wallis *H* Test

Summary Points to Remember

- Computing parametric tests requires that your dependent variable is measured at the scale level; your population is, generally speaking, normally distributed; and your sample is large enough. If any one of these conditions is not present, use one of the nonparametric tests.

- If your sample is normally distributed, you can assume your population is also.

- An idealized normal distribution of values can be represented visually as a bell-shaped curve.

- A normal distribution has a skewness and kurtosis value measured between 0.0 and 1.00.

- The chi-square test is always nonparametric since it uses nominal-level data, or ordinal-level data treated as nominal level, in both dependent and independent variables.

- Spearman's *rho* test is always nonparametric since it uses ordinal data in both dependent and independent variables.

- The Wilcoxon test is the nonparametric alternative to the paired samples *t*-test. It produces a *Z* value.

- The Mann-Whitney test is the nonparametric alternative to the independent samples *t*-test. It produces a *U* value.

- The Kruskal-Wallis test is the nonparametric alternative to the ANOVA test. It produces an *H* value.

- There is no nonparametric alternative to a post hoc test.

Case Illustration 15.1

As part of a larger research project, titled the Perceptions of Social Issues (PSI), a researcher in the United Kingdom investigated how people respond to Web-based surveys, specifically whether the mode of delivery of the survey affected the responses in any way. Two near-identical questionnaires in two distinct modes (i.e., Web based and paper based) were submitted to near-identical groups. The focus of the questionnaires was to determine health-related behavior of adolescents. Eleven items on the instrument, all relating to self-image, were measured on a 5-point ordinal-level scale (high to low), as was one final item that asked the adolescent respondents to rank themselves in one of six categories regarding the amount of cigarettes they smoked per week (*more than 20 a week* to *never smoked*). The independent variable for this study was *mode of delivery* (paper or Web), and the dependent variables consisted of the responses on the ordinal-level scales by the respondents.

The researcher reported that

the Mann-Whitney and Kruskal-Wallis tests produced probability values well above .05 in all five cases [of self-image] (thin or fat $p = .189$; tall or short for age $p = .265$; popular or not $p = .176$; easy going or serious $p = .077$; like risks or prefer safety $p = .089$. . . . There was just 1 of the 23 quantitative items where the substantive content of the answers varied fairly unequivocally between the two modes. This item investigated how many cigarettes the young people smoked per week and asked to place themselves in one of six categories ranging from *never smoked* to *more then 20 cigarettes a week*. The chi-square statistic in this instance ($\chi^2 = 21.313$, $df = 5$, $p = .001$) was corroborated by Mann-Whitney and Kruskal-Wallis tests (both with $p = .015$). On this particular item, those participants using a web-based questionnaire reported a lower level of smoking than did those using a paper-based questionnaire. (Denscombe, 2006, pp. 251–252)

Discussion. In this example, it was appropriate to use the Mann-Whitney test to compare the differences between answers on the paper surveys and the Web-delivered surveys since the researcher was comparing two independent samples that had been measured on ordinal-level instruments across an independent variable with just two categories within it. From what is presented in the methodology section of the article, however, it is not clear why the author refers to the use of the Kruskal-Wallis test, which would be appropriate only if the independent variable (*mode of delivery*) consisted of more than two categories. Perhaps the author computed the Kruskal-Wallis test as a reinforcing procedure for the Mann-Whitney test since they are related in their general orientation and purpose.

Case Illustration 15.2

A pilot study aimed at the prevention of work-related injury among clerical and office workers used a random assignment process to place the participants in either an intervention group ($N = 8$) or a control group ($N = 8$). The intervention group received 4 hours of specialized and comprehensive training relating to workplace injury prevention. One of the measurement instruments used was the Symptom Evaluation Measure that gauged the intensity of physical symptoms (e.g., eyestrain, neck pain, wrist-hand pain) on a 4-point Likert scale: *none, mild, moderate,* and *severe*. Other instruments provided nominal-level demographic data and scale-level frequency-of-occurrence data. The Wilcoxon test was computed to compare pretest and posttest intensity of symptoms. The Mann-Whitney test indicated whether the two groups were equal at the time of pretest (which is identified as *baseline* in this project). The researchers reported that

> the Mann-Whitney U test indicated group equality at baseline along studied variables of average symptom frequency and intensity, average weekly stress levels, and average weekly energy levels. . . . A Wilcoxon Signed Ranks test . . . yielded only one statistically significant difference between pre and post measures (Lower Back ache/pain frequency for Group A [intervention group]. . . . There were clinically relevant [but not statistically significant] decreases in symptom frequencies following intervention for Eyestrain/fatigue, Elbow-Forearm ache/pain, Wrist-Hand ache/pain, and Lower Back ache/pain. Upper back ache/pain frequency increased following intervention. No clinically relevant changes were noted in symptom intensities or perceived Average Weekly Stress. There was a decrease in perceived Average Weekly Energy from pre to post intervention. (Martin, Irvine, Fluharty, & Gatty, 2003, pp. 191–192)

Discussion. This is an interesting example of the combined use of the Mann-Whitney *U* test (as the ordinal-level equivalent of the independent samples *t*-test) and the Wilcoxon signed-ranks test (as the ordinal equivalent of the paired samples *t*-test). The Mann-Whitney *U* test was appropriately introduced because the researchers wished to show the equality of the experimental sample with the control sample across the three variables of average symptom frequency and intensity, average weekly stress levels, and average weekly energy levels. Thus, although they were independent samples of participants, the researchers showed at the beginning of the experiment (i.e., "at baseline") that the two groups were similar across those variables. The Wilcoxon test was then correctly computed to indicate whether there existed statistically significant changes from the pretest point to the posttest point. As presented, you can see that there was only one statistically significant change during the experiment (lower back ache/pain for the intervention group). When no significance is discovered, it is common to simply report that finding without also providing the statistical notation. However, unlike this example, and as you have seen before, it is more typical to report the actual statistical values when statistical significance is discovered.

Case Illustration 15.3

Researcher Prospero (2006) initiated a recent study of young adolescents' perceptions of their partners' behavior during a dating encounter, as well as their own reactions to their partners' behavior. Data were collected by means of a survey that presented typical dating situations in four scenarios, with participants asked two sets of questions in response to whether they perceived the stated behaviors (i.e., their own and their partners') to be either aggressive or not aggressive on a 4-point ordinal scale. Study participants were middle school students ($N = 89$) who were assumed, by school officials, to be at risk of experiencing violence in dating relationships, either as perpetrators or victims. Responses were analyzed based on gender.

The author described the statistical analysis as follows:

Mann-Whitney *U* tests were conducted to investigate gender differences in the participants' responses to the perceptions of the protagonist, as well as the behavioral expectations of the protagonist. . . . The results of the first test revealed no significant gender differences in their responses to the perceptions of the protagonist, $z = -.335$, $p > .05$. However, the results of the second test revealed significant gender differences in the participants' reporting of the behavioral responses of the protagonist, $z = -3.347$, $p < .025$. Average rankings for male and female participants were 57.60 and 39.01, respectively. (Prospero, 2006, p. 477)

Discussion. In this example, the author conducted the Mann-Whitney *U* test (as the ordinal equivalent to the independent samples *t*-test) since the responses of the participants were analyzed according to the variable *gender* with only two categories (female/male). As you can see, it is important to report the actual mean scores of the rankings (i.e., 57.60 for males and 39.01 for females) in order to assist the reader in understanding the meaning of a finding of statistical significance (i.e., the males were seen as more likely to expect aggressive responses to their own behaviors than did females). Remember that finding statistical significance in a test does not ensure absolute truth or certainty. Statistical significance translates as an assumption that the differences uncovered (in this case, that males expect more aggressive responses than females) were probably not due to chance or sampling error.

Activities Involving Alternative Nonparametric Tests

1. Using Data Set 2 (Agency Satellite Offices), compute a Wilcoxon test for the variables *future1* and *future2*. Narrate the results in a format appropriate for a formal research report. Remember to explain clearly what the results mean in reference to the two variables.

2. Using Data Set 5 (Community Social Needs Survey), compute a Mann-Whitney test for the variables *adol* as the dependent variable and *gen* as the independent variable. Then, compute a second Mann-Whitney test for the variables *coupfam* as the dependent variable and *gen* as the independent variable. Narrate the results in a format appropriate for a formal research report. Remember to explain clearly what the results mean in reference to the two variables.

3. Using the same Data Set 5 (Community Social Needs Survey), compute a Kruskal-Wallis test for the variables *ment* as the dependent variable and *emp* as the independent variable. Narrate the results in a format appropriate for a formal research report. Remember to explain clearly what the results mean in reference to the two variables.

4. Using Data Set 1 (Client Demographics and Treatments Results), compute a Kruskal-Wallis test for the variables *att2* as the dependent variable and *eth* as the independent variable. Narrate the results in a format appropriate for a formal research report. Remember to explain clearly what the results mean in reference to the two variables.

SPSS Procedures

Nonparametric Alternatives to Parametric Procedures in SPSS

When Used

This is used in situations where at least one of the following conditions exist:

1. The population values (scores) of the population are *not* normally distributed (i.e., the visual spread of the values does not approximate a *bell-shaped curve*).

2. The number of respondents is *very small*.

3. The dependent variable is measured at the *ordinal* or *nominal* level.

Wilcoxon Test as an Alternative to the *t*-Test for Paired Samples (for Two Variables, Both Measured at the Ordinal Level)

Both variables are assumed to be two measurements from the same respondents at different times or from matched samples.

SPSS Process

In either the *Data View* or *Variable View* window, do the following:

CLICK on the *Analyze* menu from the top of the window.

SCROLL DOWN and release the mouse over the *Nonparametric Tests* choice.

CLICK on 2 *Related Samples*.

CLICK on the first of two variable(s) you are interested in. Include only ordinal-level variables.

CLICK on the second of the two variable(s) you are interested in. Include only ordinal-level variables.

CLICK on the right-pointing button in the middle of the window.

NOTE that both variables appear in the box at the bottom left.

LEAVE CHECKED the *Wilcoxon* choice under *Text Type* at the right side of the window.

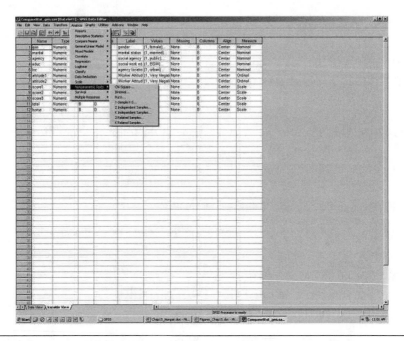

Figure 15.7   *Nonparametric Tests* Screen in SPSS

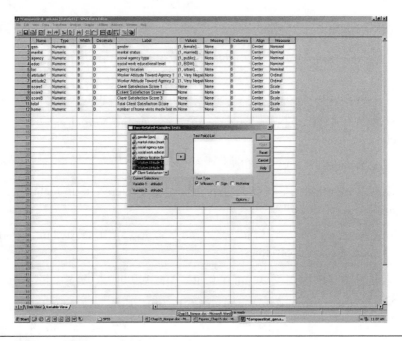

Figure 15.8   *Two Related-Samples Tests* Screen in SPSS With Variables Identified

CLICK on the *Options* button at the bottom right of the screen.

CLICK on *Descriptives* in the box labeled *Statistics*.

CLICK on the *Continue* button.

CLICK on the *OK* button at the top right of the window.

Applying the SPSS Output

From the table labeled *Descriptive Statistics*, do the following:

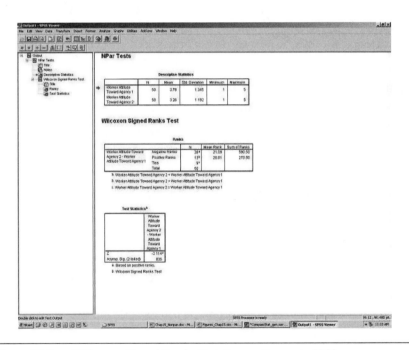

Figure 15.9   *Wilcoxon Signed Ranks Test* Output Screen in SPSS

EXTRACT the mean value and the standard deviation for each variable.

From the table labeled *Test Statistics*, do the following:

EXTRACT the *Z* value on the right side of the table.

EXTRACT the *Asymp. Sig. (2-tailed)* value directly underneath the *Z* value. If the *Asymp. Sig.* value is .05 or less (e.g., .01, .000), you have found a statistically significant difference between the two variables. This difference should be obvious when you compare the mean values of the two variables. If, however, the *Sig. (2-tailed)* value is greater than .05 (e.g., .07, .215), you have not found a statistically significant difference between the two variables.

DISREGARD any other data in the output screen.

NOTE that in this example, Figure 15.9, you have discovered a statistically significant difference (*Asymp. Sig.* or p = .035) between the workers' attitude toward Agency 1 as compared to Agency 2. Reviewing the mean ranked scores (M = 3.78 and M = 3.26), you further know that the ranking (on a 5-point ordinal scale) was higher for Agency 1 over Agency 2. Thus, you can reject your null hypothesis that there exists no difference in rankings as measured by the scales used in this situation.

Mann-Whitney *U* Test as an Alternative to the *t*-Test for Independent Samples (for One Dependent Variable Measured at the Ordinal Level and One Independent Variable Measured at the Ordinal or Nominal Level)

Remember that at any one time, you can analyze only two categories of the independent sample with this test.

SPSS Process

In either the *Data View* or *Variable View* window, do the following:

CLICK on the *Analyze* menu from the top of the window.

SCROLL DOWN and release the mouse over the *Nonparametric Tests* choice.

CLICK on 2 *Independent Samples.*

CLICK on the ordinal-level variable (dependent) in the box on the left.

CLICK on the right-pointing button in the middle of the window and move that variable to the box labeled *Test Variable List.*

CLICK on the nominal- or ordinal-level variable (independent) in the box on the left.

CLICK on the right-pointing button in the middle of the window and move that variable to the box labeled *Grouping Variable.*

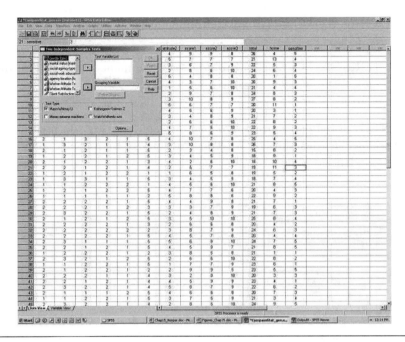

Figure 15.10   *Two Independent-Samples Tests* Screen in SPSS

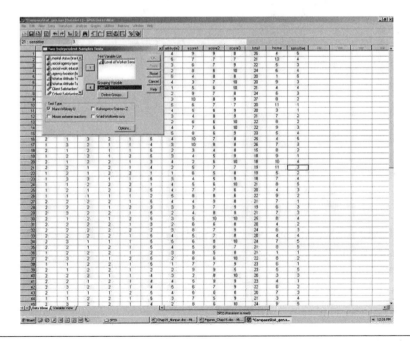

Figure 15.11   *Two Independent-Samples Tests* Screen in SPSS With Dependent
(Test) Variable and Independent (Grouping) Variable Selected

CLICK on the *Define Groups* button immediately below the *Grouping Variable* box.

ENTER in the box labeled *Group 1* the same number you used in the *Variable View* window for one category of the variable under the column labeled *Values*.

ENTER in the box labeled *Group 2* the same number you used in the *Variable View* window for a second category of the variable under the column labeled *Values*.

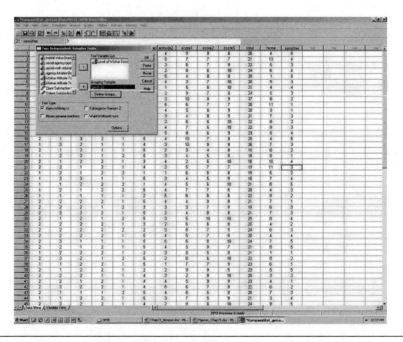

Figure 15.12   *Two Independent-Samples Tests* Screen in SPSS With Two Categories Selected for the Independent (Grouping) Variable

REMEMBER that your dependent variable may have more than two categories, but you can measure only the differences between two categories with this test.

LEAVE CHECKED the *Mann-Whitney U* under *Test Type* at the bottom left of the window.

CLICK on the *Options* button at the bottom right of the screen.

CLICK on *Descriptives* in the box labeled *Statistics*.

CLICK on the *Continue* button.

CLICK on the *OK* button at the top right of the window.

Reading the SPSS Output

From the table labeled *Descriptive Statistics*, do the following:

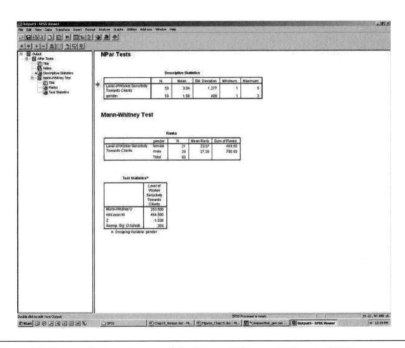

Figure 15.13   Output Screen of the Mann-Whitney *U* Test in SPSS

EXTRACT the mean value and the standard deviation for each variable.

From the table labeled *Test Statistics*, do the following:

EXTRACT the *Mann-Whitney U* value on the first line of the table.

EXTRACT the *Asymp. Sig. (2-tailed)* value toward the end of the table. If the *Asymp. Sig. (2-tailed)* value is .05 or less (e.g., .01, .000), you have found a statistically significant difference between the two categories (i.e., between Group 1 and Group 2). This difference should be obvious when you compare the mean rank values of the two categories. If, however, the *Asymp. Sig. (2-tailed)* value is greater than .05 (e.g., .07, .215), you have not found a statistically significant difference between the two categories (i.e., between Group 1 and Group 2).

DISREGARD any other data in the output screen.

NOTE in this situation in Figure 15.13 that you do not have a statistically significant difference in the mean rankings of worker sensitivity based on gender. While the mean rankings of men are slightly higher than women (27.26 for men compared to 23.07 for women), that difference is not wide enough to produce statistical significance (*Asymp. Sig.* or $p = .304$). Therefore, you should not reject your null hypothesis that gender does not influence the level of sensitivity as measured by the instrument used in this example.

NOTE FURTHER that this is also a good example of how the results can be considered "good news" when you *do not* uncover any statistical significance and therefore *do not* reject your null hypothesis. Take the results as presented, regardless of whether you discover statistical significance, and interpret those results within the context of your study. The "good news" in this situation is that the female and male workers are equally sensitive to clients, statistically speaking, since gender does not appear to be an influence on client sensitivity according to the data collected in this hypothetical study.

Kruskal-Wallis *H* Test as an Alternative for the One-Way ANOVA (for One Dependent Variable Measured at the Ordinal Level and One Independent Variable Measured at the Nominal or Ordinal Level)

More than two categories of this independent variable may be measured at any time.

SPSS Process

In either the *Data View* or *Variable View* window, do the following:

CLICK on the *Analyze* menu from the top of the window.

SCROLL DOWN and release the mouse over the *Nonparametric Tests* choice.

CLICK on the *K Independent Samples* choice.

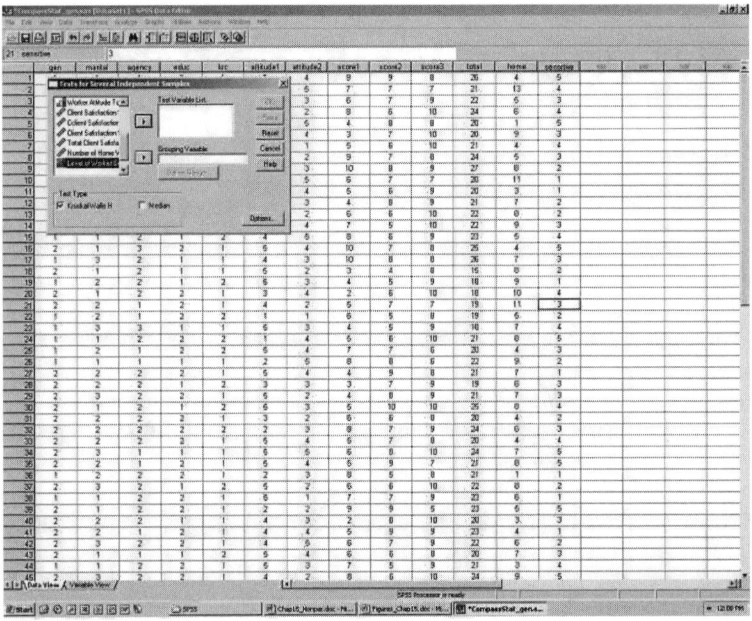

Figure 15.14   *Tests for Several Independent Samples* Screen in SPSS

CLICK on the ordinal-level variable (dependent) in the left box.

CLICK on the right-pointing button in the middle of the window and move that variable to the box labeled *Test Variable List.*

CLICK on the nominal- or ordinal-level variable that has more than two possible categories (independent) in the left box.

CLICK on the right-pointing button in the middle of the window and move that variable to the box labeled *Grouping Variable.*

CLICK on the *Define Range* button immediately below the *Grouping Variable* box.

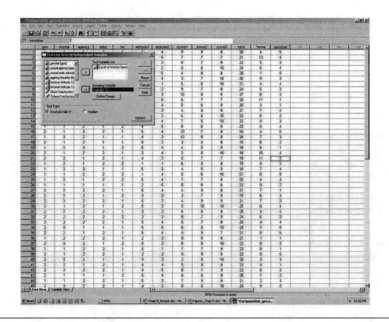

Figure 15.15   *Tests for Several Independent Samples* Screen in SPSS With Dependent (Test) Variable and Independent (Grouping) Variable Selected

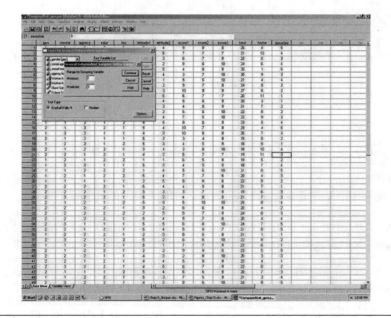

Figure 15.16   *Tests for Several Independent Samples* Screen in SPSS With Range Defined for Independent (Grouping) Variable

ENTER in the box labeled *Minimum* the first number you used in the *Variable View* window for the first category of the variable under the column labeled *Values*.

ENTER in the box labeled *Maximum* the last number you used in the *Variable View* window for the last category of the variable under the column labeled *Values*.

REMEMBER that the independent variable should contain more than two categories. If it contains only two categories, then use the Mann-Whitney *U* test.

CLICK on the *Continue* button.

LEAVE CHECKED *Kruskal-Wallis H* under *Test Type* at the bottom left of the window.

CLICK on the *OK* button at the top right of the window.

NOTE that there are no *Post Hoc Tests* options with this test.

Applying the SPSS Output

From the table labeled *Ranks,* do the following:

EXTRACT the *Mean Rank* value for each of the categories of the independent variable.

From the table labeled *Test Statistics,*

EXTRACT the *Chi-Square* value on the row to the right. As noted under the table, this *Chi-Square* value is considered the *Kruskal-Wallis H* value.

EXTRACT the *df* value on the next row down.

EXTRACT the *Asymp. Sig.* value on the last row. If this *Sig.* value is .05 or less (e.g., .01, .000), you have found a statistically significant difference between the categories of the independent variable. If, however, the *Sig.* value is greater than .05 (e.g., .07, .215), you have not found a statistically significant difference between the categories of the independent variable.

DISREGARD any other data in the output screen.

NOTE in this example, in Figure 15.17, that you have not detected any statistically significant difference (*Asymp. Sig.* or p = .083) between the categories of the independent variable (*marital status*) regarding the participants' level of sensitivity toward clients. While there exists some

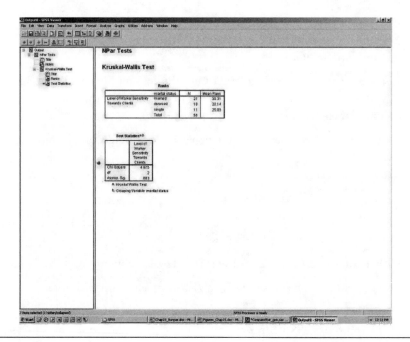

Figure 15.17   Output of Kruskal-Wallis Test in SPSS

observable difference in mean rankings between the categories ($M = 30.31$ for married, $M = 20.14$ for divorced, and $M = 25.09$ for single staff members), those differences are not large enough to warrant your rejecting your null hypothesis. Thus, your results indicate that based on the data you collected, marital status has no observable influence on the level of worker sensitivity, as measured by the study instruments.

References

Denscombe, M. (2006). Web-based questionnaires and the mode effect: An evaluation based on completion rates and data contents of near-identical questionnaires delivered in different modes. *Social Science Computer Review, 24*(2), 246–254.

Martin, S. A., Irvine, J. A., Fluharty, K., & Gatty, C. M. (2003). A comprehensive work injury prevention program with clerical workers: Phase I. *Work, 21,* 185–196.

Pinquart, M., & Sorensen, S. (2002). Older adults' preferences for informal, formal and mixed support for future care needs: A comparison of Germany and the United States. *Journal of Aging & Human Development, 54*(4), 291–314.

Prospero, M. (2006). The role of perceptions in dating violence among young adolescents. *Journal of Interpersonal Violence, 21*(4), 470–484.

Appendix A

Getting Started With SPSS

1. Opening a New SPSS File

SPSS Process

CLICK on the *Start* button at the bottom left of the computer screen.

CLICK on *Programs*.

CLICK on *SPSS 14.0 for Windows*.

CLICK on *Type in data*.

CLICK on the *OK* button at the bottom right of the screen.

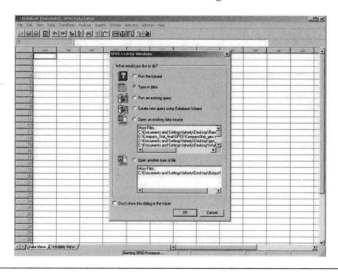

Figure A.1   *Type in data* Screen for SPSS

2. Creating New Variables

SPSS Process

MAKE SURE the *Variable View* window is clicked open at the bottom left of the screen.

CLICK in the first cell under the column labeled *Name*.

ENTER in the first cell a short abbreviated name for your first variable using no spaces or symbols (e.g., *gen* for the variable *gender*).

CLICK in the first cell under the column labeled *Type*.

LEAVE the word *Numeric* untouched.

LEAVE the number *8* untouched in the column labeled *Width*.

CLICK in the right corner of the column labeled *Decimals*.

CHANGE the number 2 to the number 0 in the column labeled *Decimals*. If the variable is expressed in two decimal points (e.g., GPA, income in dollars and cents), then LEAVE UNTOUCHED the number 2. If the variable is expressed in one decimal point (e.g., temperature in degrees), then CHANGE the number 2 to 1.

CLICK in the first cell under the column labeled *Label*.

ENTER in the first cell the full name for your first variable, using the format you want to appear in any output (e.g., *age at last birthday* for the variable *age* or *gender* for the variable *gender*). You may use whole phrases and spaces between words since the cell will expand to accommodate the length of your entry. Remember that what you enter here will appear exactly that way in any SPSS output.

NOTE: If the variable is scale level, LEAVE UNTOUCHED the word *None* in the first cell of the column labeled *Values*, then SKIP the next seven steps. If the variable is either nominal level or ordinal level, then CONTINUE.

CLICK in the first cell under the column labeled *Values*.

CLICK on the shaded square appearing in the right corner of the cell across from the word *None*.

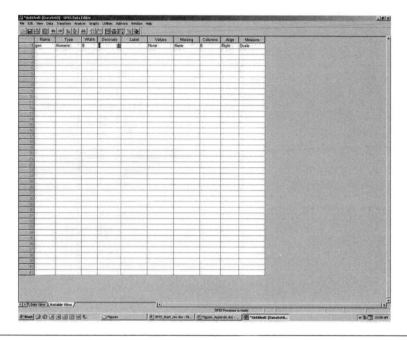

Figure A.2   Creating a New Variable Screen in SPSS

ENTER in the box labeled *Value* a number (e.g., the number 1 for the first category of a nominal variable or the number 5 for the highest category of an ordinal variable).

ENTER in the box labeled *Value Label* the name of the first category of the variable (e.g., *female* for the first category of the variable *gender* or *very satisfied* for the highest category of an ordinal variable).

CLICK the *Add* button on the left middle of the window.

REPEAT the three previous steps until all categories of the variable have been entered.

CLICK the *OK* button at the top right of the window.

LEAVE UNTOUCHED the word *None* in the first cell of the column labeled *Missing*.

LEAVE UNTOUCHED the word *number 8* in the first cell of the column labeled *Columns*.

CLICK in the first cell under the column labeled *Align*.

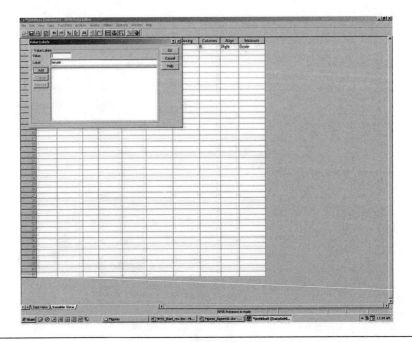

Figure A.3   *Value Labels* Screen in SPSS

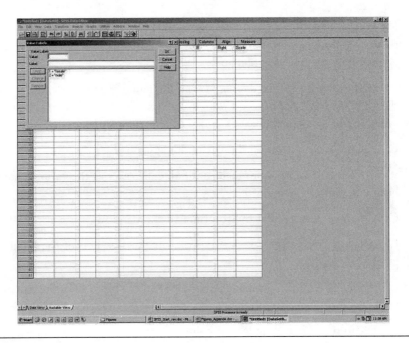

Figure A.4   Completed *Values Labels* Screen in SPSS

CLICK on the down-pointing arrow and CHOOSE by clicking on *Left*, *Right*, or *Center*. This choice decides the position for the alignment of data in each cell. This is your personal choice for visual purposes only as you work with your data. The placement chosen has no effect on any future procedure or data analysis output.

CLICK in the first cell under the column labeled *Measure*.

CLICK on the down-pointing arrow and CHOOSE by clicking on *Scale*, *Ordinal*, or *Nominal*. This choice decides the level of measurement for the variable being entered.

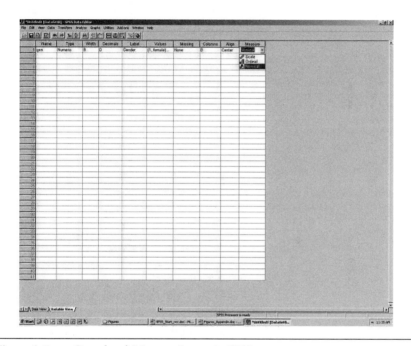

Figure A.5   Completed *Measure* Screen in SPSS

REPEAT the above steps for each variable being entered.

3. Entering New Data

SPSS Process

CLICK on *Data View* at the bottom left of the screen.

CLICK in the first cell under the column labeled with the abbreviated name of the variable (e.g., *gen* for the variable *gender*).

ENTER the appropriate number assigned (e.g., 1 for female, 5 for very satisfied, 7 for length of employment).

ENGAGE the *Enter* key, *Tab* key, or the *Down Arrow* key on the computer keyboard, or CLICK on the second cell under the column labeled with the abbreviated name of the variable.

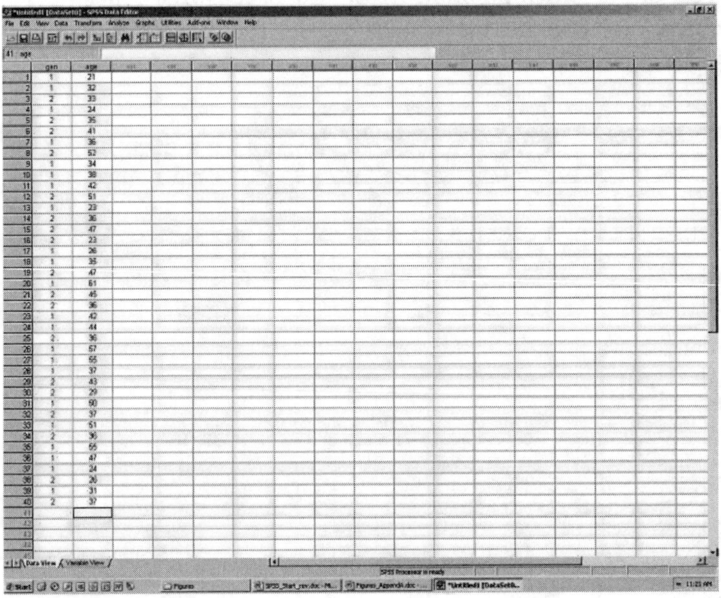

Figure A.6   Completed *Data View* Screen in SPSS

REPEAT the previous two steps until all data have been entered for all nominal or ordinal variables.

REPEAT the above steps until the numerical data for all variables have been entered.

4. Opening an Existing SPSS File

SPSS Process

CLICK on the *Start* button at the bottom left of the computer screen.

CLICK on *Programs*.

CLICK on *SPSS 14.0 for Windows.*

LEAVE UNTOUCHED the already clicked *Open an existing data source* circle.

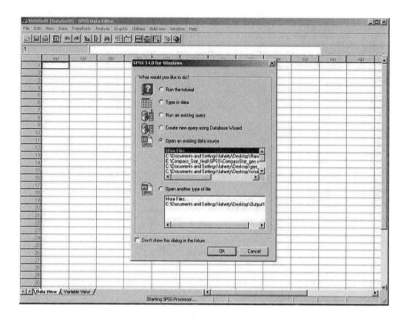

Figure A.7   Opening an Existing File in SPSS

CLICK on the SPSS file you wish to open from the list in the center of the window.

CLICK on the *OK* button at the bottom right of the screen.

5. Editing Existing Data: Selecting a Subset of Cases

SPSS Process

In either the *Data View* or *Variable View* window, do the following:

DECIDE what subset of cases you need (e.g., only *female* cases).

CLICK on the *Data* button at the top of the window.

CLICK on *Select Cases* toward the bottom of the list.

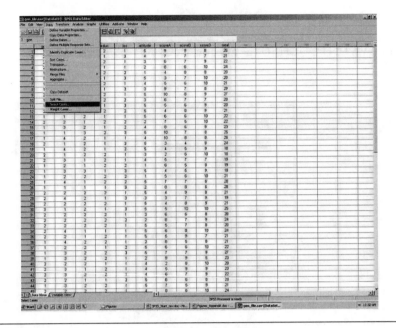

Figure A.8   Choosing *Select Cases* Screen in SPSS

From the list on the left side of the screen, CLICK on the variable in which you want to select cases (e.g., *gender*).

CLICK on the button *If condition is satisfied.*

CLICK on the *If* box immediately under this *If condition is satisfied* button.

CLICK on the *left-pointing arrow* at the top middle of the screen. Once *gen* appears in the right box on top, ADD the phrase *=1* with no spaces. You may use either the keyboard or numbers and symbols on the pad directly below the box on the top right.

CLICK on the *Continue* button at the bottom of the screen.

CLICK on the *OK* button at the bottom of the window. The *Data View* window will change so that a diagonal line will appear through the case numbers of those cases not selected (i.e., the males in this example). Any statistical analysis you now conduct will include only the female cases.

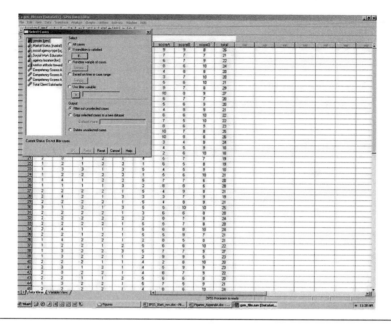

Figure A.9   *If condition is satisfied* Screen in SPSS

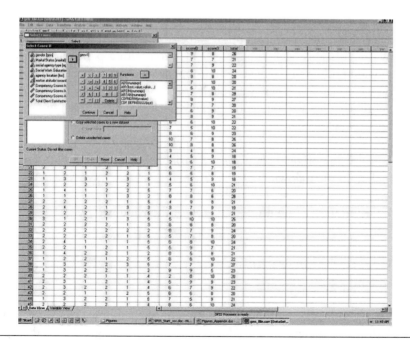

Figure A.10   Completed *If condition is satisfied* Screen in SPSS

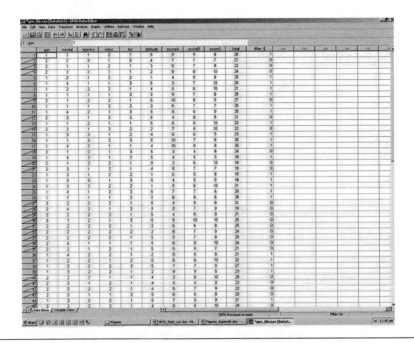

Figure A.11   Completed *Select Cases* Screen in SPSS

NOTE that a new variable appears labeled *filter_$* at the end of your list of variables. This new variable provides you with a permanent copy (if you want one) of the changes you just made with the *Select Cases* option. You can rename this new variable if you choose to save it. If you do not need to save the variable with the newly selected cases, then ignore this new *filter_$* variable.

To return to the original status of the variable *gen* including both females and males, do the following:

CLICK on the *Data* button at the top of the window.

CLICK on *Select Cases* toward the bottom of the list.

CLICK on the variable *gender.*

CLICK on *All cases.*

CLICK on the *OK* button at the bottom of the window. The *Data View* window will change so that a diagonal line will no longer appear through the case numbers of any of the cases.

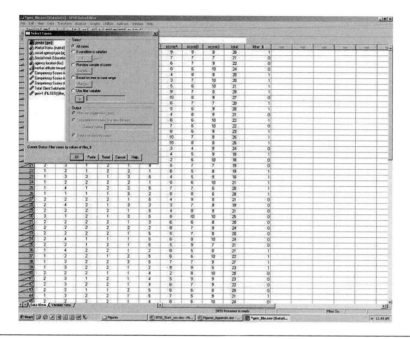

Figure A.12   Returning *Select Cases* Screen in SPSS to Original Status

Appendix B

SPSS Data Sets

Data Set 1: Client Demographics and Treatment Results (N = 57 Clients)

This file contains basic demographic data regarding clients, the type of clinician treating them, their attitudes toward treatment on a pre- and posttreatment basis, and an assessment of their progress by the clinicians from a pre-, mid-, and posttreatment perspective. You can directly download this data set at the Sage Web site (http://www.sagepub.com/fahertystudy) under the file name dataset_1.sav.

Data Set 2: Agency Satellite Offices—Expenditures, Staffing Patterns, and Outcome Measures (N = 34 Offices)

This file tracks the organizational data of a national, nonprofit social agency that supports 34 separate satellite community offices across the United States. The monthly budget data presented represent the totals of expenditures for all nonsalary items. Other data provide information about staffing patterns and program output in the form of service units delivered. Finally, there are indications of client satisfaction, the presence of advisory committees, and staff morale. You can directly download this data set at the Sage Web site (http://www.sagepub.com/fahertystudy) under the file name dataset_2.sav.

Data Set 3: Client Single-Case Evaluation (N = 32 Clients)

This data set presents the results of a series of single-case evaluations of 32 different clients in residential treatment at the same social agency. The clients evaluated were all exhibiting serious aggressive acting-out behaviors directed toward other residents and toward staff. The numerical data recorded in this file represent the number of times per week that the resident was noted in the agency daily log book for initiating negative, acting-out behavior toward either other residents or staff. Three distinct interventions, designed to minimize these negative behaviors, were introduced to the resident. The first intervention (Int1) consisted of extra time spent in typical, one-on-one counseling sessions with their assigned counselor; the second intervention (Int2) provided extra in-house and community privileges beyond the normal amount typically allotted to all residents; and the third intervention (Int3) introduced a positive reinforcement strategy wherein the resident received a monetary award of $5.00 per day for each day during which they were not entered into the agency daily log book for negative behavior. The interventions were introduced at planned intervals so as to minimize the possible cumulative effect one intervention might exert over another. Behaviors were observed during four sequential stages: (1) baseline, before the intervention began; (2) introduction phase, during which the intervention started; (3) withdrawal phase, during which the intervention was stopped; and (4) reintroduction phase, which involved the reestablishment of the intervention with the client. You can directly download this data set at the Sage Web site (http://www.sagepub.com/fahertystudy) under the file name dataset_3.sav.

Data Set 4: Client Satisfaction Survey (N = 49 Respondents)

This file presents the results of a survey from 49 respondents who are former clients of a community social services agency. Basic demographic information is provided, followed by the respondents' reaction to how responsive were the various levels of staff to their needs. A general assessment of treatment is provided along with some evaluation of the physical surroundings of the agency itself. You can directly download this data set at the Sage Web site (http://www.sagepub.com/fahertystudy) under the file name dataset_4.sav.

Data Set 5: Community Social Needs Survey (*N* = 76 Respondents)

This data set communicates information collected from the general public regarding their impressions about the ongoing needs for social services in one community. Typical demographic data were collected, as well as the respondents' perceptions along a wide range of social service needs and economic support options. You can directly download this data set at the Sage Web site (http://www.sagepub.com/fahertystudy) under the file name dataset_5.sav.

Appendix C

Outline of Common Univariate and Bivariate Statistical Procedures

Common Univariate Statistical Procedures

Nominal Level	Ordinal Level	Scale Level
Mode	Median	Mean
Frequency count	Mode	Median
Percent	Quartiles	Mode
Sum	Interquartile range	Standard deviation
	Frequency count	Range
	Percent	Minimum–maximum
	Sum	Frequency count
		Percent
		Sum
		Skewness
		Kurtosis

Common Bivariate Statistical Procedures

Two Nominal Variables	Two Ordinal Variables	Two Scale Variables	One Scale + One Nominal or Ordinal Variable	One Ordinal + One Nominal Variable
Chi-square Fisher's exact	Spearman's *rho* Wilcoxon *Z*	Pearson's *r*	*t*-Tests ANOVA Post hoc tests	Mann-Whitney *U* Kruskal-Wallis *H*

Appendix D

Outline of Common Parametric and Nonparametric Inferential Tests

R emember that to use one of the parametric tests for inferential analysis, you should have present all of the following three conditions:

- The dependent variable contains data that are measured at the scale level (i.e., interval or ratio).
- The population is normally distributed, so that the levels of skewness and kurtosis are, generally speaking, not greatly more than ±1.00.
- The sample is large enough. This is often interpreted to mean that you must have a minimum of 30 cases suitable for analysis.

If one or more of these conditions is absent, you should use one of the nonparametric tests for inferential analysis. See Chapter 15 of this book for an expanded discussion of the conditions for using parametric tests and for the differences between parametric and nonparametric inferential tests.

Parametric	Nonparametric
t-Test for paired samples	Chi-square test
t-Test for independent samples	Fisher's exact test
ANOVA	Wilcoxon signed-ranks Z test
Post hoc tests	Mann-Whitney U test
Pearson's r	Kruskal-Wallis H test
	Spearman's rho

Appendix E

Table of Random Numbers
With Instructions

A. To Create a Simple Random Sample . . .

1. Remember that a random sample guarantees that every respondent in your study population has an equal chance of being chosen for your research project. Thus, your choice of where to start the selection of respondents must be totally out of your personal control. Hence, the word *random* is used.

2. Decide who/what constitutes your study population of research respondents.

3. Obtain a list of all the respondents in your study population (e.g., a membership list of some organization) or have physical access to them (e.g., all the closed case files in Agency XYZ for 2006). This list or grouping is considered your *sampling frame.*

4. Count the exact total number of cases in your study population from your sampling frame. No estimates or assumptions are allowed.

5. Decide on your sample size (i.e., the number of people or objects from which you plan to collect your data). Remember that sample size is often dictated by your own personal resources of time, financial assets, and cooperation (i.e., are you working alone, or is this a group research project?).

6. Based on the size of your sampling frame, decide on the length of the number, in digits, of the last case in that sampling frame. For example, a sampling frame of 95 respondents requires a two-digit possible number (01 to 95), a sampling frame of 250 respondents requires a three-digit possible number (001 to 250), and so on.

7. Remember that the first possible case in a two-digit sampling frame is always 01, the first case in a three-digit sampling frame is always 001, and so on.

8. Decide what direction you will move once you enter the Table of Random Numbers (Table E.1). Your choices are the following: up or north, to the right or east, down or south, and to the left or west.

9. Ignore all the lines and spaces in the Table of Random Numbers (Table E.1). They are irrelevant to the process and are included only for your visual comfort as you work with a solid page of numbers. Ignore also the fact that the numbers are grouped together in nine-digit arrays. Think only in terms of moving through those numbers no matter how orderly they may appear or whether they continue to the next column or row. There exists absolutely no pattern in the numbers as listed, and that is why they serve this helpful function.

10. Without consciously looking, land your index finger or pen/pencil on some spot in the Table E.1.

11. Move in the direction chosen (i.e., up, down, left, or right) and note the next two-digit or three-digit number (as appropriate) that you come across. That is the number of your first randomly selected case. Ignore any number that falls above the total number of your study population (e.g., if your sampling frame contains 617 cases, ignore any number above that) and keep moving in the direction chosen.

12. Mark the specific case on your sampling frame whose number you have selected randomly.

13. When you come to the end of a column or row, simply continue sequentially onto the next row or column in any new direction. The key is to keep moving so the numbers appear without your making any conscious choice. In a sense, they select you rather than you select them.

14. When you have finished the selection of all the cases you planned for, stop the process. You have concluded the extraction of a simple random sample from your study population.

15. If you find this procedure to be especially tedious (which it probably will become if you need a sample larger than 30 or 40 respondents), you might consider using a systematic random sample, described next.

B. To Create a Systematic Random Sample . . .

The first four steps are the same as for a simple random sample.

1. Remember that a random sample guarantees that every respondent in your study population has an equal chance of being chosen for your study. Thus,

your choice of where to start the selection of respondents must be totally out of your personal control. Hence, the word *random* is used.

2. Decide who/what constitutes your study population of research respondents.

3. Obtain a list of all the respondents in your study population (e.g., a membership list of some organization) or have physical access to them (e.g., all the closed case files in Agency XYZ for 2006). This list or grouping is considered your *sampling frame.*

4. Count the exact total number of cases in your study population from your sampling frame. No estimates or assumptions are allowed.

5. Decide on a number that represents a *percentage* of your sampling frame that you want to include in your sample. Use some easily understood round number, such as 50%, 33%, 25%, 20%, 10%, or 5%. Since your sampling frame is rarely (if ever) a round number, this choice typically will yield an uneven total number in your sample. For example, a 50% random sample of 176 closed cases will produce a sample of 88; a 20% sample of a membership list of 392 members will yield a sample of 78. Do not worry about having an uneven number in your sample. Simply note this fact in the Methodology section of your final report with a statement such as, "This researcher drew a fifty percent random sample ($N = 88$) of all the client case files for Agency XYZ closed in 2006."

6. Since this is a systematic random sample, rather than a simple random sample, you will now begin to work with number *intervals* that are implied when you use percentages. Note and remember that a

50% sample produces an interval of 2 (i.e., 1 out of 2 or 1/2)

33% sample produces an interval of 3 (i.e., 1 out of 3 or 1/3)

25% sample produces an interval of 4 (i.e., 1 out of 4 or 1/4)

20% sample produces an interval of 5 (i.e., 1 out of 5 or 1/5)

10% sample produces an interval of 10 (i.e., 1 out of 10 or 1/10)

5% sample produces an interval of 20 (i.e., 1 out of 20 or 1/20)

7. Based on the size of your sampling frame, decide on the length of the number, in digits, of the last case in that sampling frame. For example, a sampling frame of 95 respondents requires a two-digit possible number (01 to 95), a sampling frame of 250 respondents requires a three-digit possible number (001 to 250), and so on.

8. To draw a systematic random sample, choose your first case number randomly (as you would in a simple random sample), then return to your original sampling frame. Mark that particular case in the sampling frame as the first selected respondent in your systematic random sample, then proceed systematically through the rest of the sampling frame according to the interval

appropriate to your chosen percentage. For example, if you chose a 33% sample size from a study population of 278 respondents for your research project, you should (1) select the first case randomly from the sampling frame, as described above; (2) mark that particular case number on your sampling frame; and (3) staying with your sampling frame, mark *every third* following case until you have a total of 93 selected cases for your sample (278/3 = 93). Specifically, if your first randomly chosen case number on the sampling frame is 134, then your second case would be 137, your third case would be 140, and so on. When you reach the end of your sampling frame, simply continue counting back at the first number. Consider the sampling frame to exist on a circular drum, like a Rolodex file. You should, in this example, end up at approximately three cases before the first case where you started since you have, in effect, come full circle through your sampling frame. Do not worry if you fail to end up with an exact interval (e.g., three cases for a 33% systematic sample) between your last numbered case and your first numbered case. A close approximation is all that is necessary since exactness depends on whether your total population number is precisely divisible by your selected interval. For example, if you draw a 25% (1/4) systematic sample from a total population of 400, then that number is equally divisible by 4 (i.e., 400/4 = 100), and you will end up exactly four places from where you began randomly. However, if you draw a 33% (1/3) sample from a total population of 400, then that number is not precisely divisible by 3 (i.e., 400/3 = 133.3). In that latter situation, you will end up *approximately* three spaces from where you began your random selection.

9. When you have finished the selection of all the cases you planned for, based on the percentage you chose, stop the process. You have concluded the extraction of a systematic random sample from your study population.

Table E.1   Table of Random Numbers

183713582	564925171	503778551	327658335
903776409	385356834	198061024	055176734
889808616	927736016	597512906	140694564
325476326	085623568	059116278	730363637
753550117	400775712	368114353	574033516
918540909	590509468	075422232	630606354
964040278	381546801	202409419	860295694
968759591	551143228	354171781	458898979
924562692	131661063	434359772	527549628
583443628	008470576	162059881	146536448
067308624	925177068	137138503	327658335
948576129	384099984	230018308	055176734
454282928	947048094	229082461	140694564
170805916	235865821	052689284	730363637
854722554	314288516	986483662	574033516
555695002	684540316	394774857	630606354
724351193	806110656	446163178	860295694
154803884	851411114	376962661	458898979
325546499	554780814	808125491	527549628
611549012	895849826	097309542	146536448
856462996	448718309	065259747	730276519
453513999	205109249	649090401	229015303
715332417	050451667	032891771	258342348
122339032	692718195	672441007	667709954
807178221	843404474	356872855	706194481
328200729	512003456	083873459	354460311
219917273	802860413	441488084	533271136
032032884	948001698	985929722	721063911
252003127	314468881	232454877	003167965
815562639	430024726	876181353	660716992

Appendix F

Glossary of Terms

Alternate hypothesis. The opposite of the null hypothesis; usually the same as the research hypothesis; also referred to as the rival hypothesis.

Analysis of variance. The formal title of the parametric test known as ANOVA.

ANOVA. The acronym for the analysis of variance statistical test of means.

Axis. A horizontal or vertical line in a graph on which values of the independent and dependent variables are plotted.

Bar graph. A visual representation of the frequency of data separated into categories; typically used to describe nominal or ordinal data.

Bell-shaped curve. The idealized visual image that occurs naturally when a large number of quantitative values are represented on a horizontal plane so that their frequency counts center around their mean, media, and modal values.

Bias. An intentional limit placed usually on a sample of respondents regarding some demographic characteristic; does not imply prejudice or discrimination in any manner.

Bivariate analysis. An analysis of the statistical relationship between two variables at the same time; usually the focus of introductory statistics textbooks.

Cause and effect. The strongest relationship between two variables; recognizable, to some degree, only by means of experimental research methodology.

Central tendency. The typical value in any data array that represents the middle position.

Chance. The likelihood of some occurrence due to random circumstances; similar to sampling error.

Chi-square test. A nonparametric test used to determine the relationship between two nominal-level variables.

Coding. In quantitative analysis, the assignment of numerical values to raw data.

Control group. In experimental research, the collection of respondents who are purposely not influenced by the independent variable; the opposite of an experimental group.

Correlation. A statistical procedure that identifies the strength and direction of the relationship between either ordinal- or scale-level variables.

Criterion variable. Another name for outcome variable.

Crosstabulation table. A diagram that visually presents the frequency distribution between two nominal-level variables; often used in conjunction with the chi-square test.

Data. Many observations; the plural of datum.

Degree of freedom. Refers to the number of ways in which the data in a statistical test can vary among (be free of) each other; depends on whether the data are measured at the nominal, ordinal, or scale level; should be included in any statistical notation provided in a report.

Dependent samples *t*-test. Another name for the paired samples *t*-test.

Dependent variable. The passive variable in contrast to the independent variable; the site of measurement of the effects of the independent variable; where the researcher looks to gauge change or variation between the variables; also called outcome variable.

Descriptive statistics. Statistical methods used simply to depict or illustrate the meaning of the data in a study without drawing any inferences.

Deviation from the mean. In any distribution of values, the variation of any value from the mean of that distribution.

Directional hypothesis. A research hypothesis stated as a prediction of a statistically significant relationship between two variables that includes the specific direction of that relationship; also called a one-tailed hypothesis.

Effect size. The strength of the relationship between variables; used frequently to compare statistical results across similar, but not replicated, research studies.

Expected frequencies. For each cell in a chi-square test, the anticipated occurrence of observations if the null hypothesis was actually true.

Experiment. A research methodology in which the researcher introduces or manipulates the independent variable and measures its effects on the dependent variable; a strict experiment requires an experimental group and a control group of respondents.

Experimental group. In experimental research, the collection of respondents who are purposely influenced by the independent variable; the opposite of a control group.

Frequency. The number of observations for a variable.

Frequency distribution. A visual display of the number of occurrences of values or value categories of variables.

F value. The output value in the ANOVA statistical test.

Grouping variable. The same as the independent variable in certain statistical tests.

Histogram. A visual representation of the frequency of data separated into their respective values; typically used to describe scale-level data.

Horizontal axis. The flat line in a graph on which values of the independent variable are plotted; typically used in conjunction with a vertical axis.

Hypothesis testing. In inferential statistics, the process of predicting characteristics of variables in a population from an observation of a sample drawn from that population; a series of sequential steps involving either the rejection or the acceptance of the null hypothesis.

Independent samples _t_-test. A parametric statistical test that compares the mean values of two samples drawn separately from a study population.

Independent variable. The active variable in contrast to the dependent variable; the variable introduced or manipulated in a study so the researcher can measure its effects on the dependent variable; also called predictor variable.

Inferential statistics. Statistical methods used to draw possible conclusions about a population of respondents by examining the characteristics of a sample drawn randomly from that population.

Interquartile range. In a distribution of ordinal or scale values, the distance between the 25th percentile point and the 75th percentile point; frequently used in conjunction with the median value (i.e., the 50th percentile point).

Interval level of measurement. Considered a part of the scale level in the SPSS computer program; in practice, typically treated as similar to the ratio level of measurement.

Kruskal-Wallis *H* test. Nonparametric alternative to the ANOVA test.

Kurtosis. In a visual frequency distribution, the amount of peakedness as an indication of the tendency of the values to gather around the center; an important determination of whether a data set is normally distributed.

Leptokurtic. A distribution of values that is excessively peaked in comparison to a normal curve; represents values concentrated closely around the mean.

Mann-Whitney *U* test. Nonparametric alternative to the independent samples *t*-test.

Mean. Another word for average; in a distribution of ordinal or scale values, the sum of all scale values divided by the number of values being considered; a measure of central tendency.

Measurement level. A way of categorizing types of data by their inherent mathematical precision; the standard list in ascending order of measurement precision is nominal, ordinal, interval, and ratio.

Measures of association. Calculations designed to indicate the strength of the relationship between two variables; also referred to as effect size; *phi*, Cramer's *V*, Spearman's *rho*, and Pearson's *r* are examples of measures of association.

Measures of central tendency. Calculations designed to provide the typical placement of values regarding their closeness to each other in a distribution; the mean, median, and mode are measures of central tendency.

Measures of variability. Calculations designed to provide the typical placement of values regarding their separateness from each other in a distribution; the range, minimum and maximum, and standard deviation are measures of variability.

Median. In a distribution of ordinal or scale values, the exact midpoint so that 50% of the values fall higher and 50% of the values fall lower in the distribution; frequently used in conjunction with the quartiles and interquartile range; a measure of central tendency.

Mode. In a distribution of nominal, ordinal, or scale values, the most commonly occurring value; a measure of central tendency.

Multivariate analysis. An analysis of the statistical relationship between three or more variables at the same time; usually discussed only in advanced statistics textbooks.

Negative relationship. In a correlation test, the same as an inverse relationship between two variables; an indication that both variables pass each other so that as one increases, the other decreases.

Negative skew. A visual description of a frequency distribution with a tail veering off to the left; a frequency distribution with many more high values than low values.

Nominal-level measurement. The lowest level of information assessment that simply names or classifies data into two or more mutually exclusive categories; also referred to as categorical measurement.

Nondirectional hypothesis. A research hypothesis stated as a prediction of a statistically significant relationship between two variables that does not include the specific direction of that relationship; also called a two-tailed hypothesis.

Nonparametric test. A statistical test of significance that analyzes nominal- or ordinal-level data, does not require the population to be normally distributed, or depends on a small number of cases.

Normal distribution. An array of values that appears as a bell-shaped curve, with generally predictable mathematical divisions.

Null hypothesis. The statement that predicts the lack of any relationship between two or more variables, stated in either a one-tail or two-tail format; the opposite of the research hypothesis.

Observed frequencies. For each cell in a chi-square test, the actual number and categorization of respondents used in the research project.

One-sample *t*-test. A parametric statistical test that compares the mean value of one sample measured against some known mean of a study population.

One-tailed hypothesis. A hypothesis stated as a prediction of a statistically significant relationship between two variables that includes the specific direction of that relationship; also called a directional hypothesis.

Ordinal level of measurement. A midlevel of information assessment that ranks or orders data into sequential categories.

Outcome variable. The same as the dependent variable in certain statistical tests.

Outlier. In a distribution of values, a score that is either extremely higher or lower than the mean and median values of the distribution.

Paired samples *t*-test. A parametric statistical test that compares the mean values of one sample measured on two occasions or of two matched samples drawn from the same study population.

Parameter. Any characteristic of a population that reflects all the members of that population; usually referred to as population parameter.

Parametric test. A statistical test of significance that analyzes scale-level data, requires the population to be normally distributed, and depends on a large number of cases.

Pearson's *r*. A statistical procedure for correlations that identifies the strength and the direction of the relationship between two scale-level variables.

Percent. A descriptive statistic that provides a value based on 100.

Percentile. In a frequency distribution, a specific point, based on 100, below which the given score falls.

Pie chart. A visual diagram of the frequency of the values or value categories of a variable presented as sections of a circle.

Platykurtic. A distribution of values that is excessively stretched out in comparison to a normal curve; represents values widely extended around the mean.

Population. An array of all the possible cases in a specific group being studied in a research or program evaluation study; typically assumed to be the *study population* rather than the total population of all possible respondents in the world.

Population parameter. Calculations computed from all the observations in a defined population under study.

Positive relationship. In a correlation test, the same as a direct relationship between two variables; an indication that both variables move in the same direction.

Positive skew. A visual description of a frequency distribution with a tail veering off to the right; a frequency distribution with many more low values than high values.

Post hoc test. A follow-up statistical test that signifies the exact relationship between multiple categories of the independent variable following the computation of an ANOVA test.

Predictor variable. The same as the independent variable in some statistical tests.

Probability. A measure of the likelihood of occurrence, stated as a p value.

p value. The numerical statement of the probability that sampling error or a chance occurrence has influenced the assumption that the variables under study are related to each other.

Quartile. In a distribution of ordinal or scale values, the exact 25th percentile point and the 75th percentile point; frequently reported in conjunction with the median value (i.e., the 50th percentile point).

Random sample. A subset of a population intentionally drawn out in a process that guarantees all cases had an equal chance of being selected; types include a simple random sample and a systematic random sample.

Range. The numerical difference between the highest and the lowest values in a distribution; often reported as a statement of the minimum and maximum values; a measure of variability.

Ratio level of measurement. Considered a part of the scale level in the SPSS computer program; the highest level of information assessment, which allows the maximum amount of statistical manipulation of the data.

Reliability. The ability of a research instrument to produce consistent results over time, in varying geographic locations, and/or with different groups of respondents; the opposite of validity.

Research hypothesis. The statement that predicts the relationship between two or more variables stated in either a one-tail or two-tail format; the opposite of the null hypothesis.

Sample. A proportion of cases that have been drawn either randomly or nonrandomly from a population under study.

Sampling error. The natural tendency of a sample to imperfectly reflect a population; the amount of predicted sampling error is used in conjunction with the assumed presence of statistical significance; also referred to as chance or chance occurrence.

Scale level of measurement. A common term in SPSS language that applies to both interval and ratio level; the highest level of information assessment that permits the most precise statistical calculation; a requirement for all inferential tests.

Scattergram. A visual representation in a graph of the relationship between two ordinal- or scale-level variables; also referred to as a scatterplot; typically used with correlation procedures.

Score. A numerical expression of a value or value category; often used interchangeably with the word *value.*

Significance level. The selected level at which you, the researcher, can reject the null hypothesis; for social science researchers, the significance level is typically .05.

Skewed distribution. A dispersal of values in which some values fall unequally above or below the mean; a statement that the distribution is not normal.

Spearman's *rho*. A statistical procedure for correlations that identifies the strength and the direction of the relationship between two ordinal-level variables.

Standard deviation. A common measure of variability around the mean; requires scale-level data and a distribution whose graphic representation approximates the image of a bell-shaped curve; typically reported in conjunction with the mean.

Statistical significance. Based on tested mathematical probability, the implication that the differences observed in the sample reflect accurately the differences found in the population from which the sample was drawn and are not due to sampling error or to chance.

Statistics. The characteristics of a sample; used as a comparison to the characteristics of a population.

Test variable. The same as the dependent variable in some statistical tests.

***t*-test.** A group of parametric statistical tests that compare mean values and draw inferences from the sample to the population.

Two-tailed hypothesis. A hypothesis stated as a prediction of a statistically significant relationship between two variables without indicating the specific direction; also called a nondirectional hypothesis.

Type I error. A statistical inaccuracy that occurs when you reject a null hypothesis in a situation where you should not reject it.

Type II error. A statistical inaccuracy that occurs when you fail to reject a null hypothesis in a situation where you should reject it.

Univariate analysis. A descriptive analysis of one variable at a time; usually the focus of introductory statistics textbooks.

Validity. The ability of a research instrument to measure precisely the phenomenon it is designed to measure; the ability of a research instrument to collect accurate information; the opposite of reliability.

Variable. An attribute that can possess different values for all respondents or cases in your research study.

Vertical axis. The upright line in a graph on which values of the dependent variable are plotted; typically used in conjunction with a horizontal axis.

Wilcoxon signed-ranks test. A nonparametric alternative to the paired samples t-test.

Index

About the Author

Vincent E. Faherty is a Professor of Social Work at the University of Southern Maine, where he has also served intermittently as Department Chairperson and Interim Director of the School of Social Work since 1988. He currently teaches at both the undergraduate and graduate levels in the areas of research methods and statistics. His formal education includes a BA in Philosophy (1960) and graduate study at St. Joseph's College and Seminary (1964), an MSW from Fordham University (1970), a DSW from the University of Utah (1976), and an MBA from the International Management Institute of the University of Geneva, Switzerland (1984). In 1986, Dr. Faherty received a Fulbright international study award and was in residency in Perugia, Italy. Prior to coming to the University of Southern Maine, he taught at the University of Missouri–Columbia and at the University of Northern Iowa. He edited *Annual Editions: Social Welfare and Social Work, 2000/2001* (2000) and has published articles in professional journals in the areas of child welfare, social work administration, social forecasting, quantitative and qualitative analysis, and social welfare history. He has also been the principal investigator on a number of federal, state, and foundation grants.